Global Film Color

Global Film Color

The Monopack Revolution at Midcentury

EDITED BY SARAH STREET AND JOSHUA YUMIBE

Rutgers University Press
New Brunswick, Camden, and Newark, New Jersey
London and Oxford

Rutgers University Press is a department of Rutgers, The State University of New Jersey, one of the leading public research universities in the nation. By publishing worldwide, it furthers the University's mission of dedication to excellence in teaching, scholarship, research, and clinical care.

Library of Congress Cataloging-in-Publication Data

Names: Street, Sarah, editor. | Yumibe, Joshua, editor.
Title: Global film color: the monopack revolution at midcentury /
    edited by Sarah Street and Joshua Yumibe.
Description: New Brunswick: Rutgers University Press, [2024] |
    Includes bibliographical references and index.
Identifiers: LCCN 2023044169 | ISBN 9781978836815 (hardback) |
    ISBN 9781978836808 (paperback) | ISBN 9781978836822 (epub) |
    ISBN 9781978836839 (pdf)
Subjects: LCSH: Color cinematography—History—20th century. |
    Color motion pictures—History—20th century. | BISAC: PERFORMING ARTS /
    Film / History & Criticism | SOCIAL SCIENCE / Media Studies
Classification: LCC TR853 .G56 2024 | DDC 777—dc23/eng/20240102
LC record available at https://lccn.loc.gov/2023044169

A British Cataloging-in-Publication record for this book is available from the British Library.

References to internet websites (URLs) were accurate at the time of writing. Neither the author nor Rutgers University Press is responsible for URLs that may have expired or changed since the manuscript was prepared.

♾ The paper used in this publication meets the requirements of the American National Standard for Information Sciences—Permanence of Paper for Printed Library Materials, ANSI Z39.48-1992.

rutgersuniversitypress.org

Contents

Global Film Color

Introduction

SARAH STREET AND
JOSHUA YUMIBE

Traditionally technological timelines date technology by invention or innovation. Timelines imply that time is a key variable, that it is the march of time which shapes history. That is the assumption behind graphing so much economic data against time. Yet things do not spread like a contagious disease, with a few people getting new technologies early, followed by increasing numbers learning from those who have them, until the rate of adoption falls as most people have them. The international spread of ownership of things shows that the diffusion of things works differently— the rate of take-up has varied enormously between countries, irrespective of how long the technology took to arrive in the first place.

—David Edgerton, *The Shock of the Old*

Color cinema has a vibrant global history. The earliest dyes used to hand-color silent films were aniline colorants sourced from around the world, largely through colonial exploitation. As various photographic color systems emerged, they had unique local histories of development as well as complex transnational legacies of production and reception. Arguably the most far-reaching transformation in color cinema occurred at midcentury. After the Second World War the widespread introduction of color to sound film transformed the look, feel, and critical reception of cinema around the world. The accessibility in the 1950s of cheaper, "monopack" stocks, which combined multiple color layers into a single chromogenic negative for easy filming, immediately expanded the potential market for color films. Yet it was not until the 1960s, during the peak of postwar youth cultures, that color became the dominant aesthetic choice for filmmakers and audiences, particularly in Europe, Japan, India, and the United States. However, the prevalence of color film stocks also varied around the world at the time. Due to asymmetrical flows of technology, the predominant adoption of color was delayed into the 1970s in countries such as Brazil, China, and Senegal. The global transition to color has been little studied, yet monopack color systems dramatically reshaped cinematic practice, leading to the normalization of color in film productions and the relegation of black-and-white cinematography from prior dominance to an anomaly.

Contextualizing the transnational circulation of technologies, David Edgerton has noted that "the rate of take-up" for a new technology fluctuates widely across countries. Edgerton's global history of technology foregrounds several themes that are central to this book's exploration of color filmmaking and processing in various national and regional contexts. Just because a technology is available in a particular locale—such as three-strip Technicolor in the United States in the 1930s, or Eastman Color in the United States and Agfacolor in Europe in the 1950s and 1960s—by no means guarantees that it will automatically be adopted in other geographic areas. While a particular technology may eventually become globally dominant, the temporality and nature of diffusion can vary immensely in differing national and regional contexts as economic inequalities, trade barriers, and cultural norms often influence uptake. In some places older modes might persist and, indeed, coexist alongside each other as "technologies do not only appear, they also reappear, and mix and match."[1] There is no single model for gauging technological diffusion, as the study of global film color in the second half of the twentieth century makes clear. Technological flows, historically as well as in our current digital milieu, are multivalent and hybrid and often guided by creative and tactical interventions.[2]

For example, as Dudley Andrew notes in his seminal article "The Postwar Struggle for Color" (1979), photographic color had a relatively late and troubled adoption in France during the sound era when compared with the United States and the United Kingdom.[3] This is surprising given that France was at the vanguard of color production during the silent era when companies such as Star Films, Pathé Frères, and Gaumont innovated and widely distributed hand-colored, stenciled, and tinted and toned films around the world. But in the post-war era that Andrew examines, ideological factors are crucial for considering the temporal disparities among countries' adoption of color. Specifically, in France, where Technicolor and Agfacolor variants competed, Technicolor was distrusted given the company's substantial control over the process through its Color Advisory Service, which advised on preproduction and production design decisions, and for its postwar association with Hollywood's growing cultural hegemony within the French film market. Technicolor was also expensive and was not widely accessible in Europe given the company's international constraints. In contrast, Agfacolor was relatively well received in the late 1940s in France, where it was thought to be more naturalistic and restrained than the supposedly saturated and garish palettes of Technicolor. But Agfacolor's quality was inconsistent at the time, which often led to noticeable color variations across reels. Further, a general lack of economic investment in the French film industry stifled domestic color technologies and productions. Given these various ideological, technical, and economic factors, Andrew rightly notes that "a color vacuum existed" in France until 1953, when developments in television colorcasting spurred the French industry to invest further in color film production.[4]

As Edgerton and Andrew make clear, researching technological change in a global context is a rewarding yet complex task given the variables. This is particularly the case when one examines film industries of the Global South, as do many of the chapters in this volume. The global focus in this book frames technical transformation in analog color stocks within the broad cultural and industrial transformations that were simultaneously taking place across a range of social practices, as well as in popular, new wave, art, and postcolonial cinemas of the era. Often these various spheres of cultural production overlapped chromatically, as James Tweedie demonstrates in his analysis of the French New Wave. Situating it in relation to the vibrant growth of consumer youth fashion of the time, he notes: "The twin demographic and cinematic new waves joined a cacophony of competing novelties, as the new man and new woman, both refashioned by mass consumption and modern technology, sped through the freshly paved streets of redesigned cities and retreated to just-constructed and furnished suburban apartments," replete with the modern and hypercolored "'nouvelle vague' of product designers and corporations like Roche Bobois and Ligne Roset."[5] The specific case studies presented in the following chapters examine such complex intersections of cultural, aesthetic, and technological factors, taking into account transnational flows, knowledge exchange and transfer, the cyclical and asymmetrical circulation of technology in a global context, as well as the accompanying transformation of color film aesthetics in the postwar decades, primarily of the 1950s, 1960s, and 1970s.

A World of Color

Literature on color cinema has expanded considerably over the past two decades, yet the majority of recent publications have focused historically and theoretically on the United States and Europe.[6] For instance, the technological and stylistic details of Technicolor have been documented and described by historians, yet there has not been an expansive study of the global experience of film color at midcentury when Technicolor gradually expanded into the world's cinemas. Andrew's earlier research usefully charts some of the ideological and cultural issues that Technicolor raised in the postwar French context, and more recently Kirsty Sinclair Dootson and Zhaoyu Zhu have traced parallel issues through Technicolor's adoption in postrevolutionary China.[7] Separately, Dootson has also carried out important work on Technicolor in India.[8] These examples are reflective of recent, growing research into the global history of color cinema, and this volume significantly expands the scope of such scholarship.[9]

Thinking globally about color, the volume's chapters in various degrees draw methodologically from media scholarship on transnationalism and Global South–North flows. The critical turn toward transnationalism, for example, has broadened the study of cinema in relation to the consequences of cross-border activities, from coproductions among different countries, to the ways in which films are complex combinations of local and global expertise, aesthetic values, and diverse cultures of reception. Yet little research has been undertaken on how color was technically relayed around the world through laboratories and official and unofficial distribution channels, or on the varying "languages" and cultural understanding of color that operate outside the Global North. Many of these approaches to color differ markedly from Eurocentric conceptions of aesthetic beauty and appropriate chromatic expression, and indeed color's cultural politics are profoundly ambivalent around the world. As Natasha Eaton has traced in the Indian colonial and postcolonial contexts, color is a "nomadic" force that, as an exploited material commodity, served both the foundation of empire and its dissolution.[10] Conceptualizing global color as an expansive, fluid phenomenon that has been largely formed by transnational exchange constitutes a shift in the field of color film. Chris Berry's observation that an adequate understanding of transnational cinema is "a long project involving different scholars and case studies, including national ones," is apposite for this book's ambition to bring midcentury color cinema centrally into the world frame.[11] Color continues to be a topic of recurrent national and international debate, encompassing critiques of its apparatus within political modernism and postcolonialism, as well as in contemporary debates about the digital restoration of analog color films. Looking to the past and future, the following chapters trace the significance of color within the differing aesthetic sensibilities and material histories of global film cultures.

A Brief History of Color Technologies

Given this book's account of global color technologies, it is important to detail here at the outset some of the key developments in color cinema as context for the technical, economic, and aesthetic transformations of the postwar period. This will also serve as a brief description of many of the technologies and processes that are referenced throughout the coming chapters.

Color was integral to the cinema at its emergence in the late nineteenth century, through hand-colored films such as the Edison Company's *Annabelle Serpentine Dance* (1895) and the Lumière brothers' *Les forgerons* (*The Blacksmiths*, 1895). Manual processes of coloring—hand coloring, stenciling, toning, and especially tinting—were used around the world throughout the silent era, as in the red stenciling found in the animated fragment of *Katsudō Shashin* (Japan, ca. 1907) and in the tinted and toned hues of *The Story of the Kelly Gang* (Charles Tait, Australia, 1906). These techniques have had ongoing uses particularly in the experimental works of filmmakers such as Stan Brakhage and Jodie Mack in the United States, the Colectivo Los Ingrávidos in Mexico, and Ignacio Tamarit in Argentina.

Photographic color systems were also developed during the silent era. Some of the earliest processes, developed primarily in Europe and the United States from the 1890s to the 1910s, were "additive" color systems, such as Friese-Green, Kinemacolor, Prizmacolor, Gaumont Chronochrome, and the initial Technicolor system, Technicolor No. I. Beginning in earnest in the late 1910s, firms such as Technicolor and Prizma also began to develop "subtractive" color systems. Both additive and subtractive processes worked on the same basic principle for filming: capturing two or three color records filmed through filters onto black-and-white negatives through specialized cameras. The difference in the systems pertains to how they subsequently produced a color image. Additive systems developed the color separations into positive black-and-white prints and then relied on a complicated—costly and often finicky—projection apparatus that would reapply the filters onto the alternating frames and composite them on-screen, producing a color image visible only during projection. In contrast, subtractive systems work to create a color image on the positive film print itself, meaning that no special apparatus is necessary for projection. Instead, complex systems of printing were developed to invert the black-and-white records into positive color film prints.

Based on its innovations to the subtractive process, Technicolor rose to prominence in the 1920s and 1930s, particularly with the development of its dye-transfer, "imbibition" method of printing films. Launched in 1927 through its two-color system, the imbibition process was a success, but Technicolor was not able to keep up with the demand for color printing, as there was a global color boom connected to the coming of sound.[12] As the company retooled for the 1930s, it continued developing its system and introduced a three-color process in 1932. Using a newly developed camera that required specialized Technicolor operators, the company was able to capture the image onto three separate negatives that contained the filtered blue, green, and red records. Its lab technicians then developed these and produced printing matrices from the positive records that were used to dye transfer the three color images onto a film print, which already contained a light grayscale image for added contrast, producing the full color image.

Technicolor as well as the other color processes and techniques just described had varying global range, particularly in the first half of the twentieth century. Additive color systems were largely constrained to their countries of origins, due to the technical apparatus needed for exhibition. For instance, Kinemacolor works were filmed and exhibited primarily in the United Kingdom and the United States, though the company had more limited, and largely unsuccessful, operations in countries such as India, France, Germany, Italy, Brazil, Canada, China, and Japan, as Luke McKernan has detailed.[13] Other additive systems had far less range in terms of production and exhibition, and the limitations were relatively parallel for subtractive systems until after the Second World War. For instance, Technicolor sought to expand globally at various points in its history. However, due to its continued reliance on its specialized cameras and operators for filming, as well as the required use of its Color Advisory Service on all productions, the company's global ambitions remained constrained throughout the 1930s and 1940s. It established a laboratory in London in 1936, and once the company became primarily a processing operation in the mid-1950s, further global expansion was attempted, with some degrees of market penetration either directly or indirectly in a number of territories including Italy, India, and China, as Dootson's chapter in this volume details. In this way Technicolor maintained a high profile in the global film market that few other color processes have been able to sustain.

What marks the postwar era is the way in which color technologies become accessible—with many variations and constraints—around the world, leading to color production becoming the global norm by the 1970s. As cheaper 35mm monopack stocks became increasingly available in the 1950s, most significantly Kodak's Eastman Color and the various Agfacolor derivatives, Technicolor's dominance as a filming technology ended, and it transitioned exclusively into postproduction laboratory processing, for negative development and imbibition printing. More than any other factor, the availability of monopack stocks as an affordable option within an expanded global market accelerated color's use across borders during the 1960s. Monopack stocks chromogenically recorded each of the primary colors onto three emulsions layered on a single base. Special cameras were not needed, and in general this made color films less expensive to produce.[14]

Experimentation with high-quality, commercially viable multilayered color film was first achieved by Agfacolor in Germany thorough the introduction of

Agfacolor-Neu in 1936. Though constrained primarily to Germany during the war, the process became the postwar basis for numerous, derivative systems, including ORWO in Wolfen, East Germany; Agfacolor in Leverkusen, West Germany; Gevacolor in Belgium; Anscocolor in the United States; Ferraniacolor in Italy; Svema (aka "Sovcolor") in the Soviet Union; and Fujicolor in Japan. The widespread adoption of the process was a result of postwar reparations, in which the Allied powers took control of Agfa-Filmfabrik in Wolfen in 1945 and by and large nullified its patent holdings. Various Allied intelligence reports on the Agfacolor process were published, making its technical specifications publicly available for adoption throughout most of the world.[15] Each of these variants, while similar, also had its own characteristics that changed over time: the West German Agfa company would merge with Gevaert in 1964, and their Gevacolor process, as well as most other Agfacolor-Neu-based systems such as Fujicolor, eventually transitioned to Kodak Eastman Color formulas.[16]

Eastman Color developed initially in the context of a collaboration between Kodak and Technicolor in the 1930s and 1940s. Kodak at first conceived of it as a quick printing stock that could be integrated as print dailies in the workflow of Technicolor productions. Following antitrust consent decrees with the U.S. Department of Justice in 1948 and 1950 that ended the formal collusion between the two companies, Kodak shifted its plans and introduced Eastman Color camera negative and print stocks in 1950. Eastman Color negatives could be used either in conjunction with Technicolor printing or printed onto less stable Eastman Color positive stock, and a number of technical improvements followed over the next decades, including reduced graininess and increased speed and sensitivity, as well as intermediate stocks for print duplication.[17] In terms of corporate branding, following its antitrust consent decree, Kodak did not initially brand its stock publicly as Eastman Color, leading to variations in its nomenclature: it was primarily referred to as Eastman Color internally at Kodak, but some laboratories, as well as critical sources, have frequently referred to it as Eastmancolor. Further, Kodak did not provide color processing services at its plants. Instead, it made the developing process public to encourage more widespread adoption among external laboratories, and as a result, many early Eastman Color films do not credit the process; for instance, Technicolor is often listed instead if its dye-transfer system had been used for printing. This did not necessarily hamper uptake, and most of the world's film industries—some more easily than others—were persuaded by the comparative ease with which these new monopack film stocks could be used for color productions.

As the following chapters make clear, technical developments in color are only a partial factor in the global surge in color cinema during the postwar era. A range of intermedial, cultural, and ideological currents also profoundly shaped color in global cinemas. As Andrew and Tweedie earlier illustrated, emerging postwar ideologies as well as new cultures of consumption greatly influenced the adoption of monopack technologies. How such factors played out beyond

France—and beyond Europe and North America—is a central concern throughout this volume, not only for the parallel histories they trace but also for the differences that emerge. For example, as Richard Dyer, Lorna Roth, Brian Winston, and others have demonstrated, moving image technologies have throughout the twentieth century embedded racial biases into their analog emulsions, as the companies and laboratories that developed them by and large prioritized the accurate reproduction of Caucasian complexions over those of people of color.[18] How this technical White bias affected the adoption and adaptation of monopack technologies in the Global South, in particular, is of concern across a number of the ensuing chapters. Finally, with regard to the intermedial dimension of color, the monopack revolution in postwar global cinemas was competitively driven by the parallel emergence of color television and colorcasting, as Susan Murray delineates in her groundbreaking *Bright Signals: A History of Color Television*.[19] The chromatic transformation of both cinema and television at midcentury was emblematic of the broader postwar landscape, steeped as it was in the alluring glamour of the culture industry, as well as in the radical hues of the new countercultures, psychedelia, and postcolonial formations.

Chapters

Beginning the volume, Kirsty Sinclair Dootson's chapter provides a comparative account of Technicolor's international reach through its postwar focus on color print processing from 1955 onward. Examining specifically the expansion of Technicolor's laboratories in France, Italy, India, and China, the chapter explores how Technicolor's renowned look and accompanying cultural values were translated across different national film styles during the era. Taking a similarly comparative approach, Josephine Diecke examines the research protocols and technical objectives in operation at Agfa's Wolfen plant during the postwar era, when it continued to operate as Agfa until rebranding as ORWO in 1964. Drawing from the company's extensive corporate records, the chapter delineates its negotiation between international standards of color quality with the prioritization of keeping its film stock affordable. This emphasis on affordability allowed for its adoption not only throughout the Eastern Bloc but also in non-aligned film markets such as India.

How color was received in different national contexts is foregrounded in many of the chapters, particularly debates on the relative merits and drawbacks of using color. In Sweden, Technicolor experienced problems in gaining acceptance. As Kamalika Sanyal's chapter details, in the early 1950s Gevacolor was for a brief time preferred as the most aesthetically pleasing stock, before Eastman Color became the dominant process. The chapter discusses the production and reception of several color films made in the 1940s and 1950s, bringing to light how Swedish critics and audiences often struggled to appreciate color. In a different context, Philip Cavendish's chapter on the Soviet Union, from 1956 to 1982, demonstrates a growing acceptance of color beginning in the 1960s. Cavendish shows how attempts to develop Soviet color stock were accompanied by many remarkable examples, particularly color adaptations of fables that were indicative of symbiotic relationships with fine and decorative arts traditions. Once again, their legacy can be discerned in subsequent color films, such as those produced by Andrei Tarkovsky. In India the import of Eastman Color stock had a lasting, remarkable impact in the 1960s. Ranjani Mazumdar's chapter discusses the aesthetic consequences, particularly for cinematographers and art directors who made a transition from black and white to color. Mazumdar argues that Bombay cinema of the decade expressed a remarkable "transnational imagination" that galvanized international and domestic tourism's imaginative force. Shifting to Italy, Elena Gipponi examines the postwar youth genre of beach movies. Her chapter tracks how these films played a pivotal role in the large-scale conversion from black and white to color in Italian cinema in the early 1960s through various film stocks and processes (e.g., Ferraniacolor, Technicolor No. V Eastman Color, and various wide-screen color stocks such as Totalscope, Dyaliscope, and Technirama). The color transition in Italy occurred from below, through low-brow production and minor popular genres that also drew attention to Italian modernization and the so-called economic miracle, exemplified in these films through the expansion of consumer culture and colored goods and materials.

Use of color by regimes such as the People's Republic of China in the 1950s involved debates about color's relationship to both realism and spectacle. Linda Zhang's chapter uses *Woman Basketball Player No. 5* (*Nülan Wuhao* 女蓝5号), directed by Xie Jin in 1957, as a case study that illuminates the development of domestic stock, which was used to celebrate technology and the regime's political ideology. Knowledge about the history of color films in China has been expanded considerably through archival initiatives such as the acquisition in 2009 of the Chinese Film Collection by the University of South Carolina. Heather Heckman, Laura Major, and Lydia Pappas analyze how the collection, transferred from the Washington, DC, embassy of the People's Republic of China, can be seen as "a project of cultural diplomacy" in which a specific selection of films nevertheless expands our understanding of various genres' aesthetic use of color. The chapter also presents case studies in the work involved in the films' preservation, as well as issues regarding dubbing, subtitling, and translation. William Carroll's chapter examines how neon light, captured using optical color, was featured to striking effect in Nikkatsu Studio's action films in Japan from 1957 to 1963. Shot in Eastman Color, these popular films brought a unique color aesthetic to the crime genre, which showcased the neon brilliance of Japanese cities in the postwar era. The chapter comments on the films' popularity in Hong Kong in the 1960s and their influence on subsequent uses of neon as captured by optical color techniques.

As several chapters demonstrate, the broad acceptance of color cinema was connected to cultures of reception as critics debated the levels of apparent visual accuracy and aesthetic impact of color films. The history of color film production and reception in Brazil is detailed in Rafael de Luna Freire's chapter. Tracing its "slow and stuttering" adoption in the 1950s and 1960s, the chapter examines both fiction and short documentary films—many of which fall into the category of useful cinema—that pioneered the use of color, as well as their critical reception in the press. Important to this account is the parallel emergence of formal and informal distribution channels of color stock in Brazil, as well as the development of Brazilian film laboratories at that time, which aided in the transformation of the Brazilian film industry. Continuing an emphasis on critical reception, Sarah Street uses Britain as a case study where critics reviewed an increasing number of color films from different countries as they became more widely circulated at film festivals. Viewing and writing about a greater number of color films brought out the varieties of screen color experimentation, challenging both critics and filmmakers to extend their descriptive vocabularies and aesthetic designs.

Color films have always shared intermedial affinities with other arts. As Kathryn Millard and Stefan Solomon discuss, this was particularly the case in Australia. Their chapter develops a set of observations through documentary, feature, and experimental films that showcase "natural color" in a particular way. This involved using color to depict the Australian landscape by drawing on traditions of Australian painting. The natural environment was a key variable in both testing and presenting color film, and specific Australian contexts were highly significant. Continuing an intermedial focus, Gregory Zinman's chapter also examines art and experimental film, specifically with regard to color field painting and the works of Paul Sharits. Focusing on the functions of monochromatic color in painting and film at midcentury, Zinman explores how these works reflected on the nature of perception, space-time relationships, and the interconnections of media. As the chapter explores, color field aesthetics are not just relevant in these historical works but also open up productive ways for thinking about contemporary, experimental digital media.

The political aesthetics of Black color design are brought out in Joshua Yumibe's chapter on African and African diasporic cinemas. Here postcolonial and diasporic color expression is remarkable and diverse, challenging color's colonial history and Western-dominated ideological associations. Through several case studies, the chapter discusses how "vivid" color works to denaturalize the primitivist prescripts of aesthetic theory while radically coding and recoding the history of chromatic Blackness.

In making these interventions into the study of global color films, the chapters interconnect even as they detail markedly diverse, midcentury cultures of production and reception as color became the dominant practice in world cinemas. The potentials of chromatic expression within genre, art, experimental, and useful cinemas are examined in detail across various national contexts.

Circulating through the studies are repeating concerns about the hegemony and politicization of color, often as an imported technology, as well as about the unequal access and technological capability regarding various chromatic processes. Covering a broad range of perspectives, the volume centers debates about transnational flows, knowledge exchange and transfer, and the asymmetrical access and circulation of film stocks, as each of the chapters traces new directions in color film aesthetics that radically transformed the moving image in various national and regional contexts. As such, color serves here as a microcosm through which to examine and reframe the broader changes that cinema underwent in the increasingly globalized, and simultaneously fractured, media environment of midcentury.

Notes

1 David Edgerton, *The Shock of the Old: Technology and Global History since 1900* (London: Profile Books, 2006), xii.
2 For a useful discussion of contemporary media flows and postcolonial "hacks," see Amit S. Rai, *Jugaad Time: Ecologies of Everyday Hacking in India* (Durham, NC: Duke University Press, 2019).
3 Dudley Andrew, "The Postwar Struggle for Color," *Cinema Journal* 18, no. 2 (1979): 41–52.
4 Andrew, 51.
5 James Tweedie, *The Age of New Waves: Art Cinema and the Staging of Globalization* (New York: Oxford University Press, 2013), 13–14.
6 For instance, see Christine Brinckmann, *Color and Empathy: Essays on Two Aspects of Film* (Amsterdam: Amsterdam University Press, 2015); Scott Higgins, *Harnessing the Technicolor Rainbow: Color Design in the 1930s* (Austin: University of Texas Press, 2007); Federico Pierotti, *La Seduzione Dello Spettro: Storia e Cultura Del Colore Nel Cinema* (Recco, Italy: Le Mani Edizioni, 2012); Sarah Street and Joshua Yumibe, *Chromatic Modernity: Color, Cinema, and Media of the 1920s* (New York: Columbia University Press, 2019); Sarah Street, Keith M. Johnston, Paul Frith, and Carolyn Rickards, *Colour Films in Britain: The Eastmancolor Revolution* (London: British Film Institute/Bloomsbury, 2021).
7 Kirsty Sinclair Dootson and Zhaoyu Zhu, "Did Madame Mao Dream in Technicolor? Rethinking Cold War Colour Cinema through Technicolor's 'Chinese Copy,'" *Screen* 61, no. 3 (Autumn 2020): 343–367.
8 Kirsty Sinclair Dootson, *The Rainbow's Gravity: Colour, Materiality and British Modernity* (New Haven, Conn.: Paul Mellon Centre for the Study of British Art, 2023), 113–145.
9 See also, for example, the articles collected in Margaret Hillenbrand, ed., "Special Issue on the Colour of Chinese Cinemas," *Journal of Chinese Cinemas* 6, no. 3 (January 1, 2012); and in Elena Gipponi and Joshua Yumibe, eds., "Cinema and Mid-century Colour Culture," special issue, *Cinéma&Cie* 19, no. 32 (Spring 2019).
10 Natasha Eaton, *Colour, Art and Empire: Visual Culture and the Nomadism of Representation* (London: I. B. Tauris, 2013), 1–14.
11 Chris Berry, "What Is Transnational Cinema? Thinking from the Chinese Situation," *Transnational Cinemas* 2, no. 2 (2010): 111–127.

12 See especially James Layton and David Pierce's account in *The Dawn of Technicolor: 1915–1935*, ed. Paolo Cherchi Usai and Catherine A. Surowiec (Rochester, NY: George Eastman House, 2015), 149–157.

13 Luke McKernan, *Charles Urban: Pioneering Non-fiction Film in Britain and America, 1897–1925* (Exeter, UK: University of Exeter Press, 2013), 111, 142.

14 See Street et al., *Colour Films in Britain*, 108.

15 See Josephine Diecke, "Agfacolor in (Inter)National Competition," in *Color Mania: The Material of Color in Photography and Film*, ed. Barbara Flückiger, Eva Hielscher, and Nadine Wietlisbach (Zurich: Lars Müller, 2020), 211–221. For the public reports prepared by the British Intelligence Objectives Subcommittee (BIOS), the Combined Intelligence Objectives Subcommittee (CIOS), and the American Field Information Agency, Technical (FIAT), see, for example, Wilhelm Schneider, *The Agfacolor process: FIAT Final Report 976* (Washington, DC: Office of Military Government for Germany, 1949); and William M. Harcourt, *Agfa Colour*, Report No. 397, Item No. 9 (London: H.M. Stationery Office, British Intelligence Objectives Sub-Committee, 1946).

16 Diecke, "Agfacolor in (Inter)National Competition," 214.

17 See details on Eastman Color in the "Technical Appendix" in Street et al., *Colour Films in Britain*, 316–329; as well as in Heather Heckman, "We've Got Bigger Problems: Preservation during Eastman Color's Innovation and Early Diffusion," *Moving Image* 15, no. 1 (March 22, 2015): 44–62. We are grateful to Heckman for further clarifications on the process.

18 Richard Dyer, *White*, Twentieth Anniversary Edition (New York: Routledge, 2017), 82–103; Lorna Roth, "Looking at Shirley, the Ultimate Norm: Colour Balance, Image Technologies, and Cognitive Equity," *Canadian Journal of Communication* 34, no. 1 (March 30, 2009): 111–136; Brian Winston, *Technologies of Seeing: Photography, Cinematography and Television* (London: BFI Publishing, 1996), 39–57.

19 Susan Murray, *Bright Signals: A History of Color Television* (Durham, NC: Duke University Press, 2018).

1

Mapping the Laboratory

Technicolor across Asia and Europe

KIRSTY SINCLAIR DOOTSON

Technicolor's brand is synonymous with American visual culture. Associated with classical Hollywood film from 1935 to 1955, three-strip Technicolor is indelibly linked to the stylistic character of that era's cinema. With its rich palette of intense saturation, produced through a combination of three-strip photography and dye-transfer printing, Technicolor connotes the lustrous extravagances of the studio era, with its vivid chromatic spectacles. Yet an advertisement for Technicolor from 1954 troubles some of these assumptions (figure 1.1). The promotion advises customers on how to appropriately credit Technicolor in twenty-six different languages listed on the right of the page. Red lines connect these Technicolor credits in Arabic, Japanese, Thai, and Serbian to disparate spots on the globe suspended at the page's center. Technicolor's trademark is emblazoned across the page in a bold yellow, which pops against the blue of the North and South Atlantic Oceans. Further lines curve and swirl around the earth, perhaps indicating the global flow of Technicolor films to locations beyond the United States. Indeed, the earth is pivoted so that the West Coast of the United States is hidden from view. The intense primaries certainly tie the image to Technicolor's Hollywood palette, and the advertisement could be interpreted as evidence of Hollywood's continued global domination in the post–World War II

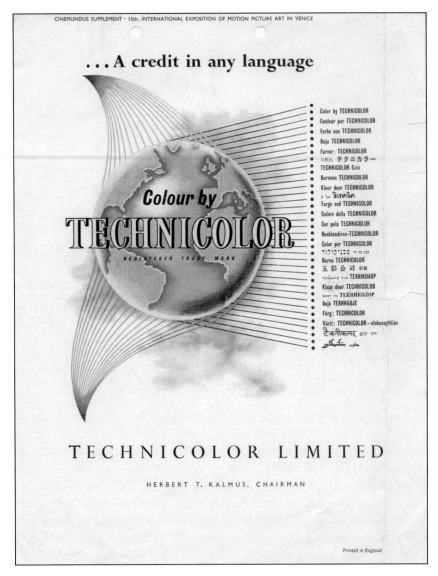

FIGURE 1.1 Trade advertisement for Technicolor Limited, 1954. (Courtesy George Eastman Museum. With permission of Technicolor Creative Studios.)

period. Yet I suggest that rather than reinforcing Technicolor's American accent, it invites us to consider how "Technicolor" was translated into different film languages.

Perhaps Hollywood is concealed because the advertisement is for Technicolor Limited, the British wing of the firm established outside London in 1936. Technicolor Limited was one of the company's European laboratories established as part of a scheme of international expansion begun in the 1930s, which accelerated in the postwar period with branches in France and Italy. At the same time, Technicolor planned laboratories in Argentina, Japan, and India, with executives forecasting in 1954 that "the spread of the Technicolor process throughout the world is inevitable."[1] This did not mean the spread of Technicolor's three-strip photographic process, however, which concluded in 1955, but the creation of an international network of color processing plants, referred to in official reports as "one global laboratory."[2]

Such confidence in Technicolor's future global domination runs counter to conventional histories of the firm, which typically conclude in 1955 with the retirement of Technicolor's three-strip cameras.[3] In 1955, Technicolor supposedly "died," defeated by the release of Kodak's Eastman Color system in 1952, as well as the other chromogenic monopack processes emerging around the world following the dispersal of Germany's Agfa patents.[4] However, the postwar period saw a global expansion of Technicolor's activities. As Bernard Happé, the technical director of Technicolor Limited, attested: "[The laboratory] side of the business was in no way diminished by the withdrawal of the three-strip cameras and in fact output increased substantially with the wider use of color by more production studios."[5] No longer restricted to processing material shot with its limited number of beam-splitting cameras, Technicolor's laboratories could now use the dye-transfer process, also known as dye imbibition or "IB," to manufacture prints from any chromogenic camera materials—a process known as Technicolor No. V.[6] This lent a clear economic rationale to Technicolor's global expansion. With the company eager to capitalize on growing international color markets and to jettison its costly three-strip cameras, the postwar decades promised a new era of global prosperity for Technicolor as a laboratory service.

Technicolor's attempts to disseminate process No. V. on a global scale throughout Europe, Asia, and South America from the mid-1950s therefore complicates a neat equation of the process with Hollywood cinema of the classical era. Rather than viewing 1955 as the end of Technicolor's American monopoly, I instead take it as the moment when Technicolor entered into an unprecedented period of international exchange and negotiation with film industries around the world, expanding the global ambitions of the firm beyond its forays into Europe in the interwar years. I therefore begin where most Technicolor histories end, taking 1955 as a point of departure for investigating the global spread of its laboratory network in the postwar period.

At stake in this reformulation of Technicolor's history is a complication of the typical associations between the technology and a particular set of cultural and political values ascribed to its brand and aesthetic. While the process was used to create a host of visual styles and by no means determined a uniform look, Technicolor, with its close association with the commercial glitz of classical Hollywood, quickly became essentialized as a byword for gawdy, vivid color and ideas of chromatic superfluity.[7] This essentialized identity also harnessed the process to a singular ideological agenda of American superficiality and capitalist consumerism. The capacity of Technicolor's process to forge idealized and glamorized flights from reality, which lent a gloss to celebrations of spectacular excess, meant it became indelibly associated with Hollywood's ideological program. Despite the range of aesthetics possible with Technicolor, the process therefore become reductively yoked to a Hollywood mode of color design and to American cultural values. Particularly in the Cold War, when Technicolor's brilliance was rhetorically opposed to the more muted hues of the Agfa derivatives favored by socialist nations, Technicolor's process carried potent ideological connotations that cemented its connections to the values of the capitalist West.[8]

Considering Technicolor's expansion into different geopolitical contexts enables an appreciation of the mutability of its meanings, which were by no means fixed. Far from simply exporting American cinematic values overseas, Technicolor's international laboratories became sites of negotiation for urgent postwar issues, including imperialism (of both a cultural and a political nature), decolonization, and political self-determination, in addition to the ideological struggles of the Cold War. But more than simply suggesting that the meanings ascribed to Technicolor's process were contingent on geographic context, I am interested in how the dispersal of the firm's technology around the world forged transnational connections between film industries, as materials, machinery, and personnel moved between these contexts. That the global spread of Technicolor's laboratory process demanded exchange and collaboration between different nations complicates any strictly nationalistic interpretation of color film in this era.

In this chapter I examine the internationalization of Technicolor's laboratory network between 1955 and 1993, to argue that the multiple meanings of Technicolor's identity were produced through this translation of the technology into different geographic, political, and cultural spheres, as well as collaboration and contact between these labs. I am equally invested in Technicolor's failed laboratory projects as in its successful ones, as these unrealized plants reveal the different social and political determinants circumscribing color cinema in these regions. What follows is therefore as much a geography as a history, organized by region rather than adhering to a strict chronology. By forging a map of Technicolor's operations, I am able not only to record the movement of Technicolor's system around the world in the past, but also chart territories ripe for scholarly exploration in the future. I draw on research about Technicolor in China, India, Scandinavia, Russia, and Britain, while highlighting the need for further work on its attempted expansion into South America and East Asia.[9] As in the Technicolor advertisement from 1954, I map the firm's operations and show how the meaning of "Technicolor" could be translated in different global film languages; unlike the advertisement, however, I suggest that it by no means carried a singular definition.

European Expansion: Société Technicolor and Technicolor Italiana

The year 1955 was a pivotal one for Technicolor. The period following the conclusion of the Second World War saw increased color film production, which boosted Technicolor's laboratory business over the subsequent decade. However, the global release of new chromogenic stocks, as well as industrial shifts toward wide-screen formats from 1953, rendered Technicolor's fleet of beam-splitting cameras obsolete. Studios were delighted their shooting schedules were no longer dictated by the availability of Technicolor cameras, and that their work would not be scrutinized by Technicolor's infamous Color Advisory Service. But Technicolor also benefited by retiring its cameras, which operated at a loss that was only recuperated by the extreme cost efficiencies of dye-transfer printing.[10] From 1955, Technicolor could therefore concentrate on the laboratory services, which had always been its primary source of income.[11]

This decision was partly motivated by the 1947 antitrust suit brought by the American government against Technicolor and Kodak.[12] For years these firms conspired to control the color film industry by cultivating artificial scarcity and keeping monopack stock from the open market. Although Kodak had produced a viable monopack stock by 1934, the firm signed an agreement with Technicolor to release it only for amateur use. This ensured Technicolor continued to dominate professional color work and to generate profits for Kodak, as Technicolor consumed vast quantities of Kodak materials. The antitrust suit tackled this collusion, forcing Kodak to make chromogenic monopack widely available, thus allowing filmmakers greater choice of laboratory for color processing. However, the government's intervention benefited Technicolor and Kodak in ways that were becoming apparent by 1955.

By this time Kodak had released Eastman Color on the open market, but the company was still profiting from the sale of materials to Technicolor, while Technicolor, following the retirement of its camera division, could focus on its lucrative laboratory services. Far from sounding the firm's death knell, 1955 signaled the beginning of a prosperous new era of Technicolor process No. V, manufacturing IB prints from chromogenic negatives. This involved the laboratory using filters to split a single camera negative into three individual gelatin matrices, which could be charged with yellow, cyan, and magenta dyes, respectively, and then transferred to a blank strip of film to recompose the full-color image. IB printing offered an advantageous economy of scale because, unlike with chromogenic printing, the only stage that involved costly and complex photochemical processing was the production of the matrices—once these were manufactured, it was possible to produce large numbers of release prints at very low cost as the colors were simply pressed onto the blank mechanically. Technicolor therefore continued to exploit both the color control and the cost

FIGURE 1.2 Trade advertisement for Technicolor showing their American and European branches, produced for the Venice Film Festival, 1950s. (Courtesy George Eastman Museum. With permission of Technicolor Creative Studios.)

efficiencies offered by IB printing, a technique so economical that laboratory workers described it as "a license to print money."[13]

This focus on processing encouraged the firm to embark on a scheme of global laboratory expansion, as overseas plants presented numerous benefits both for Technicolor and the domestic film industries they served (figure 1.2). For Technicolor these labs increased their access to overseas markets, enabling the circumvention of import tariffs and legal restrictions designed to protect certain national film industries, and also reduced shipping costs, while for foreign film industries these laboratories meant high-quality domestic processing, fewer delays, cheap release prints, and skilled employment for local economies.[14] This scheme marked a continuation of Technicolor's earlier European expansion in the interwar years, when it had planned a Berlin laboratory but failed to find investment, and had successfully opened its London plant in 1936.[15] In 1955 Technicolor continued to grow in Europe, opening its Parisian laboratory

Société Technicolor in Joinville-le-Pont, and establishing Technicolor Italiana in Rome, which was operational by 1959. These plants were intended to manufacture release prints of both American and domestic color films for distribution in Western Europe. But the French and Italian laboratories fared very differently; Société Technicolor closed within three years due to debts, while Technicolor Italiana's IB unit thrived until 1978. There are numerous reasons that could account for these disparities.

Although the French plant was 51 percent owned by French shareholders, including Pathé-Gaumont's GTC laboratory, there was resistance from within the French film industry even before the laboratory opened.[16] With France's strong protectionist policies for domestic filmmaking, particularly against American incursion, it is unsurprising that a 1953 report by the Commission Supérieure Technique argued Technicolor's expansion in France would retard the development of new, domestic processing and damage existing French color laboratories. The report maintained that the Parisian Technicolor plant would place the industry in a position of inferiority, as France would be using an outdated technology while other nations evolved new techniques for chromogenic processing.[17] Such anxieties could only have been exacerbated by the fact that half the laboratory's output consisted of American pictures for European distribution.

This speaks to the wider cultural and ideological reasons that resulted in the Joinville plant's failure. Following the conclusion of the war and France's saturation with Hollywood films, the French film industry grew increasingly antagonistic to American intervention, and Technicolor was viewed as part of Hollywood's plans for European colonization. Dudley Andrew has argued that in postwar France, an ideological opposition to American cultural imperialism was therefore articulated through an aesthetic distaste for Technicolor's supposedly gaudy palette.[18] The preference of French filmmakers for the muted, subtler hues of Agfa derivatives like Belgian Gevacolor connoted a political position of anti-Americanism as much as an aesthetic bias, and possibly accounts for the failure of the Société Technicolor to secure sufficient work to become viable.

By 1958, Technicolor closed the Parisian laboratory, as shareholders could not recoup investments in the face of debts totaling 450 million francs.[19] However, Herbert Kalmus suggested the failure of the plant had less to do with the French film industry than its Hollywood counterpart. Because American films accounted for half the Parisian laboratory's work, the downturn in color production in America (triggered by wide-screen systems, independent production, and smaller budgets) meant less work for the European Technicolor laboratories.[20] While the British laboratory remained buoyant through its distribution networks in the British Empire, and the Italian laboratory had a robust slate of domestic work, the French laboratory, located in a territory with heightened resistance to American film and a lack of support from the domestic industry, failed to withstand this downturn.

The year after the French plant closed, the Italian laboratory began generating profits. Its establishment was incentivized by new import taxes on foreign films in Italy, which could be circumnavigated through a domestic processing laboratory, but there was also much domestic work to sustain the plant.[21] British technicians suspected that the lower cost of labor also made Italy an attractive location, as ongoing union disputes with the London laboratory may have encouraged Technicolor to seek a cheaper European alternative.[22] Indeed, by the 1960s Technicolor Italiana was intruding upon the British laboratory's market, distributing prints to eighteen countries across Europe, Africa, and Asia.[23]

Technicolor Italiana's success was partially marked through its significant diversification for Technicolor's operations, as the laboratory excelled in developing new techniques, including the Technirama wide-screen process, and the ENR developing process, which enabled richer blacks and drastic desaturation (departing from Technicolor's historical associations).[24] However, the laboratory also became a site where filmmakers developed new expressive applications for the conventional look of IB prints. For instance, in Dario Argento's iconic *giallo* film *Suspiria* (Italy, 1977), one of the last films made using Italy's dye-transfer unit and produced in close collaboration with the laboratory, the brilliant saturation of the process was exaggerated to heighten the film's hysteria. Inspired by Disney's Technicolor animation *Snow White and the Seven Dwarfs* (William Cottrell and David Hand, U.S., 1937), the film transforms the bold primaries of Technicolor's palette from the joyful hues of a children's fairy tale into a nightmarish vision by exacerbating the intensity of their juxtapositions. Appropriately for this gory title, the laboratory adjusted the IB process to let the colors "bleed."[25] By reinterpreting the affective impact of Technicolor's vivid palette, *Suspiria* exemplifies how filmmakers used Technicolor's heritage look for innovative ends in different geographic, historical, and generic contexts, creating new hybrid color styles through the international circulation of the process. Moreover, it suggests Technicolor's decentralized laboratory network created spaces for aesthetic experimentation that would be impossible if all materials were processed centrally through the Hollywood plant.

Despite the eventual success of the Roman laboratory, Italy was not considered Technicolor's priority for international expansion. From the mid-1950s, Technicolor articulated its ambitions to grow beyond Europe and North America, reporting plans to establish laboratories in Buenos Aires and Tokyo.[26] These plans were undoubtedly motivated by the expansion of color production in territories where Technicolor hoped to stake claims. The company acknowledged that "the spread of Technicolor all over the world must prevent the spread of some other color process with accompanying solidification of our position everywhere," and it is very likely that its international diversification was driven by competition from within other domestic film industries.[27]

It is possible that Argentina's shift into color with the Ferraniacolor feature *Lo que le pasó a Reynoso* (*What Happened at Reynoso*, Leopoldo Torres Ríos, 1955) prompted Technicolor's interest in this market, as well as increased American location shooting across South America, which the firm saw as "the 'good neighbor' policy ... being advanced visually through the medium of color by Technicolor."[28] In Japan, Toyo Laboratory's move into Eastman Color processing in 1953 with the release of *Jigokumon* (*Gate of Hell*, Kinugasa Teinosuke, 1953) may have similarly aroused Technicolor's ambitions to expand in the region.[29] As Jasper Sharp notes, Toyo's laboratory in Tokyo attracted sufficient color work to expand into a second plant in Kyoto by 1955, processing films made all over East Asia, and Technicolor would have been eager to capitalize on this burgeoning market.[30] It is unclear how far these plans advanced, however, particularly as it was not Japan or Argentina but India that was cited as a top priority for the firm's global expansion in the 1950s.[31] Yet several factors made Technicolor's attempted entry into India particularly fraught, despite great enthusiasm from the domestic industry.

Technicolor's Agents in India: Ramnord Research Laboratories

The circumstances of Technicolor's planned expansion in India are complicated by the political situation in the early decades of Indian independence from British colonial rule, which ended in 1947. By the 1950s, India was in a unique position as a newly independent nation that was also home to the world's second-largest film industry. Color was important both as an instrument for self-representation and as a symbol of prestige, but India had produced only a small number of color features to date.[32] Technicolor saw the potential in this new market, and by 1952 a headline in Technicolor's in-house journal claimed, "India Called Active Field for Technicolor."[33]

The Indian press excitedly discussed this opportunity, noting an Indian Technicolor laboratory would "obviate the necessity of processing Technicolor films in London or in Hollywood."[34] The proposed laboratory would make India less reliant on Britain, important economically, as foreign exchange was strictly controlled, and politically, as the nation was forging its independent identity.[35] Indeed, color laboratories were identified as crucial for a self-sufficient national film industry in a 1951 advisory report for the Indian government.[36] The report lamented India's lack of high-grade photographic chemicals and printing machines, urging development in this area.[37] India's broadcasting minister therefore held talks to discuss a possible new Bombay lab with Technicolor's Kay Harrison, who also addressed a film seminar headed by Prime Minister Nehru on his 1955 trip to the subcontinent.[38]

While the French industry had seen a Technicolor laboratory as a form of cultural imperialism, for the Indian industry, eager to modernize and globalize at this time, it could celebrate the nation's new independence. In India the color laboratory become a site for negotiating new postcolonial identities, particularly because color had been so central to the British regime in India, where the brutal extraction of dyes, pigments, and textiles had fueled the economy of empire.[39] The heightened political salience of color in Anglo-Indian relations is important to remember when considering the British Technicolor laboratory continued to print Indian color films throughout the 1950s, including Mehboob Khan's *Aan* (*Savage Princess*, 1952) and *Mother India* (1957), as well as V. Shantaram's *Jhanak Payal Baaje* (1955) and *Navrang* (1959).[40] Establishing a Technicolor laboratory in India would not only economize on costs and reduce delays but also restore the control over color to Indian filmmakers.

This combination of political and technological factors made Technicolor's attempted expansion in India extremely delicate. As Technicolor executives noted in 1956, the Swadeshi movement of protectionist policies established by the Indian government (to weaken Britain's economic power in India) made it difficult for foreign companies to operate there if their business threatened a local trade.[41] Technicolor was concerned that, given the new availability of monopack technologies, domestic color processing would soon emerge in India. Indeed, by 1952 Ambalal Patel, the chief importer of Gevacolor stock in India, had established a plant for processing the material in Bombay. *Pamposh* (*Lotus of Kashmir*, 1953), the debut Indian film made with the process and directed by Ezra Mir, had also received acclaim at the 1954 Cannes Film Festival.[42] Technicolor was eager to establish itself in India before Patel's business gained sufficient momentum to prevent Technicolor's intrusion into the market. Technicolor also needed to offer something unavailable at local laboratories, namely, its IB process, to ensure it could compete without government interference through the Swadeshi system.

However, there was also hesitancy about establishing an Indian IB plant when the future scale of color production in the country was undetermined. Technicolor executives expressed concern that India might not generate sufficient business to warrant the expensive establishment of a laboratory there.[43] One solution was to establish three-strip cinematography in India, thereby utilizing the cameras made obsolete by monopack stock, stimulating Indian color production, and offering Technicolor a way of "keeping the door open until the potentialities of this growing market can be better assessed."[44] Technicolor had already begun experimenting with domestic three-strip production in India from the early 1950s. Films, including the international coproduction of Jean Renoir's *The River* (1951) and Sohrab Modi's *Jhansi Ki Rani* (1953), operated as training grounds for Indian film workers eager to learn this specialized process.[45] The Indian cinematographers who worked on *The River* (Ramananda Sengupta) and *Jhansi Ki Rani* (M. N. Malhotra and Y. D. Sarpotdar) trained at Technicolor in London, a precedent followed by cinematographers Radhu Karmakar and V. K. Murthy.[46] This transnational exchange of expertise complicates any strict division between European, American, and Indian conceptions of color, underscoring how these new kinds of international Technicolor pictures were produced through the productive contact between these industries.

The first domestically produced three-strip Technicolor film in India, *Jhansi Ki Rani*, for example, told the story of India's first war of independence, underscoring how this color technology could be used to articulate a new sense of freedom from British colonial control. However, the film was printed at the London Technicolor laboratory, which had also trained the cameramen, and numerous British Technicolor experts also worked on the production.[47] This scenario highlights the complexity of geopolitical considerations here, proving Priya Jaikumar's assertion that the reductive labels of "hegemonic versus resistant" film practices overlook the productive negotiation of multiple political and aesthetic forces at work.[48] For instance, the vivid shades of red used throughout *Jhansi Ki Rani* are indicators of Britain's imperial control of the country, displayed on uniforms, maps and flags, but also celebratory facets of Hindu culture when used in the rani's wedding ritual. These colors were the product of Indian cameramen, designers, and technicians working in Bombay, as well as laboratory staff working in England; they were symbols of freedom and liberation but also of a continuation of Britain's exploitation of Indian color as a source of income.

In 1956, three years after the Indian release of *Jhansi Ki Rani*, Technicolor Limited signed an agreement with Ramnord Research Laboratories of Bombay appointing them "Agents of Technicolor."[49] The aim was to use this local laboratory for "front end" services until the local market grew sufficiently competitive, at which point Ramnord would expand into IB printing. Until then, Ramnord would process chromogenic negatives and send them to London for dye-transfer printing, ensuring Britain retained a foothold in the Indian market during this growth period.[50] This resulted in color credits like those found in the opening titles of the hugely successful *Gunga Jumna* (Nitin Bose, 1961), which states that the film was "Processed at Technicolor Ltd. London through Ramnord Research Labs. Ltd. Bombay" (figures 1.3 and 1.4). The dazzling palette that became synonymous with Hindi cinema in the 1960s (discussed in this volume by Ranjani Mazumdar) was therefore partially facilitated through Technicolor's IB process, before domestic chromogenic processing became the norm.

This planned Bombay IB laboratory never emerged, however, as Technicolor decided that India, which produced fewer than ten color features a year by the early 1960s, presented insufficient work to justify the construction of a dye-transfer plant.[51] Furthermore, by this time there were three Indian laboratories capable of domestic chromogenic processing when Gemini in Madras added its services to those offered by Film Center and Ramnord. Subsequent plans in the 1970s to open a dye-transfer facility in Madras also never moved beyond the initial planning stages.[52] However, it was East Asia rather than South Asia that would host a new IB processing plant in this decade.

FIGURE 1.3 Opening credits to *Gunga Jumna* (Nitin Bose, India, 1961, reproduced in black and white).

FIGURE 1.4 *Gunga Jumna* (Nitin Bose, India, 1961).

Technicolor's "Chinese Copy": The Beijing Film Laboratory

As a result of declining print runs, Technicolor retired its IB machines in Hollywood in 1975 and in London and Rome in 1978. However, 1978 was also the year China manufactured its first IB prints at the Beijing Film Laboratory. While this was not an official Technicolor laboratory operating under the firm's formal trademark, Technicolor had manufactured the laboratory's equipment and trained the laboratory staff, forging what was described as a "Chinese Copy" of Technicolor's process, offering yet another example of hybrid and transnational practice.[53]

China first approached the British laboratory in 1971 when a delegation of officials traveled to London to discuss purchasing its printing system, and by 1973 Technicolor Limited had been contracted to construct a dye-transfer plant in Beijing. The Chinese government was interested in Technicolor's IB process because the system offered an ideal solution to the challenges posed by its film industry during the Cultural Revolution (1966–1976). During this time filmmaking was entirely state operated, and primarily limited to producing filmed recordings of the *yangbanxi*, or eight revolutionary model stage works. These colorful performances of opera and ballet were explicit propaganda vehicles for promoting Maoist ideology across China, which glamorized and spectacularized the revolutionary ideology of the Communist Party.[54] While China had a long history of color filmmaking (discussed in Linda Zhang's chapter in this volume) and various technologies at its disposal, Technicolor's IB system would enable the government to cheaply mass-produce these dazzling films in unparalleled quality for distribution all over China.

This desire to adapt Technicolor's process was not simply practical but profoundly symbolic at a time when color technologies were politically freighted during the Cold War. While Technicolor's process may have seemed incompatible with the demands of the socialist film industry through its associations with capitalist America and Hollywood spectacle, this was precisely what made it so desirable to China's government. The *yangbanxi* could take the vivid palette of Technicolor's process and weaponize it against the West, using its rich intensity to promote the communist cause. Technicolor's palette conveyed the rule of *hongguanglian* (red, shiny, and bright), a vivid aesthetic that embodied the utopian aspirations of the Cultural Revolution and permeated visual culture at this time.[55] The planned use of Technicolor's IB system to print the *yangbanxi* therefore highlights yet another way the meaning of this palette could be reimagined for radically different purposes when located in a new sociopolitical and geographic context.

By the time Beijing's IB plant was operational in 1978, however, Mao had died and the Cultural Revolution concluded. The Beijing IB unit was therefore subsequently deployed to manufacture the kind of commercial films that emerged in China in line with Deng Xiaoping's economic reforms (discussed in this volume by Heather Heckman, Laura Major, and Lydia Pappas). Yet the Beijing Film Laboratory's IB unit, operational until 1993, continued to offer a utopian political promise not to Chinese communist filmmakers but to African American directors.

As John Akomfrah recalls, the American filmmakers Julie Dash and Arthur Jafa were fascinated by the possibilities of China's dye-transfer plant, which they planned to visit in the 1980s, in his words "not simply to retrieve an archaic technique but also . . . to re-inscribe the black figure in the photochemical matrix."[56] It was the delicate color calibration possible with IB printing that intrigued Dash and Jafa, as it could potentially be refined to correctly reproduce the chromatic nuances of Black skin, so often distorted by laboratories to privilege White flesh tones.[57] Indeed, Technicolor's legacy in Hollywood was imbricated with histories of anti-Blackness and racialized violence, yet this "Chinese Copy" of Technicolor's system offered Black filmmakers the opportunity to redress these asymmetries of power.[58] As the last place operating Technicolor's dye-transfer system, the Beijing Film Laboratory was therefore imbued with a political promise quite different from those imagined by Mao's regime, offering American filmmakers the possibility to challenge the racist biases built into the laboratory system.

Conclusion

Returning to the advertisement with which I began this chapter, it becomes clear that the "translation" of Technicolor into multiple global film languages was a complex process that demanded the navigation of different sets of expectations in each region: legal, governmental, aesthetic, and ideological. Far from simply exporting a standardized Technicolor brand throughout the world, this era marks Technicolor's fraught negotiation with a multitude of factors that gave the process unique characteristics in each region. But because these laboratories were part of a global network of exchange (of matrices, technicians, and ideas), they forged collaborations that resulted in films that evidenced not only distinctive national Technicolor styles but also hybrid transnational color aesthetics. Technicolor's plan to cultivate "one global laboratory" from the 1950s, far from producing a singular homogeneous unit, resulted in a series of heterogeneous spaces of interchange and collaboration. These laboratories illuminate how a single process could be deployed in divergent manners: as a symbol of postcolonial independence, a sign of American cultural imperialism, an instrument for fighting anti-Black racism, or a weapon for communist supremacy in the Cold War. These meanings do not contradict or conflict with one another. Instead, they underscore the multivalent meanings of Technicolor's corporate identity, visual aesthetic, and political valence in the newly globalized system of color filmmaking from the 1950s.

Notes

1 Report to the Board of Directors of Technicolor Limited, June 4, 1954, Technicolor Corporate Archives, George Eastman Museum, Rochester (hereafter Technicolor Archives).

2 Annual Report, 1969, Technicolor Archives.

3 One notable exception is Richard W. Haines, *Technicolor Movies: The History of Dye Transfer Printing* (Jefferson, NC: McFarland, 1993).

4 Russell Merritt, "Crying in Color. How Hollywood Coped When Technicolor Died," *Journal of the National Film and Sound Archive* 3, no. 2/3 (2008): 1–16.

5 Bernard Happé, *80 Years of Colour Cinematography* (London: British Kinematograph, Sound and Television Society, 1985), 15.

6 See Barbara Flueckiger, Timeline of Historical Film Colors, "Technicolor No. V," 2012, https://filmcolors.org/timeline-entry/1445/.

7 On British Technicolor's departure from this aesthetic, see Sarah Street, *Colour Films in Britain: The Negotiation of Innovation, 1900–55* (London: Palgrave Macmillan/British Film Institute, 2012), 51–67.

8 See Dudley Andrew, "The Postwar Struggle for Color," *Cinema Journal* 18, no. 2 (1979): 41–52.

9 On Britain, see Street, *Colour Films in Britain*; on China, see Kirsty Sinclair Dootson and Zhaoyu Zhu, "Did Madame Mao Dream in Technicolor? Rethinking Cold War Colour Cinema through Technicolor's 'Chinese Copy,'" *Screen* 61, no. 3 (Autumn 2020), 343–367; on Russia, see Philip Cavendish, "The Political Imperative of Color: Stalin, Disney, and the Soviet Pursuit of Color Film, 1931–45," *Russian Review* 78, no. 4 (2019): 569–594; on Sweden, see Kamalika Sanyal's chapter in this volume.

10 Report to the Board of Directors of Technicolor Limited, June 5, 1950, Technicolor Archives. According to lab workers, members of the camera department could be redeployed to other areas of the firm, for instance, becoming contact men for the labs or working in the electrical department. Laboratory technician Les Ostinelli, interview, November 5, 1992, interviews made by the Broadcasting, Entertainment, Communications and Theatre Union Oral History Project (hereafter BECTU), https://historyproject.org.uk; Stan Sayer, interview, February 20, 1992, BECTU.

11 On IB as the cornerstone of Technicolor's finances, see James Layton and David Pierce, *The Dawn of Technicolor, 1915–1935* (Rochester, NY: George Eastman House, 2015), 221.

12 See Heather Heckman, "We've Got Bigger Problems: Preservation during Eastman Color's Innovation and Early Diffusion," *Moving Image* 15, no. 1 (July 9, 2015): 44–61.

13 This phrase recurs in interviews with Technicolor staff, specifically Paddy O'Gorman, interview, July 31, 1992, BECTU; Wilfred Brandt, interview, November 11, 1991, BECTU; and Len Runkel, November 9, 1988, BECTU.

14 Detailed in "Technicolor Plans for Expansion Abroad," *Technicolor News and Views* 14, no. 4 (December 1952): 2.

15 On Berlin, see Sarah Street and Joshua Yumibe, *Chromatic Modernity: Color, Cinema and the Media of the 1920s* (New York: Columbia University Press, 2018), 239.

16 Béatrice de Pastre, "Présentation du Fonds Jean Vivié aux Archives françaises du film du CNC," *1895 Revue d'Histoire du Cinéma,* no. 71 (Winter 2013): 275–282, 295–296. My thanks to David M. Evans for the French translation.

17 Reproduced in de Pastre.

18 Andrew, "Postwar Struggle for Color."
19 See de Pastre, "Présentation du Fonds Jean Vivié," 281; letter from Herbert Kalmus to Mr Flaud, July 1, 1958, Technicolor Archives.
20 Letter from Kalmus to Flaud.
21 O'Gorman interview; Frank Littlejohn interview, June 13, 1989, BECTU.
22 On strikes at Technicolor Limited, see Technicolor Limited Minutes of Directors' Meetings, March 24, 1954, Technicolor Archives.
23 "50 Golden Years of Technicolor," special edition, *Technicolor News and Views* (1965).
24 ENR was named after its designers Ernesto Novelli ('EN') and Raffaele Raimo ('R'). On ENR, see Blain Brown, *Cinematography: Theory and Practice* (Oxford: Taylor and Francis Group, 2011), 250; on Technirama, see Haines, *Technicolor Movies*, 106–107.
25 Luciano Tovoli quoted in Stanley Manders, "Terror in Technicolor," *American Cinematographer* 91, no. 2 (February 2010): 74.
26 "Technicolor," *Motion Picture Daily* 77, no. 95 (May 16, 1955), 5.
27 Report to the Board of Directors of Technicolor Limited, October 28, 1949, Technicolor Archives.
28 "Location Companies from Hollywood Roam the Hemispheres to Bring the World in Color by Technicolor to Screens," *Technicolor News and Views* 14, no. 2 (July 1952): 2.
29 On Toyo, see Jasper Sharp, "Japanese Widescreen Cinema: Commerce, Technology and Aesthetics" (PhD diss., University of Sheffield, 2013), 204; on *Gate of Hell*, see Sarah Street, "The Monopack Revolution, Global Cinema and *Jigokumon/Gate of Hell* (Kinugasa Teinosuke, 1953)," *Open Screens* 1, no. 1 (June 6, 2018).
30 Sharp, "Japanese Widescreen Cinema," 204.
31 "Technicolor," 5.
32 Including *Sairandhri* (V. Shantaram, 1933), shot on Agfacolor and processed in Germany, and *Kisan Kanya,* shot and processed in India using Cinecolor (Moti Gidwani, 1937). See Gulzar, Govind Nihalani, and Saibal Chatterjee, *Encyclopedia of Hindi Cinema* (New Delhi: Encyclopedia Britannica, 2003), 253–254.
33 "India Called Active Field for Technicolor," *Technicolor News and Views* 14, no. 4 (December 1952): 7.
34 "Plan to Set Up Technicolor Laboratory: Producers Enter into Agreement," *Times of India*, April 24, 1955, 3.
35 On foreign exchange, see Priya Jaikumar, *Where Histories Reside: India as Filmed Space* (Durham, NC: Duke University Press, 2019), 234–286.
36 *Report of the Film Enquiry Committee* (India Press: New Delhi, 1951).
37 *Report of the Film Enquiry Committee*, 74.
38 "Lok Sabha Questions," *Times of India,* August 3, 1955, 11; "State Control of Film Marketing Suggested," *Times of India,* March 5, 1955, 1. I use the colonial names Bombay and Madras here rather than Mumbai and Chennai to adhere to the historical terminology of the period.
39 See Natasha Eaton, *Colour, Art and Empire: Visual Culture and the Nomadism of Representation* (London: I. B. Tauris, 2013).
40 Film Center processed *Mother India*'s Gevacolor negative; Technicolor Limited manufactured release prints.
41 Minutes from a meeting between Mr. Chattopadhaya of Ramnord Laboratories and Technicolor representatives, August 23, 1956, Technicolor Archives.
42 "Patel's 'Pamposh': A Poem in Celluloid [*sic*]," *Times of India*, January 18, 1953, 3; Frederick Foster, "India's First Feature in Gevacolor," *American Cinematographer* 35, no. 8 (1954): 414–416.

43 Report to the Board of Directors of Technicolor Limited, October 8, 1956, Technicolor Archives.

44 Chattopadhaya meeting minutes; Report to the Board of Directors of Technicolor Limited, October 8, 1956.

45 On *The River*, see Jaikumar, *Where Histories Reside*, 125–180. I explore India's relationship to Technicolor further in Kirsty Sinclair Dootson, *The Rainbow's Gravity: Colour, Materiality and British Modernity* (London: Paul Mellon Centre for Studies in British Art, 2023), 129–145.

46 On Malhotra and Sarpotdar, see *Jhansi Ki Rani* souvenir program, William K. Everson Collection, New York University; on Sengupta, see Jean Renoir, *Renoir on Renoir: Interviews, Essays, and Remarks*, trans. Carol Volk (Cambridge: Cambridge University Press, 1989), 242; on Radhu Karmakar, see *The First 25 Years, Indian Cinematography* (Mumbai: Western Indian Cinematographers Association, 1993), 5, accessed November 24, 2023 at https://www.muraleedharanck.com/research; on V. K. Murthy, see Raqs Media Collective and C. K. Mualidharan, the History and Practice of Cinematography in India project, interview with V. K. Murthy, 1999, https://www.muraleedharanck.com/research.

47 "Months of Research and Years of Planning behind India's First Picture in Color by Technicolor," *Jhansi Ki Rani* Supplement, *The Times of India*, January 18, 1953, p. II.

48 Priya Jaikumar, *Cinema at the End of Empire: A Politics of Transition in Britain and India* (Durham: Duke University Press, 2006), 21.

49 Report to the Board of Directors of Technicolor Limited, October 8, 1956.

50 Chattopadhaya meeting minutes.

51 Report to the Board of Directors of Technicolor Limited, October 8, 1956; Ambalal Patel, "A Plea for Protection," *Sports and Pastime* 17, no. 40 (October 12, 1963), 52.

52 Letter from Paul W. Fassnacht to Mr. S. Krishnaswami, Chitra Art Productions, Madras, June 6, 1973, Technicolor Archives.

53 "Deposition of Richard J. Goldberg," April 5, 1990, Technicolor Archives.

54 See Chris Berry, "Every Colour Red? Colour in the Films of the Cultural Revolution Model Stage Works," *Journal of Chinese Cinemas* 6, no. 3 (September 2012): 233–246,

55 As Zhu highlights in Dootson and Zhu, "Did Madame Mao Dream in Technicolor?," 349.

56 John Akomfrah, "Digitopia and the Spectres of Diaspora," *Journal of Media Practice* 11, no. 1 (March 2010): 23.

57 On calibrating for Whiteness, see Genevieve Yue, *Girl Head: Feminism and Film Materiality* (New York: Fordham University Press, 2020), 33–72. Also see Dootson, *The Rainbow's Gravity*, 14–17.

58 On Technicolor's long entanglement with racialized color, see Xin Peng, "Colour-as-Hue and Colour-as-Race: Early Technicolor, Ornamentalism and *The Toll of the Sea* (1922)," *Screen* 62, no. 3 (September 1, 2021): 287–308.

2

"Keeping Your Enemies Closer"

Strategies of Knowledge
Transfer at the East German
Filmfabrik Wolfen

JOSEPHINE DIECKE

The Agfacolor process, introduced in 1936 by the German Agfa corporation at the Filmfabrik Wolfen, was the first subtractive, multilayer chromogenic film stock. Founded in 1867 as a colorant manufacturer, Agfa was part of the IG Farben conglomerate from 1925 to 1945. Its Wolfen plant, which had been built in 1909, was the exclusive producer of Agfa film stock through the end of World War II, and it continued producing film for Eastern Bloc nations after the war. With the postwar division of Germany and the ensuing breakup of IG Farben, the West German Agfa-Werke was founded as a subsidiary of Farbenfabriken Bayer AG, which opened a new plant for photochemical film production in 1949 in the British-occupied city of Leverkusen, at the site of a former Agfa photographic paper factory.[1] Each factory, in Wolfen and Leverkusen, produced its own Agfacolor derivatives under the same name, but through separate corporations.[2] This ended in 1964 when Wolfen sold the rights for the Agfa brand to Agfa-Werke in Leverkusen and changed its company's name to ORWO, which is an acronym for "ORiginal WOlfen." In the same year, Agfa-Werke merged with Gevaert of Belgium, after six years of negotiations, forming Agfa-Gevaert N.V. in response to a wave of Western European corporate mergers in the photochemical industry.[3] Although this caused the Agfacolor name to disappear with the production end at the Leverkusen plant of Agfacolor negative CN5 in 1968, the basic formula lived on in the form of the Wolfen Orwocolor and Orwochrom films.[4] The Leverkusen products, on the other hand, increasingly adopted the innovations that Kodak's color film processes brought to the market beginning in 1950 through the introduction of Eastman Color negative and positive film stocks, as well as its photographic processing systems.

In most histories of color cinema, the later, postwar materials from the Wolfen Agfa-ORWO company have been considered only in passing, if at all, especially in comparison with Western competitors such as the U.S. Eastman Kodak (Kodachrome, Ektachrome, and Eastman Color), the West German–Belgian Agfa-Gevaert (Gevacolor and Agfa XT), and the Japanese Fuji (Fujicolor).[5] These processes were intricately connected, yet also distinct in their end products. Both Agfa-Gevaert and Fuji, for instance, based their systems initially on the original Agfacolor process but increasingly adopted Eastman Color's monopack innovations to revise their own. The chromogenic process that is the basis of these stocks relies on the development of multilayer dyes on a single, monopack filmstrip.[6] The colors are produced by means of dye couplers, and these color-forming substances are either embedded in several different layers in the emulsion (as with Agfacolor and Eastman Color) or added during film development (Kodachrome). The composition of dye couplers is responsible for the specific look of a film stock, giving each unique saturation levels and color palettes that can provoke a variety of realistic and spectacular effects, as well as reproduce diverse skin tones with varying degrees of fidelity.

Among these various chromogenic stocks, however, Wolfen's continued use and development of the Agfa process has not yet been examined in detail. This can be attributed in part to the fact that the Cold War brought numerous political barriers that made exchanges between the Western and Eastern Blocs difficult if not impossible. Yet, the lack of interest in the development of Agfacolor and Orwocolor at Wolfen is also rooted in a skewed, overly teleological focus on the aesthetic factors of color stocks, such as their satisfying and accurate color renditions, as well as on economic considerations, including a film stock's compatibility with existing equipment and processing techniques.

For example, in *A History of Motion Picture Color Technology*, Roderick T. Ryan praises the monopack film stocks Fujicolor, Gevacolor, and Ferrania-color, whose success he attributes to their ongoing technical and aesthetic "progression":

> They were all developed and used successfully in Europe and/or Asia before their introduction in the United States. In general, their acceptance by American laboratories and production companies has been favorable. An

important factor in this acceptance was their compatibility with existing equipment and processes. In a single processing machine a laboratory could process Eastman Color Print Film, Gevacolor Print Film, Fujicolor Print Film, or Ferrania Color Print Film without changing solutions. This has stimulated competition both in pricing and in quality. . . . Each of the four film manufacturers whose products are mentioned above has contributed significantly to the state of the art technology of color motion pictures. A review of any one of these processes indicates a steady progression towards improved quality and simplification of process techniques.[7]

According to Ryan, standardizing a color film stock to existing technical requirements (chemical compatibility in processing laboratories) would have been the biggest goal for a company and by and large determined the perceived *quality* of its product. Such a quality assessment was based on a comparison of different chromogenic film stocks and their underlying chemical compatibility. This compatibility relied on the exchange of knowledge among international competitors within the Western Bloc and shaped the global spread of color film processing during the Cold War. However, the case of Wolfen's Agfacolor and Orwocolor stocks demonstrates how one-sided such quality assessments of color film stocks were in the West.

Supplementing and revising standard narratives about postwar color, this chapter focuses on the technical, cultural, and institutional history of the Agfacolor and Orwocolor processes in order to highlight an alternative set of strategies and circumstances of knowledge transfer that existed in the Eastern Bloc as well as nonaligned countries of the postwar era. In the face of ideological agendas, Wolfen's employees aimed to keep their politically framed enemies closer by setting up strategies of knowledge transfer to monitor international technical developments. As the historian Stefan Wolle has pointed out, in East Germany there was no need to explain who was meant by the "enemy" (*Feind*) or the "class enemy" (*Klassenfeind*, a common Cold War term for enemies of the working class).[8] The German Democratic Republic (GDR), established in 1949, relied on the perpetual notion of an imaginary enemy from the West as a means of legitimizing and stabilizing its rule, while also motivating corporations such as Filmfabrik Wolfen to monitor closely their Western competitors.

The first section of the chapter presents the background against which Agfacolor's quality was measured in relation to competing processes such as Eastman Color and Fujicolor. The second section focuses on the process of quality control and observation at Filmfabrik Wolfen. In the final section, information retrieval with the neo4j graph database is employed to explore selected departments and scientists who oversaw in-house products at the company, while also monitoring their corporate and political competitors.

Reputation of Low Quality

The example of Agfa/ORWO shows that the historiographical discourse on "quality standards" for color technologies has depended strongly on specific political and cultural contexts. Due to the emerging divide between the Eastern and Western Bloc nations, Wolfen's economic conditions after the transition to the Soviet occupation zone in 1945 were closely tied to the centralized requirements of the socialist regime. This intensified in 1950 with the entry of East Germany—the newly established GDR—into the Council for Mutual Economic Assistance (CMEA), the Eastern Bloc technical and economic consortium founded in 1949. The quality of technical production as well as the quantity that could be produced by any company depended strongly on external factors decided through the consortium, such as political agreements and annual economic and technical plans, which were at times opaque. International competitors were not supposed to find out about internal problems within the CMEA, so even factory employees, such as those at Wolfen, were not allowed to criticize the consortium's policies publicly without fear of consequences. This led to various technical discrepancies. For instance, the evaluation of color film stocks likely differed significantly in official and unofficial discourses. In the case of the latter, Agfacolor's positive connotation in the early postwar years, particularly for its responsiveness to natural light, was eventually replaced by an ever-louder disapproval regarding its quality during the Cold War period, especially within the Eastern Bloc. Attracting less serious attention in the West was one thing, but also revealing that Eastern Bloc technologies could not keep up qualitatively weakened the idea of the superior socialist collective.

Agfacolor/Orwocolor at Wolfen was notorious for its apparent technical flaws, such as its distinctive color rendition of shifted red and green tones, its rather dull and muted look, and its uneven application of emulsion. However, less known outside of Wolfen were its corporate problems: the company had to navigate unreliable supply agreements and a lack of communication among its socialist trading partners, as archivists Anna Batistová and Tereza Frodlová have highlighted within the Czech context.[9] Also in the Czechoslovak Socialist Republic (CSSR), the more readily available Wolfen Agfacolor/Orwocolor was compared unfavorably with color stocks from the West, in particular Eastman Color. Regarding the factors for quality comparison in the 1950s and 1960s, Batistová notes:

> [The] quality of the eastern Agfa stock was low. In various tests conducted in the period, Czechoslovak technicians found the definition of Agfacolor positive materials 50 per cent lower than that of Eastman Color, while the sensitivity of the emulsion was uneven, sometimes in the same reel. Up to 10 per cent of the Agfacolor material was sent back to Wolfen as faulty every

year. Reports from the period comment on the low quality of the color stock causing problems during shooting and processing. . . . Proof of this is evident in the poor color saturation in scenes with lower intensity of light (for example night scenes) and changes of color during dissolves which are visible on the surviving prints and recently released digital copies of some films.[10]

As Batistová's assessment of Agfacolor's user experience in the CSSR shows, the quality of color film stocks was primarily equated with aesthetic and technical properties—color definition and saturation levels, as well as consistency and stability.

However, the successful production and distribution of chromogenic color film stock was not only driven by aesthetic qualities. Economic factors depended decisively on the transnational exchange of material components for building specialized casting machines for producing the film base and for acquiring the chemicals for film processing. Although transnational specialization within production lines was discussed early on within the CMEA, many member states sought the way out of their economic problems through national solutions or in increased exports to hard currency countries, notably after the wave of mergers in the West, as in the case of Agfa-Gevaert and Ferrania-3M in 1964.[11] Thus, the USSR also began to build up its own processing plants in the mid-1960s and consequently faced the GDR and other member states increasingly as competitors in the film and photographic market. Instead of pursuing long-term, international plans for the division of labor and resources among members of the CMEA, East Germany was forced to rely heavily on raw materials and chemical intermediates from Western Bloc nations as well as from Japan after the 1960s.[12]

Another example for one of the aforementioned national solutions is Wolfen's trading deal with India. Thanks to bilateral agreements beginning in the 1970s between the GDR and India, Orwocolor film stocks became deeply intertwined with Indian film production and influenced a generation of filmmakers working with the material, which was otherwise being increasingly squeezed out of the markets of nonsocialist countries in the 1970s and 1980s.[13] Günther Gromke, an employee of the Technische Kundendienst (Technical Customer Service) working for ORWO in India at the time, describes the conditions of the international collaboration in a documentary from 2010: "There was a bilateral agreement between India and the GDR. It was not settled in foreign currency, but it was mutually settled. That was a barter, if you like. So we bought coffee, tea, bone meal, shellac and such things, largely natural products, and we sold [our raw film stocks] too and that was set off against each other. In this respect, this was also very attractive for the Indians, the Indians as well lacked foreign exchange at that time."[14] Taking this "barter" into account, Gromke also admitted that ORWO's greatest strength in India was not its aesthetic potential but its low cost compared with competing color film stocks that were thought to be of higher quality but were more expensive at the time. Referring to the direct comparison,

Gromke, on the other hand, cites an analogy that illuminates the technical and local realities in India: "It had to work with the material, of course. But it didn't have to be the very best. And that's the way we sold. As our representative in Bombay used to say: 'There are people who sell air conditioners, and there are people who sell this fan that hangs in the living room. Of course an air conditioner is better, it is also more expensive, but a lot of people get along with the fan. And we sell fans.'"[15] Gromke points out that ORWO was focused on the mass production of compatible materials to cope with the demands, rather than on the highest quality standards. Indeed, quality is a relative term here, grounded less on aesthetic absolutes than on practical needs. That is why Wolfen—metaphorically speaking—successfully produced fans instead of air conditioners. India also benefited from ORWO's need for favorable trade-offs and thus was able to build its own film production on the cheaper color film stock, in particular for its release prints.

Global Spread and Observation

In 1945, before the Russians arrived in East Germany to take over, the American Combined Intelligence Objectives Sub-Committee (CIOS) and the British Intelligence Objectives Sub-Committee (BIOS) compiled detailed summaries of the seized technological secrets and patents from Agfa and made them publicly available.[16] For instance, with the help of former Agfa employee Wilhelm Schneider, the American Field Information Agency, Technical (FIAT) published a report that detailed the chemical formula and workflows of the Agfacolor process.[17] With this, they promoted Agfacolor's subsequent use and adaptation at least on paper, which the Soviets took even further by bringing German scientists such as Kurt Meyer to Shostka in Ukraine to get the Wolfen laboratory machinery that had been moved there up and running.[18] Afterward, the Agfacolor formulas spread from Wolfen in Germany and were adapted to other processes such as Ferraniacolor, Sovcolor, and Fujicolor.[19] Although it remains to be clarified to what extent Agfacolor influenced the development of the Eastman Color process, there are clear parallels in the operating principles of both processes. However, competitive research was certainly being carried out on both sides before and after the war, demonstrably at Agfa already during the introduction of Kodachrome in 1935.[20]

But it was not only the Agfacolor formulas and materials that circulated in this manner immediately after the war. In 1950, Kodak introduced its next major initiative with Eastman Color negative 5247, which had many international adopters, of both the chromogenic stock and its processing solutions.[21] Even the newly constructed Agfa plant in Leverkusen, West Germany, made Kodak-compatible stocks in the 1970s and 1980s that had higher sensitivity and detail for color reproduction than its Agfa-based formulas.[22] The international competition, which had increased dramatically with the global spread of Kodak stocks and Agfa derivatives, was felt on the ground in Wolfen. Although Orwocolor raw stocks never imitated Kodak's innovations—such as using hydrophobic, oil-soluble Kodak couplers, especially in combination with the new Developer Inhibitor Releasing (DIR) coupler technology—local scientists and engineers watched the progress of their competitors closely, as revealed by surviving research reports from the Wolfen film factory.[23]

Nicolas Le Guern notes regarding industrial research and knowledge transfer that "two opposite fundamental practices control the management of knowledge: secrecy and transfer of knowledge."[24] Often, such control mechanisms occur simultaneously behind the closed doors of research and development laboratories and do not reach the general public. As Le Guern has stated, the more open companies were with their research findings, the easier it is for us today to trace where and how the departments obtained their knowledge.[25] This was not the case at Filmfabrik Wolfen, but the gap in public discussion of its findings is countered by a large cache of inspection reports that have survived in the Wolfen archives, mostly from the period of 1945 to 1990, illustrating the industrial research into color going on at the plant.

Wolfen pursued a meticulously standardized evaluation process in its scientific departments for comparing the quality of so-called *Konkurrenzfilme* (competitor films) and *Fremdfilme* (foreign films) with those of its in-house products. The goal was to assess the respective values of the company's Agfacolor and subsequent Orwocolor stocks in comparison with international competitors. These evaluation processes at Wolfen can be subsumed under the category of *competitor research* through their systematic analysis of the strengths, weaknesses, and developmental and market potentials of rival companies' products.[26] Relevant market data and scientific knowledge were systematically collected, processed, interpreted, and presented so that Wolfen was able to consciously "act" and not just "react."[27]

After the German reunification in 1989, former employees of the ORWO plant in Wolfen started to create *Karteikarten* ("index cards") in 1994 to catalog the remaining research reports from the former Wolfen factory, which was privatized in 1990 and closed in 1995. These cards are now housed in the archives of the Wolfen Museum of Industry and Film. Each index card contains metadata with regard to a research report's unique *Nummer* ("number"), *Abteilung* ("department"), *Titel* ("title"), sometimes also an old *Berichts-Nr.* ("report number"), *Autor[en]* ("author[s]"), and the *Datum* ("date[s]"), of publication. The archive also used *Deskriptoren* ("keyword tags") to group the research records according to specific recurring topics, as documented in card No. 494, which lists keywords for *Forschung* (research), *Strukturanalyse* (structural analysis), *Colormaterial* (color material), *Positivmaterial* (positive material), *Fremdmaterial* (foreign material) and *Farbkuppler* (color coupler) (figure 2.1). Thanks to these indicators, the index cards lead to the associated research reports that contain the actual information about completed analysis methods, film stocks and components involved, and the results of these steps (figure 2.2).

```
Database : ARCHIV              12.04.1994                    Seite   4
```

NUMMER	*494*
ABTEILUNG	HA Color, Abt. Analytik
TITEL	Abtrennung der Farbkuppler aus Color-Positivfilmen der Konkurrenz in für die Strukturanalyse ausreichenden Mengen, 1. Untersuchungen an Eastmancolor-Positiv. Typ 5385, Teil 1 (DTP *1974* – 8.6.5.1.). Notiz
BERICHTS-NR.	137/74
AUTOR(EN)	Rundnagel
DATUM	20.09.74
DESKRIPTOREN	Forschung. Strukturanalyse. Colormaterial. Positivmaterial. Fremdmaterial. Farbkuppler

FIGURE 2.1 Index card of the Wolfen research report No. 494.

However, cross-referencing these index cards and reports through the keywords in their analog form would be difficult and time-consuming given the nonrelational nature of the single documents. Accordingly, to facilitate my research, I scanned more than 37,000 of these documents, including the index cards and research reports.[28] With the help of these scans, instead of just asking specific questions about persons and film stocks involved in single research reports, I have been able to look at broader connections across the reports by drawing on materials from the departments that were most familiar with the production of raw color film, such as the Departments of Research (Forschung), Emulsion Manufacturing (Emulsionierung), Testing Laboratory (Prüfstelle), and Technical Control Organization (Technische Kontrollorganisation).

In working through Wolfen's archive of index cards and reports, it becomes clear that the company dedicated itself to quality control and observation in almost every field of work. Members of the Technische Kundendienst department traveled abroad or received test films from their on-site representatives, who then analyzed them in their research laboratories to identify the components used. For instance, in one report regarding a business trip to Hungary in 1973, the Wolfen researchers returned with film stocks from ORWO and Kodak to compare their compatibility with different print materials. In this case, the task was to compare the result of printing Eastman Color 5254 and Orwocolor NC3 negatives on Eastman Color 5381 and Orwocolor PC7 positive stocks with regard to the visibility of scratches.[29]

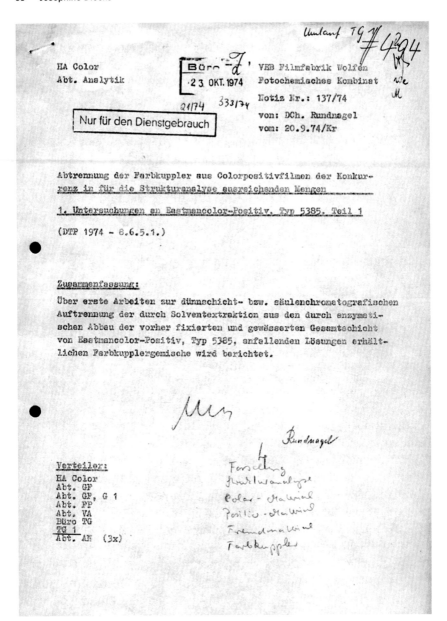

FIGURE 2.2 First page of the Wolfen research report No. 494.

Further debates on the quality of domestic Agfa/ORWO film stocks were held in the Technische Kontrollorganisation. The department was tasked with checking the manufacture of domestic products and associated components. The archived in-house reports provide excellent insight into the quality issues of the color film materials from Wolfen. In parallel, the investigations of the Forschungslaboratorien ("Research Department") monitored the quality of foreign film stocks by analyzing their material components, from the film base to the color couplers. This was followed by a thorough quality comparison of competing products with the in-house film materials, carried out at the Hauptabteilung Color (HA Color) (Main Color Department) and the Analytik (Analytics Department), according to qualitative and economic criteria. The scientists compared not only single raw films but also entire series of competing film stocks from the same period, demonstrating their systematic approach. These assessments were dependent on close, technical observation and comparison, which were carried out in the strictest secrecy and at regular intervals.

Analyzing and Visualizing Agfa/ORWO's Foreign Film Stock Inspection

To understand Agfa/ORWO's underlying dynamics of competitor observation, it is helpful to closely read, interpret, and situate individual sources, activities, and developments in historical and political contexts, as demonstrated in the first section of this chapter. It is possible to address previous gaps in Cold War narratives by tracking the aforementioned competitive research in Wolfen through selected contemporary production sources. For this reason, this section examines the observation and transfer movements from and to the Wolfen film factory. Systematically analyzing the digital scans of Wolfen's index cards and research reports allows us to shift focus from individual research initiatives to the company's industrial research process itself.

Taking a quantitative as well as a qualitative approach to the materials, I uploaded 2,710 index cards of the Forschungslaboratorien into the graph database and network visualization tool neo4j.[30] Looking for transnational connections in the manufacturing of chromogenic color film processes served the primary focus of the investigation. In the first step, the index cards were converted into machine-readable files with the help of optical character recognition (OCR). Then, each index card was converted through a Python script into a JSON file that identified keywords in the index cards, which became metadata for search categories.

In the next step, the individual JSON files were combined into a collective JSON that was then imported into neo4j. This open-source software provides a graph database management system; a language to query the database, called Cypher; and visual interfaces. With the help of these components, the tool offers several approaches for data research and visualization that can help establish complex relationships across large archives. Specifically with the Wolfen material, intricate connections can be traced through keyword queries across multiple index cards, reports, and research departments that would otherwise be obscured. For instance, returning to index card No. 494, one can pose the neo4j query: "What kind of keyword values are connected to the index card no. 494?" The information documented on the index card is then broken down into a new

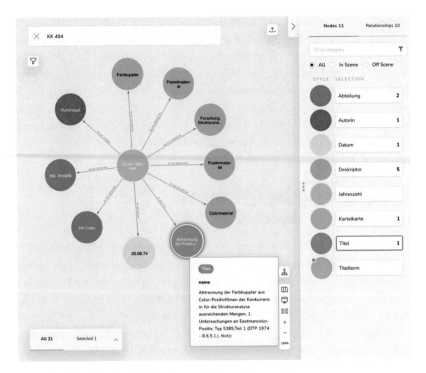

FIGURE 2.3 Visualization of the index card No. 494 in neo4j browser.

arrangement of relationships (composed of graphical nodes and edges), leading to a cross-referenced report by Karl-Heinz Rundnagel, who analyzed an East-man Color positive film stock in 1974 (figure 2.3).

Rundnagel wrote reports for multiple Wolfen departments, including the Analytics Department (Analytik), which focused on *Fremdmaterialprüfung* (foreign film inspection), the examination and evaluation of film stocks from other countries. These studies were marked with the keyword *Fremdmaterial* in the index cards. By far the most reports with this keyword were written by Mr. Rundnagel, with 63 reports out of 164 (38 percent), followed by R. Jantos with 11 reports (7 percent) and Hans-Martin Barchet with 8 reports (5 percent). Between 1967 and 1990, Wolfen's employees repeatedly wrote research reports on third-party materials, of which Rundnagel was a key contributor, especially in the 1970s.

The importance of foreign film research is evident from the frequency with which the *Fremdmaterial* keyword also shows up in index cards and reports from multiple departments: representatives of the HA Color wrote the most reports with the keyword *Fremdmaterial*, with 59 reports out of 164 (36 percent), directly followed by the Hauptabteilung Filmforschung (HA FF) (Main Department Film Research) with 44 reports (27 percent). And the Abteilung Analytik

(Analytics) with 42 reports (26 percent). Since the Analytics Department was named differently in different index cards, it also reappears in other constellations as Analytik with 9 reports (5 percent) or as part of the Hauptabteilung Grundlagenforschung (HA GF) with 7 reports (4 percent) and HA FF with 2 reports (1 percent).

Also, Rundnagel wrote most of his reports for HA Color (33 reports out of 101), Analytik (37 reports), and HA FF (20 reports). He and other authors in the Analytik department devoted a large amount of their research to the topic of *Fremdmaterial*: for Rundnagel, it is the most frequently used keyword across his files, and it was the second most frequent for Analytik. The report titles also reveal which companies and film materials were examined in combination with the testing of competing film stocks. Kodak materials, which were referred to as "Eastman," "Eastmancolor-Positiv," "Eastmancolor," or "Eastmancolor-Print," were particularly common. However, film stocks from Agfa-Gevaert ("Gevacolor-Positiv," "Gevacolor"), Svema ("Schostka"), Fuji ("Fujicolor-Positiv," "Fujicolor"), and Ferrania ("3M-Color-Positivfilm," "3M-Color-Positiv") were among the subjects of the "competitor film test reports," demonstrating the diversity of countries, methods, and products that Wolfen's research departments were interested in as objects of investigation.

In addition to these title terms, it is also possible to draw attention to further corporate relationships through selected keywords such as *Dienstreise* (business trip) and *Kooperation international* (international cooperation) across various departments and authors. Therefore, another helpful aspect of this quantitative approach is the ability to map search results from different queries simultaneously. In this way, collaborations between East Germany and other countries can be identified not only from the qualitative close reading of individual reports but also from the systematic analysis and mapping of report titles and descriptors.

The same applies to written reports on individual competitors, as, for example, with Fuji Photo Film. In querying neo4j about the number of reports by ORWO's Forschungslaboratorien that mention the name Fuji either in their titles or in the keywords, the graph database returns nine reports (green nodes) that are linked to six different report titles (blue nodes) and two different keywords (pink nodes). Figure 2.4 shows the network character of these connections with a total of seven authors (red nodes) and eight departments (purple nodes) involved in the reporting on Fuji.[31] These findings testify that research into Fuji film stocks at Wolfen spanned both black-and-white and color materials and involved scientists associated mostly with the department HA Color in the 1970s and 1980s. By shifting to a close reading of these nine reports, it is possible to distinguish among the different inquiries they were carrying out. Thematically, the reports covered, for example, the detailed component analysis of several Fuji positive and negative film stocks with a special focus on color raw materials. Specifically, the chemical composition of dye couplers, their arrangement within

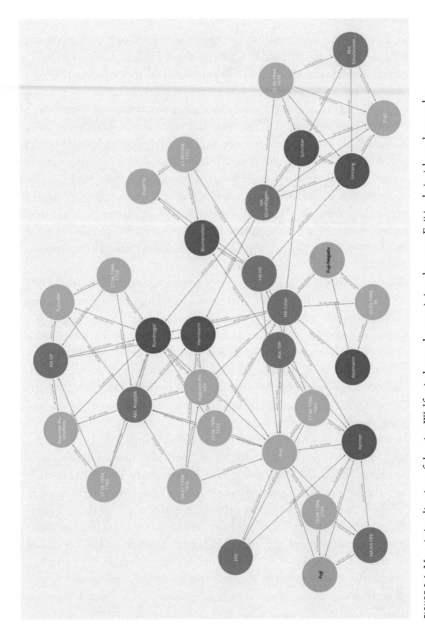

FIGURE 2.4   Neo4j visualization of the nine Wolfen index cards containing the name Fuji in their titles or keywords.

the multilayer filmstrips, and their effect on color rendition were of particular interest.[32] In addition, Wolfen's scientists compared some of the analyzed Fuji film stocks directly to film materials from other competitors, for instance, to the ones of the Soviet Svema company and to the products of Dupont, Kodak, and Agfa-Gevaert.[33]

By shifting scale again and zooming in on the summary of report No. 1622, we understand the extent to which Wolfen systematically approached its foreign film inspection on a global level. On June 18, 1974, Rundnagel examined the Fujicolor positive type 8822 in direct comparison with Svema's SU Color positive ZP-10. In his conclusion, he states:

In order to achieve the quality of the best color positive films on the world market, it is not possible to ignore the previously mentioned requirements such as

- *a lower application of silver*
- *improved color couplers*
- *higher sharpness*
- *more suitable emulsions for color positive materials*

A comparison of the Fujicolor positive, type 8819, tested in 1970, with the new Fujicolor positive, type 8822, now under investigation, shows that the Japanese company has followed this path purposefully and successfully over the past four years. In the befriended Soviet Union, too, efforts have been made to develop an improved positive material with the new SU Color positive ZP-10, although it must be said that this film, which is already world-class in its sharpness, still has to be improved in some other properties. When creating a new color positive material, the above-mentioned "main tasks" should be given special attention.[34]

Rundnagel's assessment is particularly interesting because it specifies the technical and aesthetic criteria—such as sharpness, color rendition, and a low silver content—that he and other scientists assigned to the color films of international competitors. As the case of Fuji film stocks indicates, Agfa/ORWO's employees analyzed and compared Eastern and Western processes equally. Moreover, the judgement of these film stocks focused exclusively on the technical and chemical components and did not hold back with criticism against political allies such as the Soviet Svema company. Even though the scientists focused predominantly on technical and aesthetic qualities, they did not make such drastic comparisons as those made by Günther Gromke regarding fans versus air conditioners. Indeed, the sociopolitical and cultural significance and personal associations of the Wolfen color films are rather less apparent from these documents. However, the index cards and reports certainly invite further close reading and cross-referencing to find out, for example, in which criteria the Wolfen film stocks did or did not stand up with competitors, and whether and to what extent the impression of falling behind the competition manifests itself over a longer period of time.

With the help of digital tools and methods, it is possible to find more of such interrelated patterns and research questions across such large archives of images and written sources. Tools such as neo4j can assist in the process of visualizing and understanding the various factors of film stock manufacturing from micro-, meso-, and macro-analytical perspectives. However, only by combining qualitative and quantitative approaches can a more complex and accurate picture be unlocked. This requires an iterative process and balancing between defining and finding research questions, as well as visualizing and interpreting sources and findings within complex, multilevel relationship structures.

Drawing on the case of Wolfen's research reports, it can thus be shown that the internal investigations appear as politically dominated debates only from a macro-level perspective. Seen from close up at the micro level, in contrast, it becomes clear that ideological agendas played a secondary role for Wolfen's staff when it came to evaluating quality criteria. Instead, research reports on foreign film stocks mainly addressed their technical components, revealing the staff's professional curiosity on the one hand while, on the other, illustrating the development of contemporary technological standards that informed the Wolfen plant.

Conclusion

As is apparent in the Wolfen plant's research reports, the history of chromogenic monopacks is one of constant transnational exchange of knowledge and products. But as these film stocks traveled the world, their reputations did not always rest on their aesthetic qualities but also were tethered to cost considerations and beneficial trade deals that made them accessible, as with Wolfen's Agfa/ORWO stocks in India. Such connections have been little mentioned in historical accounts of color cinema because, as the decades progressed, particularly into the 1980s, Eastern Bloc film stocks such as Wolfen's Agfacolor and Orwocolor developed along their own technical parameters, which increasingly diverged from Western Bloc standards. By and large, Western standards were being set by Kodak, particularly with regard to lab development processes and the color coupling system. Nevertheless, the film production plant in Wolfen, even as it pursued its own path, spared no expense or effort in keeping its politically framed enemies (*Klassenfeinde*) closer by monitoring the progress of these competitors.

In Wolfen, however, the quality assessment of foreign materials usually confronted a dilemma. On the one hand, Wolfen's technicians recognized the aesthetic and economic strengths of competitors such as Kodak; on the other hand, Western standards could not be easily integrated into the ideologically controlled planned economy. This eventually led to considerable frustration, especially for the employees. Nevertheless, Wolfen's technicians continued the cycle of observation, knowledge exchange, and adjustment and adaptation when feasible. But with each new investigation, Wolfen fell increasingly behind the Western competition. Its former research director Herward Pietsch blamed this on what he called the *Randbedingungen* (limiting conditions), an indirect criticism of the Eastern Bloc political situation of the GDR in the 1970s. Speaking in terms not found in the actual research papers, he notes: "Our people are not more stupid than the others. They can do their work at least as well as them, we have a good school system.... We have excellent colleges that are well equipped, which also produce sufficiently well-educated academics; and we have good basic research. So there is the question: Why and for what reason do we have such problems? It cannot be up to the individuals! ... So it's just about limiting conditions that make it easier for others."[35] The varied individuals and companies involved in Cold War surveillance of Western technologies were in many instances slight, yet in other industrial circumstances they were extensively organized, as the case of Wolfen's research reports and corresponding index cards demonstrates. German reunification and the dissolution of the GDR brought many archival sources to light that had previously been kept in secrecy. The legacy of Wolfen's archive is far from complete, but it offers a heterogeneous picture of the official and unofficial chromatic proceedings behind the Iron Curtain.

Notes

1 Silke Fengler, *Entwickelt und fixiert. Zur Unternehmens- und Technikgeschichte der deutschen Fotoindustrie, dargestellt am Beispiel der Agfa AG Leverkusen und des VEB Filmfabrik Wolfen (1945–1995)* (Essen: Klartext-Verlag, 2009), 66–70.
2 Josephine Diecke, "Agfacolor in (Inter)National Competition," in *Color Mania. The Material of Color in Photography and Film*, ed. Barbara Flückiger, Eva Hielscher, and Nadine Wietlisbach (Zurich: Lars Müller, 2020), 213–214.
3 Fengler, *Entwickelt und fixiert*, 135.
4 Gert Koshofer, "Die Agfacolor Story," in *Weltwunder der Kinematographie. Beiträge zu einer Kulturgeschichte der Filmtechnik. Fünfte Ausgabe*, ed. Joachim Polzer (Berlin: Verlag der DGFK, 1999), 102.
5 See, for instance, Roderick T. Ryan, *A History of Motion Picture Color Technology* (London: Focal Press, 1977); Brian Coe, *The History of Movie Photography* (Westfield, NJ: Eastview Editions, 1981); Gert Koshofer, *Color: Die Farben des Films* (Berlin: Wissenschaftsverl. Volker Spiess, 1988); and Jack H. Coote, *The Illustrated History of Color Photography* (Surbiton, Surrey: Fountain Press, 1993).
6 The term *chromogenic* is derived from the chromogenic reaction between the dye couplers (forming cyan, magenta, and yellow in individual layers) and the oxidized color developer (in the developing bath). The processing of chromogenic negative film consists of several steps: (1) a *color developer* reduces the silver halide crystals that have been exposed to light so that a metallic silver image appears; the oxidized developer reacts with the dye couplers around unexposed silver halide, resulting in the formation of visible color dyes in each emulsion layer; (2) a *bleach* converts the developed metallic silver into silver halide; (3) a *fixer* removes the remaining silver halide, which can then be recovered from the fixer bath; (4) *washing* the film removes fixer bath residues and silver complex compounds; (5) a *stabilizing* bath

contains a wetting agent to prevent dry spots on the surfaces of the processed film, and formaldehyde to improve the stability of the dyes. See Regula Anklin-Mühlemann and Rudolf Gschwind, *Script zur Vorlesung Farbphotographie* (Basel: Universität Basel, 2001), 84–98.

7   Ryan, *History of Motion Picture Color Technology*, 181.

8   Stefan Wolle, "Das Feindbild der Stasi. 'Der Gegner ist überall . . . ,'" in *bpb: Bundeszentrale für politische Bildung*, October 20, 2016, https://www.bpb.de /themen/deutsche-teilung/stasi/222243/das-feindbild-der-stasi/.

9   Anna Batistová, "Glorious Agfacolor, Breathtaking Totalvision and Monophonic Sound: Colour and Scope in Czechoslovakia," in *Color and the Moving Image: History, Theory, Aesthetics, Archive*, ed. Simon Brown, Sarah Street, and Liz Watkins (New York: Routledge, 2013), 47–55; and Tereza Frodlová, "In the Colours of Agfacolor: Introduction of Colour to Czechoslovak Cinema of the 1940s and 1950s," in *Czech Cinema Revisited: Politics, Aesthetics, Genres and Techniques*, ed. Lucie Česálková (Prague: Národní filmový archiv, 2017), 276–301.

10 Batistová, "Glorious Agfacolor," 49.

11 Fengler, *Entwickelt und fixiert*, 189–190.

12 Fengler, 190.

13 As Fengler has elaborated, with a world market share of 3 percent, Wolfen ranked seventh in the international photographic industry in 1973, but by 1985 the market share of ORWO products in nonsocialist countries had fallen to less than 0.1 percent. However, in some developing countries, it remained at 2 percent of the market, and in India and Algeria it was as high as 10 to 15 percent. See Fengler, *Entwickelt und fixiert*, 221–222.

14 Günther Gromke in Anne Schmidt, *ORWO. Die Geschichte einer Filmfabrik*, 2010, TC 00:32:11–00:32:47, trans. Josephine Diecke.

15 Günther Gromke in Anne Schmidt, *ORWO. Die Geschichte einer Filmfabrik*, 2010, TC 00:33:20–00:33:50, trans. Josephine Diecke.

16 D.A.W. Adams u. a., "I.G. Farbenindustrie: The Manufacture of Intermediates and, Colour Formers' for Agfa Farbenfilm," in *BIOS Final Report* (London: British Intelligence Objectives Sub-Committee, 1946); G. C. Brock, "Agfa Film Factory Wolfen," in *CIOS Report* (London: Combined Intelligence Objectives Sub-Committee, 1945); Wilhelm Schneider, *Wegweiser zum Agfacolor-Verfahren für Jedermann, FIAT Final Report 976* (Wolfen, February 1946), No. 1023, AIFM, Bibliothek Industrie- und Filmmuseum Wolfen; Alice Lovejoy, "Celluloid Geopolitics: Film Stock and the War Economy, 1939–47," *Screen* 60, no. 2 (June 1, 2019): 224–241.

17 See Schneider, *Wegweiser zum Agfacolor-Verfahren für Jedermann.*

18 See Industrie- und Filmmuseum Wolfen e.V., Hrsg., *Die Filmfabrik Wolfen. Aus der Geschichte, Heft 13* (Wolfen: Industrie- und Filmmuseum Wolfen e.V., 2004), 13.

19 See Koshofer, *Color.*

20 Josephine Diecke, "Qualitätsfilm aus Wolfen: Die diskursive Konstruktion von Agfacolor und Orwocolor im globalen Spannungsfeld, 1936–1990" (PhD diss., University of Zurich, 2022), 72–81.

21 On the history of Eastman Color, see John Waner, *Hollywood's Conversion of All Production to Color Using Eastman Color Professional Motion Picture Films* (Newcastle: Tobey, 2000); Heather Heckman, "Undervalued Stock: Eastman Color's Innovation and Diffusion: 1900–1957" (PhD diss., University of Wisconsin–Madison, 2014).

22 See Fengler, *Entwickelt und fixiert*, 222.

23 The archival collection of the Industrie- und Filmmuseum Wolfen includes thousands of contemporary research papers, pictures, posters, cameras, and memorabilia from the period of 1909 to 1994; see Industrie- und Filmmuseum Wolfen, "Der Archiv- und Bibliotheksbestand," accessed October 1, 2021, http://www.ifm-wolfen.de/de/das_archiv.html.

24 Nicolas Le Guern, "Contribution of the European Kodak Research Laboratories to Innovation Strategy at Eastman Kodak" (PhD diss., De Montfort University, 2017), 51.

25 Le Guern, 73.

26 Alexander Magerhans, *Marktforschung: Eine praxisorientierte Einführung* (Wiesbaden: Springer Gabler, 2016), 265.

27 Magerhans, 266.

28 This research was carried out as part of the project "Film Colors: Technologies, Cultures, Institutions," funded by the Swiss National Science Foundation at the University of Zurich.

29 See Wolf-Dieter Sende, "Zum Bericht über die Auslandsdienstreise nach Budapest vom 24.10.1973 bis 1.11.1973," HA Color, 1.11.1973, AIFM 1980.

30 This step was accompanied by the data scientist Marcel Förster in the framework of the research project "Digital Cinema-Hub: A Research Hub for Digital Film Studies," at the Philipps-Universität Marburg.

31 For comparison, the same search query for Kodak returns fourteen index cards, and that for Eastman, thirty-six.

32 See, for example, Rainer Redmann, "Untersuchungen zu Einflußfaktoren der Entwicklungskinetik bei Color-Negativmaterialien," HA Color, 19.12.1974, AIFM 35; Karl-Heinz Rundnagel, "Analytik organischer Bauelemente in Fremdmaterialien 7. Isolierung der Farbkuppler des Fujicolor Positivfilms LP 8816, Notiz," HA GF, Abt. Analytik, 19.06.1987, AIFM 1758; and G. Herrmann, "Konkurrenzfilm-Prüfbericht, Untersuchung von Fujicolor-Positiv, Typ 8822, der Firma Fuji Foto Film Co. Ltd., Tokyo (Japan) und SU Color-Positiv ZP-10 vom Chemiewerk Schostka (SU), Notiz," Abt. Analytik, 14.08.1974, AIFM 1916.

33 See, for example, Blumenstein, "Konkurrenz- Scanner-Filme LS 600 (Fuji), CSL 4 (Du Pont), SO 267 (Kodak), S 710p (Agfa-Gevaert) im Vergleich zum ORWO-Material FO 65, FO 7, FN 60, FO X—Fremdfilmvergleich," HA HS, 21.10.1987, AIFM 1722; and C. I. Renner, "Fremdfilmvergleich 107/87, Vergleich des Kontaktfilmes der Fa. Fuji mit einem entsprechenden Film der Firma Agfa-Gevaert und Filmen des fototechnichen Sortimentes des FCK, Notiz," HA HS FPE, 29.10.1987, AIFM 2189.

34 Karl-Heinz Rundnagel, "Konkurrenzfilm-Prüfbericht, Untersuchung von Fujicolor-Positiv, Typ 8822, der Firma Fuji Foto Film Co. Ltd. Tokyo (Japan) und SU Color-Positiv ZP-10 vom Chemiewerk Schostka (SU), Notiz zum Detailthema 8.6.5.3.—DTP 1974," HA Color, Abt. Analytik, 18.06.1974, AIFM 1622.

35 Herward Pietsch in Schmidt, *ORWO. Die Geschichte einer Filmfabrik*, TC 00:30:15–00:31:00, trans. Josephine Diecke.

3

"We're Not in Sweden Anymore"

Technicolor's Brief Venture in Swedish Cinema

KAMALIKA SANYAL

Technicolor is arguably the most influential color film technology in the history of cinema, including its influence on subsequent color film processes. After the initiation of the three-color subtractive process in 1932, it was successful, especially in Hollywood and the United Kingdom, and its popularity spread worldwide.[1] However, some European countries did not share the same enthusiasm for Technicolor, not least because the processes required special cameras, on-set technicians, and the "Technicolor package" that included a color consultant to advise on "appropriate" colors.[2] In Sweden, film companies tried to utilize monopack and dye-transfer techniques in their high-budget and highly publicized releases, but these films were unable to make Technicolor processes a norm. This chapter is an archival study that draws on journalistic and critical reviews, correspondence, and promotional materials to investigate the production, promotion, and reception of three Technicolor Swedish films: *Tant Grön, tant Brun och tant Gredelin* (*Aunt Green, Aunt Brown and Aunt Lilac*, 1947), *Lappblod* (*Sámi Blood*, 1948), and *En djungelsaga* (*The Flute and the Arrow*, 1957).[3] A Gevacolor film, *Eldfågeln* (*The Firebird*, 1952), is also taken into consideration as an example of possible competition posed by "local" color processes to Technicolor.

Before Technicolor

Since the 1910s, some Swedish feature films were produced using applied color such as the tinting method. The conversion to sound films occurred in Sweden much earlier than the adoption of photographic color. The first Swedish talkie, *Säg det i toner* (*The Dream Waltz*, 1929), was received with moderate enthusiasm, and throughout the 1930s the Swedish industry mainly focused on patenting various sound systems.[4] On the other hand, the progress of film color in Sweden was nonlinear and slower, and as in other film industries was often met with skepticism.[5] The Technicolor Corporation patented its two-color film system in Sweden as early as 1922.[6] There is no archival evidence, however, that any films were produced in Sweden using two-color Technicolor. In the 1940s, multiple Swedish patents were requested by Technicolor inventor J. M. Andreas for improved color film processing.[7]

Only a few photographic color live-action short films were released before the first feature film in color, *Klockorna i gamla sta'n* (*The Bells in Old Town*, 1946), and these are preserved at the archives of the National Library of Sweden: a *journalfilm* (journal film), an amateur nonfiction film, a home movie, and seven advertisements are available in digitized format. The journal film *Stockholm i färger* (*Stockholm in Colors*, 1933), is perhaps the earliest preserved photographic Swedish color film. It was made using a two-color, 35mm film process, but the specific system is unknown. It was distributed by the largest Swedish film production company, AB Svensk Filmindustri (abbreviated as SF).[8] The amateur film *Sommarstad* (*Summer City*, 1939) was made using Kodak Kodachrome 8mm; the types of color processing used for the rest of the short films are unknown.

According to John W. Boyle, the cinematographer of the two-color Cinecolor Hollywood documentary *Sweden, Land of the Vikings* (1934), the crew enjoyed the collaboration of the company AB Hasselblad Fotografiska, George Eastman's representatives in Sweden.[9] They maintained "excellent 16 mm processing plants" and provided 16mm film and equipment for processing.[10] This supports the assumption that some resources for color film production were available in Sweden at that time, but the demand for domestic color features was simply not yet evident.

In 1946, multiple film production companies took initiatives to produce color feature films. AB Europa Film undertook production of a musical, titled *Klockorna i gamla sta'n*, using two-color Cinecolor.[11] In the same year, Filmo and Hamberg Studio together decided to introduce the latest Technicolor monopack process in Sweden with *Lappblod*, a big-budget feature. Also in 1946, SF experimented with monopack in a children's short film, *Tant Grön, tant Brun och tant Gredelin*, which was released in 1947.

Gevacolor: A Scandinavian Color?
Color Experimentation and Sweden

While Technicolor was one of the most significant players in the domain of color film, from the 1920s to 1960s there were constant domestic attempts around the world to develop other color film systems. Extensive literatures are available on numerous British film inventors' experimentations with color film systems; on the widely circulated Agfacolor of the German-speaking region; on the efforts in China in the 1960s to develop water-soluble monopacks; and on French experimentations in film color.[12]

No comprehensive evidence to date has been found that a domestic film color system was ever developed in Sweden. John Belton argues that film color is not just about aesthetics, since economic demands also influence its development.[13] In the 1930s, significant socioeconomic reforms took place in Sweden. After the Second World War, film business was declining, and in 1948 the entertainment tax was raised from 24 percent to 39 percent of the income from ticket sales.[14] The struggling film industry was always small in comparison with those in other European countries.[15] In the spring of 1951 there was an industry-wide strike or "film stop." After 1958 the frequency of production of color and wide-screen films in Sweden fell markedly for two reasons: first, the costs of these visual effects were extraordinarily high (the budget of a color film was easily twice that of a black-and-white one); second, after television was introduced in Sweden, the black-and-white television sector was not enthusiastic about buying color films.[16] These factors would appear to demonstrate that there was no particular interest in developing a Swedish photographic color process that would have required expensive experimentation and investing in many high-budget color features. Nonetheless, in the early 1950s the Scandinavian film industry, as well as the press, began to pay attention to Gevacolor. The Gevacolor process, developed by Gevaert Photo-Producten N.V. in Belgium, was the one of the most popular color processes used in the French film industry until 1955.[17] It was an affiliate of the German Agfacolor, and there were technical similarities between the two processes. Later, the two companies merged to form Agfa-Gevaert N.V. in 1964.

Sarah Street comments that through the decades in British cinema there has been a national investment in making a case for a "specifically British deployment of color."[18] While Gevacolor was not invented in the Nordic region, the idea of a region-specific style of deployment is relatable when it comes to Gevacolor and its Nordic press reception. In 1951, for example, Nordisk Film Teknik in Denmark became the first Scandinavian laboratory to upgrade to color duplication. The lab processed Gevacolor, which was reported as having "soft and natural colors, in opposition to the harsh and eerie colors of the American Technicolor system."[19] Another report asserted that this color film system was, therefore, "especially well-suited for Scandinavian colors."[20] *Herr Arnes penningar* (*Sir Arne's Treasure*, 1954), a Swedish Gevacolor film, received positive reviews for the color photography being technically perfect, and Gevacolor was praised as sober and *fullgoda* (satisfactory).[21]

However, Gevacolor enjoyed popularity in Sweden for only a few years. In 1951, *Elddonet*, a thirty-two-minute stop-motion animation short film for children, was produced by SF. After *Eldfågeln* (1952), only two feature films were made entirely in Gevacolor: *Ingen mans kvinna* (*No Man's Woman*, 1953) and *Herr Arnes penningar. Karin Månsdotter* (1954) had its "prologue" in Gevacolor. One of the national newsreels titled *Veckorevy 1953-06-08* was shot in Gevacolor and distributed as "the first color film report completely produced in Sweden."[22] But when Eastman Color entered Sweden in 1954 with *Gula Divisionen* (*The Yellow Squadron*, 1954), the process quickly became the primary choice of Swedish filmmakers for color filming and printing.

Glorious Color . . . for Children? *Tant Grön, tant Brun och tant Gredelin* (1947)

SF started filming *Tant Grön, tant Brun och tant Gredelin* in the summer of 1946. The film is based on the first book of a beloved children's series that tells the tale of three aunts in the 1840s who are distinguished by their personalities and the color of their clothes: green, brown, and lilac. The film portrays the aunts as follows: Aunt Green takes care of the garden; Aunt Brown works in the kitchen and bakes treats; Aunt Lilac sits in the drawing room, plays the spinet, and does embroidery. Uncle Blue is a regular visitor at their house in a small cozy village. The plot revolves around the aunts losing their dog, and in the process of finding it, they meet Peter and Lotta, two sweet orphan children, and take them under their wings. The film has a "Technicolor look" (as defined by Scott Higgins), with carefully planned, vivid contrasting hues for the attire and sets.[23]

From 1942 until the mid-1950s, Technicolor used a certain procedure in which Kodachrome 16mm was used as the raw stock for films, which was then blown up to 35mm Technicolor projection prints. Kodachrome was a chromogenic color system, and Kodachrome raw stock could be used in a typical camera, unlike the large, bespoke beam-splitter cameras required for Technicolor. Interestingly, Technicolor avoided mentioning the name Kodachrome when referring to this technology in its communications to the press and stockholders. Phrases such as "an experiment in monopack," "the monopack procedure" and "Technicolor monopack" were used instead.[24] The veteran cinematographer Roland Sterner confirms that in August 1946, *Tant Grön* was produced using this method: "The film was made on 16 mm reversal film with a single camera. . . . All the materials were sent to England to be developed and blown up, to a 35 mm negative. It took a year before we saw the results of our work."[25]

A careful study of the production-time reports from the set of *Tant Grön* suggests that the engagement of the press helped it to become an anticipated release.[26] It was described as "this country's first fairy tale film, THAT TOO

IN COLOR!"[27] While reporting from the set, the film journalist Marco Polo hoped that as the popular aunts were photographed in color by SF, it "surely could be a captivating story."[28] In 1946, the company published a two-page advertisement with preproduction sketches and a note summarizing the upcoming film.[29] Around the time of the film's release, SF ran page-wide advertisements in *Biografbladet*,[30] and *Biografägaren*,[31] and a smaller one in *Filmjournalen*.[32] The company's branding is clearly visible—mostly promoting *Tant Grön* not as the first Technicolor film in Sweden but as "SF's first color film."[33] In addition, *Tant Grön* continued to be publicized with full-page advertisements sometime after its release (figure 3.1).[34]

Despite being a short film, *Tant Grön* received significant exposure from mixed reviews by journalists, writers, and critics, including Margareta Sjögren,[35] Lill (Ellen Liliedahl),[36] and Robin Hood (Bengt Idestam-Almquist).[37] Lill found the colors to be clear and brilliant and hence interesting enough for children.[38] The reviewer of *Arbetaren* found the color to be "consistently successful, fresh and natural."[39] *Aftontidningen* referred to the color as *kletiga* (sticky) and postcard-ish, while acknowledging that for fairy tales color could be used vividly.[40] Hood wrote that the "blurry and unsatisfactory" color did not serve any narrative purpose and was used dramatically only once.[41] The review in *Ny Dag* was scathingly critical, stating that only children might like "the roaring optical cacophony of Technicolor."[42] According to Colombs of *Dagens Nyheter*, the color was rather "stark and nuanced," and in the wide shots, color flowed out and it became difficult to perceive the details.[43] In contrast, the US-based *Variety* commented: "Excellent Technicolor enhances the film's story considerably."[44] Nils Beyer of *Morgontidningen* penned that it was a simple and exciting film for a five-year-old, with images that are "dripping with color," and the reviewer of *Aftonbladet* remarked rather brutally: "We would not talk about the colors. . . . In some kind of eagerness to get as many color clicks as possible on each frame, they have mostly succeeded in creating a garish and inharmonious color mess."[45]

It is possible that the presence of color in the name of the film title itself influenced some aesthetic decisions by the filmmakers, and the same also brought in additional attention and expectations of the critics. The color was perceived as unsatisfactory or unsuccessful when the film was scrutinized not as a short film for young children but just as a color film. As a result of the extensive promotion and critical prominence given to *Tant Grön*, Technicolor's debut in Sweden certainly created a stir.

"'Cause You Give Me Technicolor Dreams": *Lappblod* (1948)

Technicolor's attempt at winning Sweden over backfired with *Lappblod*. The film is a love story about the Sámi man Arvi and the Sámi woman Aino against the winter backdrop of the beautiful Swedish Lapland (figure 3.2). *Lappblod*'s budget was initially reported as half a million kronor, which later rose to approximately

FIGURE 3.1 The three titular aunts in *Tant Grön, tant Brun och tant Gredelin* (*Aunt Green, Aunt Brown and Aunt Lilac*, 1947). The short film enjoyed significant exposure as a color film adaptation of a beloved narrative but received mixed reviews for its color. (Courtesy of AB Svensk Filmindustri and Svenska filminstitutet.)

1 million kronor.[46] At the time, a typical black-and-white Swedish film budget was around 250,000–300,000 kronor or higher.[47] The head of Technicolor's technical department visited the first day of shooting in April 1946, and Technicolor exercised its usual assertive control on the cinematography.[48] It is not clear whether the film was shot using 16mm or 35mm raw stock, but the single-strip monopack process was mentioned in reports.

FIGURE 3.2 Arvi, the protagonist, with his love interest, Aino, in *Lappblod* (*Sámi Blood*, 1948). The outdoor scenes in Technicolor were praised, while every other aspect of the film was lambasted by the critics. The failure of *Lappblod* had pivotal repercussions for Technicolor films in Sweden. (Courtesy of AB Svensk Filmindustri and Svenska filminstitutet.)

In 1946, in advance of the film's release, headlines in the press referred to *Lappblod* as the first Swedish color film.[49] The contender, *Klockorna i gamla sta'n*, was not mentioned in any of these reports. Shooting required harsh white light that required a power of 180,000 watts and 900 amperes, or more than double the illumination for ordinary film.[50] In November 1946, twelve members of the crew suffered from gas poisoning from the lighting and had to spend several days in the hospital. The magazine *Ny Tid* attributed this unfortunate incident to color film: "The brightness of color film must be more than twice as strong, i.e., 150,000 watts against the usual 70,000. It has been possible to use carbon instead of ordinary arc-light lamps and in doing so, such a strong carbon oxide has been produced that the staff have been surprised by the dangerous gas one by one during the recording."[51]

Lappblod was reported to be released in "two versions," one obviously in Swedish and another one in English, in a hope to increase the foreign market for Swedish film.[52] As in most of the Technicolor films of 1933–1949, Natalie Kalmus was credited as a "color consultant" for *Lappblod*. At the time Technicolor did not have a self-sufficient laboratory in Sweden; ultimately the delay associated with postproduction was crucial for *Lappblod*'s "race" with *Klockorna*. The Cinecolor copying process of *Klockorna* was completed in Hollywood,[53] and the film was finally released on December 30, 1946, thus winning the title of the "first Swedish color feature film."

It was reported that *Lappblod* would be developed in the United States,[54] and then sent to the film laboratory in London for copying and printing.[55] Multiple reports and communications from Technicolor Limited (the UK company of the Technicolor Corporation based in the United States) in 1946 and 1947 confirm that the postproduction stage was hindered by problems associated with damage on color negatives in many scenes and other miscellaneous errors.[56] According to a report on May 22, 1947, from Technicolor's F. N. Busch, there were many "unusable" scenes in which the color appeared to "shift."[57] A telegram from Busch dated November 4, 1947, shows that there were also issues with rolls of film being over the permitted length, and "impossible" instructions regarding "dissolves," "opticals," and "fades."[58] A December 1947 report of *Expressen* bemusedly pointed out that even this year it was "Christmas without *Lappblod*."[59] Technicolor's laboratories in New Jersey, Hollywood, and London had an "incredible work backlog" in 1948 when they processed forty-six U.S. and ten UK films.[60] Finally, they also finished *Lappblod*, which was premiered on June 26, 1948. The saga of technical difficulties featured in the film's promotional leaflet.[61]

Lappblod was the first high-profile color film that was filmed in and based on Swedish Lapland. Technicolor's monopack photographed the outdoor scenes beautifully; looking at them even now evokes wonder, with miles of white snowy regions and herds of reindeer. In contrast, the facial colors of the actors in indoor scenes look unimpressive, partly because of the problematic makeup mentioned earlier. According to most of the reviews, Technicolor captured the beauty of the Swedish mountain region very well.[62] *Skånska Dagbladet* mused: "The color is very hard and bright, and rarely evokes any mood. But we have seen many American color films, which have not been more pleasing to the eyes, so the Swedish color film techniques do not have to feel depressed."[63] However, almost all journalistic reviews and later scholarly studies lambasted the screenplay, the direction, and the performances of most of the actors.[64] *Lappblod* was such a commercial failure that Landsorganisationen i Sverige, the parent organization of Filmo, lost millions of kronor, which was "a scandal in the film world," and the following year Filmo went bankrupt.[65] As the film historian Leif Furhammar puts it, the production company and the director targeted not only Sweden but also an international market that was "completely uninterested in a Swedish mountain romance."[66] Given that the film was promoted so extensively, its utter failure showed that neither Swedish film journalists nor audiences were ready to accept color film just for the sake of the visual grandeur.

"Paint the [Film]Town Red": Technicolor-Inspired *Eldfågeln* (1952)

> And today one really might say that there is color on Swedish films. But, as a matter of fact—the first real Swedish film in color is still to come!
> —COLOUR OF SWEDISH FILM (Promotional
> Material; Stockholm: Terrafilms Produktions, 1952)

An account of Swedish color cinema would not be complete without a brief mention of Hasse Ekman's *Eldfågeln* (*The Firebird*, 1952), which was made using Gevacolor. A ballet segment, *Meeting with a Stranger*, was recorded and printed in Paris, during the Swedish film industry's strike in 1951. The producer Lorens Marmstedt was so impressed with the outcome that he decided to produce a color feature film on ballet and include *Meeting with a Stranger* as part of it. Eventually, *Eldfågeln* was produced, and the postproduction was completed at Denham in the United Kingdom.[67]

Eldfågeln is a love story of a Swedish prima ballerina and an Italian opera singer (figure 3.3). The cinematographers Göran Strindberg and Hilding Bladh experimented boldly with Gevacolor. Scott Higgins comments that "a Technicolor production engages us in the unfolding of a complex and determined design," and *Eldfågeln* claims similar attention.[68] In this film with melodramatic moments and skilled dance sequences, red is present in almost every other frame—from costumes to red flowers in a vase. Often other bright colors like blue and silver are used, making the film visually engaging. Apart from actor-singer Tito Gobbi's vocal performances, the ballet segments are the most interesting for their use of contrasting colors, long shadows, and the impressive sight of Ellen Rasch dancing, wearing a fiery red dress in the climax.

FIGURE 3.3 A moment from one of the ballet performances in *Eldfågeln* (*The Firebird*, 1952). The surreal imagery, contrasting hues, shadows, and dance movements made creative use of film color. (Courtesy of AB Svensk Filmindustri and Svenska filminstitutet.)

An English promotional publication for the film clearly states that *Eldfågeln* is influenced by Powell and Pressburger's famous Technicolor film *The Red Shoes* (1948).[69] *Eldfågeln* was promoted as an international color film with lead actors and locales of Sweden and Italy. According to Fredrik Gustafsson, red is the film's primary color, hence it is not only the ballet settings that connect the two films but also the expressive use of color, especially "a striking, bold and vibrant red that sometimes gives the film the impression of having been shot in 3D."[70] Furhammar comments that *Eldfågeln* is the first Swedish film in which color was used in an artistic manner.[71]

Despite *Eldfågeln's* bold use of color, extensive promotion, and international releases, Swedish media in the 1950s remained unimpressed. Robin Hood was the only critic who appreciated the quality of the dance.[72] The bold statement at the beginning of this section was echoed in Hood's review. Apart from Lill writing in *Svenska dagbladet*, both the color and the film were dismissed by reviewers as unsuccessful, with occasional interesting moments.[73] Nils Beyer, a critic for *Morgontidningen*, found the color to be largely uneven; he remarked that it could be politely considered as a student work.[74] The *Arbeteren* review criticized the director Ekman, asserting that while he wanted to make another *The Red Shoes*, he had overestimated his artistic power.[75] Contemporary critics were also "extremely hostile" toward international collaborations.[76] Hood claimed that they were being unfair toward the film's artistic qualities.[77] It is intriguing that while scholars would later consider the film to be significant in the history of Swedish color, at the time of its release *Eldfågeln* did not make an impact on Swedish film culture, either as a color film or as a film about performance art.

The Color Exotic: *En djungelsaga* (1957)

After *Lappblod*, the Technicolor processes were absent from Sweden until 1957, when *En djungelsaga* (*The Flute and the Arrow*) was released. This was a long period of absence, given that in 1949 only forty-nine three-strip Technicolor titles in English were released. By contrast, only fifteen complete Swedish color feature films (fiction) were released in 1949–1957: eleven were produced using Eastman Color; three in Gevacolor; and *En djungelsaga*, a wide-screen film, in Technicolor. *En djungelsaga* is a visually immersive and emotionally involving drama with documentary-like visuals and a "voice of god" narration that tells a story of the Muria tribe in the Bastar district of Bihar, India. The small village is subject to regular attacks from a leopard, and a hunter and his family become directly involved with this dangerous situation (figures 3.4 and 3.5).

In the 1930s and 1940s, the earlier versions of Technicolor systems were used to make short documentaries including "Technicolor specials," a notable series of short two-strip Technicolor live-action documentaries produced by Warner Bros. After that, film databases affirm that, in the 1940s, globally only a handful of feature-length documentaries were made using Technicolor's three-strip method. However, the development of monopack boosted the possibilities for outdoor shooting, and a significant number of documentaries used this process until the early 1950s.[78]

By the time *En djungelsaga* was produced, the technology had advanced to Technicolor V dye transfer, with Eastman Color negatives as raw stock and Technicolor 35mm dye-transfer printing technique. The film was made at a point in time that demonstrated, according to Anna Westerståhl Stenport, "the spectacular cinema cultures in 1950s Scandinavia."[79] There was a worldwide shift in the 1950s toward new technologies, including color, wide-screen formats, and 3D, trends that affected production, audience priorities, and critical assessment in Sweden, where in the mid-1950s Eastman Color was quickly becoming the popular color option. Yet, *En djungelsaga* was produced using Technicolor V— an expensive choice considering the costs of the "Technicolor package" and

FIGURE 3.4 Muria hunter Ginjo guarding the rice field during night watch in *En djungelsaga* (*The Flute and the Arrow*, 1957). He holds a flute decorated with cowrie, something many Muria hunters carry and play.

FIGURE 3.5 Chendru, the lively young protagonist from the Muria tribe, smiles at the camera behind the scenes of *En djungelsaga* (*The Flute and the Arrow*, 1957). This image was widely used for promotion and inspired one of the film posters. (Courtesy of AB Svensk Filmindustri and Svenska filminstitutet.)

postproduction. AgaScope, the wide-screen camera technology developed in Sweden, was also utilized. Both decisions aligned with the idea that *En djungel-saga* was a large-scale project aiming for a grand spectacle.

The press reports during the production highlighted the practical challenges involved in shooting a color film in a jungle, and during monsoon time filming had to be stopped.[80] The filming lasted from February 1955 to June 1957 with few gaps, using around 6,000 kilograms of filming equipment.[81] An additional difficulty was that the color film stocks were to be sent to London for developing within ten days of shooting; otherwise, the color would be "enlarged,"[82] a term possibly used to mean a smudge-related defect. Personnel at the production company AB Sandrew-Ateljéerna (commonly known as Sandrews) were as nervous about the color developing as they were about being in the forest.[83]

Examining the program pamphlets has been vital to understand Technicolor's role in promotion, region-wise. In the English-language cinema program, the focus is on the famed color system, with "Technicolor" printed diagonally across the page, right over the details of the crew, in large, bold red font and capital letters, resembling a handstamp. The content of the program focuses on Arne Sucksdorff's image as a star documentary filmmaker.[84] One of the Swedish programs elaborates Sucksdorff's achievements, filmography, and film philosophy, without mentioning many details of the film itself.[85] Another program includes positive excerpts from the premiere reviews and a paragraph on Sucksdorff's experience of making the film.[86] These testify to the popularity gained by Sucksdorff as an "auteur." Among the programs aimed at continental European audiences, the German cinema program includes no mention of Technicolor on the front page, only that *En djungelsaga* was a color film in wide-screen AgaScope.[87] The Danish program promoted the child actors and the wilderness as the main attractions, and less importance was given to Technicolor, which was only mentioned on the inside.[88]

The film's color and cinematography were hailed by Swedish reviewers as masterful, "radiantly" and "dizzyingly" beautiful.[89] Some predicted that the film would lead to an international breakthrough.[90] Nominated for a Palme d'Or at the Cannes Film Festival in 1958, *En djungelsaga* became a crucial example of attempting to introduce "the exotic elsewhere" to the Swedish audience.[91] Evidently, Technicolor was the ideal medium to capture the wild nature and indigenous Indian lifestyle in bright, dazzling colors.

The Technicolor films discussed in this chapter received significant exposure in the press. *Tant Grön* was a short film, yet it was reviewed by all the major newspapers; *Lappblod* was a largely publicized bilingual feature film in which color footage of Swedish Lapland was a highlight; *En djungelsaga* was the critically and commercially successful high-budget fairy-tale-like narrative of a far-off land. However, *Lappblod*'s economic failure and critical lambasting were fatal for Technicolor's attempt to really succeed in Sweden. The complexity of the huge cameras (these were in use until 1953, after which Technicolor started using Eastman Color negatives); the special lighting arrangements and potential dangers that eventually caused accidents; the absence of a local laboratory and delays in overseas postproduction; and the tremendous overall expenses made Technicolor monopack and Technicolor V undesirable to Swedish filmmakers and producers. By comparison, the Gevacolor system gained prominence around the period 1951–1954. Also, notably, in 1948 Technicolor had a huge workload to serve the U.S. and UK film sectors, and there was no evidence of any serious intention to expand into continental Europe.[92] Nevertheless, Technicolor's defining feature—the careful design of screen color—inspired filmmakers like Hasse Ekman and resulted in the ballet film *Eldfågeln*, which was at the time a unique cinematic experience. Technicolor also saw success with Sucksdorff's exotic chronicle, but by then the "glory" had faded. After seven years, Technicolor had another release in Sweden, *Blåjackor* (*Sailors*, 1964), but given that the popularity of the Technicolor monopack as well as the Technicolor film process in general had waned, it was possibly a delayed release. Almost none of the press reports focused on the film's color.[93] Around the same time, it is surprising how rapidly Eastman Color gained acceptance in the film industry: while from 1946 to 1954 only four Swedish films were produced using various color processes, thirty-two Eastman Color films were made during the period 1954–1959. The frequency of Eastman Color releases increased even more in the next decade, and eventually in 1967 *Elvira Madigan* won critical acclaim and financial success on an international level. The famed director Ingmar Bergman also accepted Eastman Color after an austere absence of color in his oeuvre. The partial use of color in *Alla dessa kvinnor* (*All These Women*, 1964) did not leave a mark; however, in *En passion* (*The Passion of Anna*, 1969) and especially in *Viskningar och rop* (*Cries and Whispers*, 1972), Bergman successfully experimented with color and cinematic language.

Technicolor thus had a truly limited stint in the Swedish film scene. The complexity of the production and postproduction phases, and the accessibility (both technically and economically) of other color processes like Gevacolor and Eastman Color in good part explain that history. Additionally, the general skepticism of the Swedish press and the film industry regarding film color during the late 1940s and early 1950s, and the shocking financial and critical failure of the first Technicolor feature, certainly also were among the principal factors behind Technicolor's brief endeavor in Sweden.

Notes

1   Sarah Street, *Colour Films in Britain: The Negotiation of Innovation, 1900–55* (London: Palgrave Macmillan/British Film Institute, 2012).
2   "George Eastman Museum—Color Advisory Service," George Eastman Museum, n.d., accessed November 30, 2021, https://www.eastman.org/technicolor/company /color-advisory-service.

3   *Lappblod* does not have a formal English title; the Swedish title is translated here. *Lapp* denotes the inhabitants of the Sapmí region. It is important to note that the inhabitants prefer the word *Sámi* over the derogatory term *Lapp*.

4   Tytti Soila, "Sweden," in *Nordic National Cinemas,* ed. Gunnar Iverson, Astrid Soderbergh Widding, and Tytti Soila (London: Routledge, 1998), 135–220.

5   John Belton, "Introduction: Colour Film," *Film History: An International Journal* 12, no. 3 (2000): 339–340.

6   D. F. Comstock, SE63411, 63411 (Kungl. Patent-och Registreringsverket, issued 1922), https://was.prv.se/spd/pdf/FqA4j3V7rB608KKJ4aHscA/SE214039.C1.pdf; D. F. Comstock, SE66528, 66528 (Kungl. Patent-och Registreringsverket, issued 1924), https://was.prv.se/spd/pdf/2OI5kTkw1FnSfAo8BkBrHw/SE66528.C1.pdf.

7   J. M. Andreas, SE118133, 118133 (Kungl. Patent-och Registreringsverket, issued 1947); J. M. Andreas, SE126692, 126692 (Kungl. Patent-och Registreringsverket, issued 1949).

8   "Stockholm i Färger (1933)," Svensk Filmdatabas, accessed August 20, 2021, http://www.svenskfilmdatabas.se/en/item/?type=film&itemid=85102.

9   Cinecolor is a two-color subtractive film process invented by William T. Crespinel in 1932—not to be confused with the additive two-color Cinecolor/Cinecolour of 1925 or Cinécolor of 1928. See Barbara Flückiger, "Cinecolor (subtractive 2 color)" Timeline of Historical Film Colors, 2012, https://filmcolors.org/timeline-entry/1297/.

10 John W. Boyle, "Kodacolor Gives Life to Travel Films," *American Cinematographer,* June 1934, 86–97.

11 "Nu Filmas," *Filmjournalen,* no. 32 (1946): 8; "Post," *Filmjournalen,* no. 33 (1946): 2.

12 See, for example, Street, *Colour Films in Britain*; Dirk Alt, "'Front in Farbe': Color Cinematography for the Nazi Newsreel, 1941–1945," *Historical Journal of Film, Radio and Television* 31, no. 1 (2011): 43–60; Josephine Diecke, "Agfacolor in (Inter) National Competition," in *Color Mania: The Material of Color in Photography and Film,* ed. Barbara Flückiger, Eva Hielscher, and Nadine Wietlisbach (Zurich: Lars Müller, 2020), 211–221; Zhaoyu Zhu, "Weaponised Colour: A Brief History of the Dye-Transfer Process in China's Cultural Revolution," Colour and Film: British Association of Film, Television and Screen Studies: Special Interest Group, 2019, https://colourandfilm.com/2019/01/23/weaponised-colour-a-brief-history-of-the-dye-transfer-process-in-chinas-cultural-revolution-by-zhaoyu-zhu/; and Dudley Andrew, "The Postwar Struggle for Color," *Cinema Journal* 18, no. 2 (1979): 41–52.

13 Belton, "Introduction: Colour Film."

14 Soila, "Sweden."

15 Arthur Elton, "Part I. The Small Countries," in *The Film Industry in Six European Countries: A Detailed Study of the Film Industry in Denmark as Compared with That in Norway, Sweden, Italy, France and the United Kingdom,* ed. Film Centre London (Paris: UNESCO, 1950), 17–84.

16 Leif Furhammar, *Filmen i Sverige: En Historia i Tio Kapitel Och En Fortsättning,* 3rd ed. (Stockholm: Dialogos and Svenska Filminstitutet, 2003).

17 Andrew, "Postwar Struggle for Color," 49.

18 Street, *Colour Films in Britain.*

19 Thomas C. Christensen, "Post-production at Nordisk Films Kompagni," in *100 Years of Nordisk Film,* ed. Lisbeth Richter Larsen and Dan Nissen (Copenhagen: Danish Film Institute, 2006), 5, http://primo.kb.dk/primo-explore/fulldisplay?docid=DFI01000035277.

20 Danish newspaper reports quoted in Christensen.

21 Filmson, Ramek, and Oldin cited in Kamalika Sanyal and Eduard Cuelenaere, "The Colour Remakes of Swedish Classics in the 1950s: Production, Promotion and Critical Reception in the Context of Technological Innovation," in *European Film Remakes*, ed. Eduard Cuelenaere, Gertjan Willems, and Stijn Joye (Edinburgh: Edinburgh University Press, 2021), 117–129.

22 "Veckorevy 1953-06-08 (1953)," Filmarkivet.se, accessed November 30, 2021, https://www.filmarkivet.se/movies/veckorevy-1953-06-08/.

23 Scott Higgins, *Harnessing the Technicolor Rainbow: Color Design in the 1930s* (Austin: University of Texas Press, 2007).

24 Barbara Flückiger, "Technicolor Monopack/Kodachrome Professional Type 5267/ Eastman Monopack 7267," Timeline of Historical Film Colors 2012, https:// filmcolors.org/timeline-entry/1302/.

25 Roland Sterner, "De Första Svenska Färgfilmerna," *Film Sound Sweden*, accessed December 29, 2017, http://www.filmsoundsweden.se/backspegel/fargfilm.html.

26 Hn., "Sagofilm På Röda Kvarn," *Arbetaren*, December 20, 1947; Maja-britta, "Tanter i Färg," *Filmnyheter*, no. 11 (1946): 15–16.

27 "Sagofarbor i Sigtuna," *Aftontidningen*, August 10, 1946.

28 Marco Polo, "'Tant Grön, Tant Brun Och Tant Gredelin,'" *Aftontidningen*, August 16, 1946.

29 Svensk Filmindustri, "Ur Rune Lindströms Skissbok," *Filmjournalen*, no. 37 (1946): 12–13.

30 Svensk Filmindustri, "Film Advertisement—SF—Tant Grön, Tant Brun Och Tant Gredelin," *Biografbladet* 28, no. 4 (1947).

31 Svensk Filmindustri, "Film Advertisement—SF—Tant Grön, Tant Brun Och Tant Gredelin," *Biografägaren* 22, no. 9/10 (1947).

32 Svensk Filmindustri, "Film Advertisement—SF—Tant Grön, Tant Brun Och Tant Gredelin," *Filmjournalen*, no. 19 (1947).

33 Only one SF program of *Tant Grön* mentions it as "den första svenska färgfilmen i Technicolor" (The first Swedish color film in Technicolor); Svensk Filmindustri, "Nu Kommer—Tant Grön, Tant Brun Och Tant Gredelin" (Svensk Filmindustri, 1947).

34 Svensk Filmindustri, "Slagnummer! Tant Grön Tant Brun Och Tant Gredelin," *Biografägaren* 23, no. 1 (1948).

35 Margareta Sjögren, "Tant Grön Tant Brun Och Tant Gredelin," *Expressen*, December 20, 1947.

36 Lill [Ellen Liliedahl], "Tant Gron, Tant Brun Och Tant Gredelin," *Svenska Dagbladet*, December 20, 1947.

37 Robin [Bengt Idestam-Almquist] Hood, "RODA KVARN: Tant Grön, Tant Brun Och Tant Gredelin," *Stockholms Tidningen*, December 20, 1947; Sjögren, "Tant Grön Tant Brun Och Tant Gredelin"; Lill [Ellen Liliedahl], "Tant Gron, Tant Brun Och Tant Gredelin."

38 Lill [Ellen Liliedahl], "Tant Gron, Tant Brun Och Tant Gredelin."

39 H.N., "Sagofilm På Röda Kvarn."

40 Bast., "Tant Grön, Tant Brun Och Tant Gredelin," *Aftontidningen*, December 20, 1947.

41 Hood, "RODA KVARN: Tant Grön, Tant Brun Och Tant Gredelin."

42 Snapp, "Tant Gron, Tant Brun Och Tant Gredelin," *Ny Dag*, December 20, 1947.

43 Colombs., "Röda Kvarn: 'Tant Grön, Tant Brun Och Tant Gredelin,'" *Dagens Nyheter*, December 20, 1947.

44 Winq., "Tant Gron, Tant Brun Och Tant Gredelin ('Aunt Green, Aunt Brown and Aunt Lilac') (SWEDISH-MADE) (COLOR)," *Variety*, February 18, 1948.

45 Nils Beyer, "Tant Grön, Tant Brun Och Tant Gredelin," *Morgontidningen*, December 20, 1947; Peo., "'Tant Grön, Tant Brun Och Tant Gredelin' På Röda Kvarn," *Aftonbladet*, December 20, 1947.

46 Sveriges Dyraste Film: I Varldrens Minsta Ateljé," *Aftonbladet*, April 1, 1946; Ton., "Första Färgfilmen Går Lös På 1 Milj.," *Expressen*, November 1, 1946.

47 "Feature Film, 1949: Prison," Ingman Bergman Foundation, accessed November 29, 2021, https://www.ingmarbergman.se/en/production/prison; Ton., "Första Färgfilmen Går Lös På 1 Milj."

48 "Svensk Långfilm i Färg Påbörjas i April," *Expressen*, March 14, 1946.

49 Theo., "Första Svenska Långfilmen i Färg Spelas In," *Ny Dag*, 1946; "Första Svenska Långfilmen i Färg," *Dagens Nyheter*, May 14, 1946; "Sveriges Första Färgfilm Vållade Gengasförgiftning," *Ny Tid*, November 2, 1946; Ton., "Första Färgfilmen Går Lös På 1 Milj."

50 "Sveriges Dyraste Film: I Varldrens Minsta Ateljé."

51 "Sveriges Första Färgfilm Vållade Gengasförgiftning."

52 "I FÄRG," *Morgontidningen*, June 23, 1946.

53 "I FÄRG."

54 Theo., "Första Svenska Långfilmen i Färg Spelas In"; Ton., "Första Färgfilmen Går Lös På 1 Milj."; "Sveriges Dyraste Film: I Varldrens Minsta Ateljé."

55 "Sveriges Dyraste Film: I Varldrens Minsta Ateljé."

56 F. N. Busch, "Technicolor Limited—Rapport Angående Felaktigheter å Negativen," *Technicolor Limited*, October 4, 1946; F. N. Busch, "Technicolor Limited—Den 11 December 1946," *Technicolor Limited*, December 11, 1946; "Technicolor Limited—Den 17 December 1946," *Technicolor Limited*, December 17, 1946; George Gunn, "Technicolor Limited—Den 28 Avril 1947," *Technicolor Limited*, April 28, 1947.

57 F. N. Busch, "Technicolor Limited—Den 22 Maj 1947," *Technicolor Limited*, May 22, 1947.

58 F. N. Busch, "Telegram Från Technicolor," November 4, 1947.

59 Ton., "Julen Utan Lappblod," *Expressen*, December 7, 1947.

60 Andrew, "Postwar Struggle for Color."

61 Filmo, "Produktions Uppgifter—Lappblod," 1948.

62 Kajax., "Fjällkolportage i Färg," *Ny Tid*, October 5, 1948; B-ff., "Royal: 'Lappblod,'" *Arbetaren*, June 28, 1948; Puck, "En Bra Film, Som Kunde Ha Varit Mycket Bättre," *Dagsposten*, June 27, 1948.

63 Svall., "Capitol: Lappblod," *AB Skånska Dagbladet*, November 30, 1948.

64 B-ff., "Royal: 'Lappblod'"; Alfa., "Lappblod På Royal," *Aftonbladet*, June 27, 1948; Puck, "En Bra Film, Som Kunde Ha Varit Mycket Bättre"; Jerome, "Royal: 'Lappblod,'" *Dagens Nyheter*, June 27, 1948; Rochelle Wright, "Dramatic Setting, Melodramatic Story: Lappblod," in *The Visible Wall: Jews and Other Ethnic Outsiders in Swedish Film* (Carbondale: Southern Illinois University Press, 1998), 153–157, https://books.google.fr/books?id=oH_06bh2XgwC; Furhammar, *Filmen i Sverige*.

65 "LO Förlorar Miljon På 'Lappblod': SKANDAL i Filmvärlden," *Aftonbladet*, December 14, 1948.

66 Furhammar, *Filmen i Sverige*.

67 Fredrik Gustafsson, *The Man from the Third Row: Hasse Ekman, Swedish Cinema and the Long Shadow of Ingmar Bergman* (New York: Berghahan Books, 2016).

68 Scott Higgins, *Harnessing the Technicolor Rainbow: Color Design in the 1930s* (Austin: University of Texas Press, 2007).

69 "COLOUR OF SWEDISH FILM."

70 Gustafsson, *Man from the Third Row.*

71 Furhammar, *Filmen i Sverige.*

72 Robin Hood [Bengt Idestam-Almquist], "Royal: Eldfågeln," *Stockholms Tidningen,* August 13, 1952.

73 Pressreaktion Svensk filmografi, "Eldfågeln (1955)," Svenska Filminstitutet, n.d.

74 Nils Beyer, "Eldfågeln," *Morgontidningen,* August 13, 1952.

75 Lasse Bergström, "Utan Eld Och Vingar Eldfågeln På Royal," *Arbetaren,* August 13, 1952.

76 Gustafsson, *Man from the Third Row.*

77 Hood cited in Astrid Söderbergh Widding, "Eldfågeln The Fire Bird," in *The Cinema of Scandinavia,* ed. Tytti Soila (London: Wallflower Press, 2005), 111–117.

78 Flückiger, "Technicolor Monopack/Kodachrome Professional Type 5267/Eastman Monopack 7267."

79 Anna Westerståhl Stenport, "Opening up the Postwar World in Color: 1950s Geopolitics and Spectacular Nordic Colonialism in the Arctic and Africa," in *Nordic Film Cultures and Cinemas of Elsewhere,* ed. Anna Westerståhl Stenport and Arne Lunde (Edinburgh: Edinburgh University Press, 2019), 105–125.

80 "Sucksdorffs Jaktdrama," *Dagens Nyheter,* June 28, 1955.

81 Sandrews, "En Djungelsaga (Swedish Program 1)" (Stockholm: Sandrews, 1957).

82 Ler., "Arne Sucksdorff Hemma Med Vilddjur i Bagaget," *Svenska Dagbladet,* June 28, 1955.

83 Gerd Osten, "Svensk Documentärfilm," *Östgöten,* October 15, 1957.

84 Sandrews, "The Flute and the Arrow" (Sandrews, 1957).

85 Sandrews, "En Djungelsaga (Swedish Program 2)" (Sandrews, 1957).

86 Sandrews, "En Djungelsaga (Swedish Program 1)."

87 UFA, "Dschungelsaga" (UFA, 1957).

88 Gefion film A/S, "En Junglesaga" (Gefion film A/S, 1957).

89 Press review excerpts in Sandrews, "En Djungelsaga (Swedish Program 1)."

90 Staffan Tjerneld cited in Emil Stjernholm, "Mobility and Marginalization: Arne Sucksdorff's Documentary Authorship in India and Brazil," in *Nordic Film Cultures and Cinemas of Elsewhere,* ed. Anna Westerstahl Stenport and Arne Lunde (Edinburgh: Edinburgh University Press, 2019), 67–75.

91 Stenport, "Opening up the Postwar World in Color."

92 Andrew, "Postwar Struggle for Color," 48.

93 "Blåjackor (1964)," Svensk Filmdatabas, accessed September 14, 2021, http://www .svenskfilmdatabas.se/sv/item/?type=film&itemid=4693#.

4

"Risk versus Conformity"

Soviet Color Film, 1956–1982

PHILIP CAVENDISH

The microscopic and mesmerizing exploration of icon paintings attributed to the eponymous hero of Andrei Tarkovsky's *Andrei Rublev* (1966) constitutes a landmark in the history of Soviet cinema. The significance of the sequence, which lasts some eight minutes and studies eleven paintings in total, lies less in the resort to color film technology per se; after all, the Soviet film industry had been releasing works in color from 1931 onward, and Tarkovsky's graduate diploma film, *The Steamroller and the Violin* (*Katok i skripka*, 1960), had been shot in color by the very same camera operator, Vadim Iusov.[1] Rather, it resides in the fact that a director with serious artistic pretensions, one who had already achieved international recognition courtesy of *Ivan's Childhood* (*Ivanovo detstvo*, 1962), had come to recognize that Soviet color film stock had become sufficiently sophisticated to render with reasonable fidelity the nuances of Russia's most celebrated religious artworks. The adoption of Soviet anamorphic wide screen necessitated a fragmentary presentation of Rublev's icons. Nevertheless, as Iusov himself subsequently confirmed, their overarching compositional dynamic and religious symbolism were less important to Tarkovsky than the brushstrokes, surface textures, decorative details, flowing lines, and chromatic palette.[2] The sequence constitutes a spiritual epiphany, the elevation of the raw material of quotidian reality, one scarred by brutality, violence, degradation, and hardship, into the sublime and luminous transparencies of art. Even if, from a purely technical point of view, the transition from black and white to color has been executed by means of a dissolve, rather than an editing cut, there can be little denying the immediacy of its impact: it is a ravishing and radical assault on the senses.

From an aesthetic point of view, the trajectory of Soviet cinema during the 1960s and 1970s is partly characterized by the gradual embrace of color after a period—the Khrushchev Thaw (1956–1964)—when black-and-white cinematography had been regarded as the more appropriate medium with which to interrogate the post-Stalinist condition. The growing acceptance of domestic color film stock—or Svema, as it was named after 1965, deriving from the Russian for "light-sensitive materials" (*svetochuvstvitel'nye materialy*)—enhanced the aesthetic potential of cinema and made possible, among other modes of inquiry, the filmic investigation of the fine-arts and folk-arts traditions.[3] For those interested in successive iterations of Svema during this period, in other words, the degree to which refinements in the production and processing of the film stock gradually improved its sensitivity, it would be sufficient to examine three documentary shorts by Sergei Parajanov, a director best known internationally for *Shadows of Forgotten Ancestors* (*Tini zabutykh predkiv*, 1964) and *The Color of Pomegranates* (*Tsvet granata*, 1969). The first of these shorts, *Golden Hands* (*Zoloti ruky*), released in 1957 by the Dovzhenko Film Studio in Kyiv, features a multiplicity of works by contemporary artists specializing in the Ukrainian folk-decorative tradition, among them two still lifes, *Exuberance* (*Buinaia*, 1946–1947) and *Watermelon, Carrot, Flowers* (*Garbus, morkva, kvity*, 1951), by the peasant artist Kateryna Bilokur. The second, *Hakob Hovnatanyan*, which dates from 1967 and was commissioned by the Yerevan Newsreel-Documentary Film Studio, derives its title from the pioneer of secular portrait painting in nineteenth-century Armenia (figure 4.1). The third, *Arabesques on a Theme of Pirosmani* (*Arabeski na temu Pirosmani*), released in 1985 by the Georgia Documentary Film Studio, offers a microscopic analysis of "neo-primitivist" paintings by Niko Pirosmanashvili, a self-taught artist and craftsman from the region of Kakheti, eastern Georgia, whose works were "discovered" by the Russian Futurists at the beginning of the twentieth century. Along with *Vasilii Surikov* (1959), a biographical feature film directed by Anatolii Rybakov, which incorporates several fragments of the artist's epic canvases, and *The Artist Petrov-Vodkin* (*Khudozhnik Petrov-Vodkin*, 1967), a documentary short by Iakov Mirimov dedicated to a modernist artist best known outside Russia for *The Bathing of a Red Horse* (*Kupanie krasnogo konia*, 1912), these works might be regarded as textbook illustrations of the degree to which Soviet color film stock during this period could accurately register the chromatic variations and tonal nuances of paintings and art forms belonging to different movements, schools, and stylistic traditions.

It is important to emphasize at this early juncture that critical appreciation of such masterpieces depends to a certain extent on the existing state of the camera negatives and release prints: depending on conditions of preservation and exhibition, color film stock is subject over time to chemical decomposition, with

FIGURE 4.1 Hakob Hovnatanyan, *Portrait of Shushanik Nadinyan* (1840–1850), National Gallery of Armenia. (Permission courtesy of the National Cinema Centre of Armenia.)

different processes decaying in different ways, and to different degrees. Recent 4K digital restorations of *Hakob Hovnatanyan* and *Arabesques*, for example, while undeniably representing a miraculous improvement on the versions previously available, do nevertheless raise important questions in relation to establishing with confidence the chromatic properties of the original negatives and first-generation release prints.[4] In relation to the digital restoration of *Andrei Rublev*, undertaken in 2008 with great fanfare by Mosfil'm as part of a larger millennial preservation project, Iusov later observed that it had achieved a degree of technical perfection far in excess of the film stock (Svema) that was available to him at the time.[5] Further complications arise in relation to establishing with precision the film stocks actually employed on Soviet color productions during the post-Thaw era. The reason for this uncertainty lies in the decision taken toward the end of the 1960s by Goskino, the state body with oversight of the film industry, to permit limited imports of Eastman Color.[6] Since the collapse of the Soviet Union, it has become clear that this initiative gave rise to an energetic and (at times) acrimonious debate within the filmmaking establishment about the relative virtues of Eastman Kodak versus Svema. Andrei Konchalovsky, for example, who coauthored the screenplay for *Andrei Rublev* and directed several critically acclaimed films during the 1960s and 1970s, has trenchantly dismissed Svema as "shit."[7] Others, like Levan Paatashvili, the camera operator who worked successfully with the film stock on Konchalovsky's very own *Lovers' Romance*

(*Romans o vliublennykh*, 1975), have contested that, while Svema undeniably required enormous reserves of patience and expertise, as well as regular testing (because successive batches could be inconsistent in terms of sensitivity), it was reasonably serviceable.[8] One film from this period, *The Bonus* (*Premiia*, 1974), a quasi-documentary feature film directed by Sergei Mikaelian, was photographed using both film stocks on the grounds that they responded differently to the fluctuating lighting conditions in the venue in which the action was ostensibly taking place (a daylong Communist Party meeting in an administrative building overlooking a construction site). The decision by Vladimir Chumak, the camera operator, to shoot with Kodak during the day and Svema in the evening reversed the conventional wisdom about the respective sensitivities and latitudes of the two film stocks.[9] It implies, furthermore, that there may have been a degree of snobbery on the part of those who preferred the foreign product. An abundance of evidence, some published contemporaneously, attests to a perceived hierarchy of privilege within the Soviet filmmaking community at this time.[10] This insinuates that there were favored directors, or those with the necessary personal contacts, or those whose films were potentially exportable, and thus capable of earning foreign currency, who conspired to gain access to Kodak while those less fortunate were forced to struggle with Svema.

The challenge for the film historian lies in the fact that the decision to import Kodak was concealed from the public because it implied Soviet technological backwardness. Archival records, if they indicate the film stock, which is rare, tend to be misleading on this count. The knowledge that Tarkovsky's *Solaris* (1972) and *Mirror* (*Zerkalo*, 1974) were filmed with Kodak has emerged only thanks to interviews given by Iusov since the collapse of the Soviet Union, and a private journal kept by Tarkovsky that was published for the first time in 1993 and only in French translation.[11] By the same token, it is only courtesy of Konchalovsky's memoirs and his posthumous eulogy to Georgii Rerberg, the camera operator on the films in question, that it has been possible to confirm that *A Nest of Gentlefolk* (*Dvorianskoe gnezdo*, 1969) and *Uncle Vania* (*Diadia Vania*, 1970), two of the most impressive screen adaptations of literary classics during the post-Thaw period, were shot with Eastman Color.[12] The digital restoration of *The Color of Pomegranates*, undertaken in 2014 by Martin Scorsese's Film Foundation as part of its World Cinema Project, has confirmed the use of Eastman Color for the camera negative (Parajanov complained bitterly to his managers at Armenfil'm that his camera operator had been forced to spend six months testing "defective" Svema before shooting had even begun).[13] The critical response to this restoration on the part of some specialists demonstrates the exceedingly complex nature of the task.[14]

Debates about the properties of film stocks, whether domestic or foreign, were not the only factors that determined the approach to color cinematography in the Soviet Union, but they certainly shaped the critical discourses that emerged during the Thaw and beyond. These discourses evolved with the passage of time in line with successive iterations of the film stock; the relaxation of official cultural policies as a result of the Thaw, which encouraged a greater degree of formal experimentation; and trends in the international sphere, for example, the public embrace of color by respected auteur figures like Michelangelo Antonioni, Federico Fellini, and François Truffaut, many of whose films, even if they were not available to the Soviet public, had been watched by students at the All-Union State Institute of Cinematography (VGIK).[15] To some extent, the broad parameters of these discourses had been established much earlier, indeed, as early as 1945, a landmark year because it signaled the moment when, courtesy of the Red Army occupation of the I. G. Farben factory in Wolfen, eastern Germany, the Soviet film industry had gained access to the patents for the Agfacolor monopack process, which had been available for 35mm since 1939. Several symbolically significant documentaries, among them *Berlin Conference* (*Berlinskaia konferentsiia*) and *Victory Parade* (*Parad pobedy*), both released in the summer of 1945, were photographed using existing stocks of Agfacolor. Their technical quality was sufficiently impressive to persuade Sergei Eisenstein to experiment with a single color episode in the second part of *Ivan the Terrible* (*Ivan Groznyi*, 1946), although for censorship reasons this could not be released until 1958.[16]

Coupled with these momentous events, and prompted by the simultaneous acquisition of a large quantity of feature-length fiction films in color from the Berlin Reichsfilmarchiv, the months of September and October 1945 witnessed the convening of a special conference in Moscow dedicated to the challenges of color cinematography. In addition to industry officials, the participants included prominent film directors, camera operators, production artists, laboratory specialists, and members of the creative intelligentsia, among them art historians.[17] By and large, these participants were unimpressed by the films screened at the conference; indeed, in the case of the art historians present, the reaction verged on the scathing.[18] The limitations of the color technologies on display were universally recognized: the degree of artifice, the distortion of natural color toward the blue-green end of the spectrum, the tendency toward oversaturation (largely the result of exposure requirements), and the absence of volume and aerial perspective. Participants roundly condemned the haphazard and tasteless orchestration of color in the domain of set and costume design, creative approaches that privileged vividness at the expense of tonal nuance, and the frequent lack of color dramaturgy. The speeches of the delegates made little attempt to distinguish between the different properties of Technicolor and Agfacolor, the former tending toward blocks of saturated, unvariegated, and "cardboard-like" color, the latter characterized by paler, softer tints and pastel shades.[19] These attitudes notwithstanding, it was accepted that the new technology might potentially be appropriate for specific artistic purposes, for example, animation and "live-action" adaptations of folktales and magical tales, where "naive," "primitive," and nonrealistic color might be warranted.[20] For some delegates, notably Alexander Dovzhenko, famous for his poetic masterpiece *Earth* (*Zemlia*, 1930), the lure of color as a technological novelty and uplifting "attraction," especially in view of the deprivations of war, was irresistible.[21] Such sentiments appeared very much to reflect the official line. The opening day of the conference witnessed the announcement of a massive investment in color film production by Ivan Bol'shakov, president of the Committee for Cinematic Affairs; indeed, 50 percent of output for the following year was earmarked for such productions.[22] Several films released during the late-Stalinist period (1945–1953), for example, *The Stone Flower* (*Kamennyi tsvetok*, 1946), a "live-action" screen adaption of a Uralic folktale published by Pavel Bazhov in 1938, won international awards for their cinematography.

If the late-Stalinist period subsequently came to be regarded as one of relative color abundance, the Thaw period, by contrast, was characterized by color "fear."[23] The statistics are revealing. In 1956, the year of Khrushchev's "Secret Speech," fifty color films were released in the Soviet Union; seven years later (i.e., one year before Khrushchev's removal from power), that number had dwindled to three.[24] The reasons for this rapid decline are various. The artifice and distortions of the film stock, coupled with the expense, had given rise to an attitude of repudiation. This is best illustrated by the advice given to the actress Iia Savvina by Andrei Moskvin, the camera operator responsible for shooting the color sequence in *Ivan the Terrible*: "If you have a poor screenplay, shoot in color, wide screen. If the screenplay is average, shoot in black and white, wide screen. If the screenplay is good, shoot in black and white, 4:3. The exceptions prove the rule."[25] For the Thaw generation, perhaps unconsciously imbibing Eisenstein's view (based on the technology available to him at the time) that color film was a "vulgarian," a "tyrant," and a "disobedient instrument in the hands of the master and experimenter," the crudity of color had become tarnished by its associations with the "monumental style" and rose-tinted varnishing of late-Stalinist cinema.[26] Bearing in mind the artistic imperatives of the Thaw, which encouraged a more honest engagement with social problems, a more nuanced examination of emotional and psychological dilemmas, and the privileging of the private over the public, color cinematography was treated as something alien and surplus to requirements. The quasi-documentary conceits of Italian neorealism, several examples of which had been showcased at a film festival in Moscow in October 1956, also exerted a magnetic attraction. Even beyond the formal ending of the Thaw in 1964, and the increasing hostility on the part of industry officials and the state apparatus toward "new wave" aesthetics, which resulted in scores of films being mutilated or shelved during the 1970s, reservations about the relevance of color were persistent. Tarkovsky, for example, in an interview recorded in 1970, referred to color as "one of the most serious problems in cinema. And one that has not entirely been resolved."[27] He was referring primarily to theoretical and conceptual concerns—during the interview he expressed his preference for "invisible" color—but the inadequacies of Svema were still causing profound concerns. Two years later, one of the pioneers of

Soviet color film technology in the 1930s, the camera operator Fedor Provorov, criticized the low sensitivity rating of Svema (65 ASA) and argued that, from a purely technical point of view, this rendered virtually impossible the shooting of scenes in the evening and at night.[28] In 1973, Ionas Gritsius, the camera operator who had photographed Grigorii Kozintsev's award-winning *Hamlet* (1964) and *King Lear* (1970), argued that the deficiencies of Svema meant that black-and-white cinematography was by no means doomed to extinction.[29] In 1975, at a time when color accounted for around 90 percent of all new releases,[30] the camera operator Viacheslav Egorov characterized the unreliability of Svema as a "sword of Damocles" that was "hanging over the heads ... of film-units."[31] In his view, this had given rise to collective risk aversion and "visual stagnation."[32]

If Svema was universally regarded as an imperfect aesthetic instrument at this time, this did not mean that color could not be exploited creatively and satisfyingly for specific artistic purposes and in relation to particular generic categories. By and large, from the late 1950s onward, color was reserved for the sphere of the fabular or fantastic: screen adaptations of folktales and magical tales (both Russian and non-Russian), adventure films for children and young adults, science-fiction fantasies, and screen adaptations of literary works characterized formally by elements of folk stylization. A parallel trend can be detected in the vogue for biographical films about writers, poets, painters, and composers, the majority of them belonging to what the veteran screenplay writer and film critic Mikhail Bleiman dubbed the "archaic" or "poetic school."[33] A third category lay in the sphere of screen adaptations of canonical literary texts that, because they were well known internationally, were potentially earmarked for export; occasionally, as evidenced by Sergei Bondarchuk's *War and Peace* (*Voina i mir*, 1965–1967), this category crossed into the zone of the historical epic or costume drama. In addition to these categories, and increasingly so with the passage of time, color was deployed for comedies of everyday life and contemporary social or psychological dramas, but this exploitation, with one or two notable exceptions, remained naturalistic for the most part.

One of the more remarkable color études in Soviet cinema of the 1960s and 1970s is Mikhail Kalik's *The Child in Search of the Sun* (*Chelovek idet za solntsem*), released by the Moldova Film Studio in 1961. Like Tarkovsky's *Andrei Rublev*, this film operates according to the principle of metamorphosis, but here quotidian reality is elevated into the realms of the poetic not by virtue of the icon-painter's brush but by means of the child's observational gaze. Shot on Svema for the most part in the Moldovan capital of Chişinău, Kalik's film constitutes an exercise in estrangement: the discoveries of the protagonist, a seven-year-old boy called Sandu, played by Nika Krimus, relate not only to the gradual expansion of his domestic environment but also to his experience of the world beyond its boundaries as a visual, sensory phenomenon. The importance of color as an instrument of perception is established right at the beginning of the film when Sandu and his friends contemplate the city's horizons from the roof of an apartment block: several point-of-view shots convey Sandu's amazement on beholding the world via colored filters. Building on this revelation, the film subsequently treats color as an immediate and palpable presence rather than a relatively imperceptible background. Numerous objects, many of them distinctively colored, are registered by the child's consciousness: advertising posters, balloons, fruit and vegetable stalls, traffic lights, flowers, goldfish, neon lights, a disco ball, the recently mown sward of a football pitch, and a setting sun. In the vicinity of these colors, more restrained and subtle chromatic environments, for example, the cascading waterfall at Valea Morilor Park in central Chișinău, are registered with greater awareness. At times, the film feels like a quasi-scientific tutorial on the changing perception of color in different light conditions and material environments. Reflected light from the surfaces of balloons, for example, demonstrably transforms the colors of objects in close proximity. Raindrops splashing onto the windscreen of a lorry, and a jet of water sprayed directly onto the camera lens from a hose act as prisms by means of which colors are intensified. An overcast sky subdues the chromatic environment of the street on which Sandu encounters a funeral procession and is thus forced to confront the fact of human mortality. Kalik's film was welcomed on its release as a "ciné-poem," but this designation does not quite do justice to the perceptual nature of its quest and what one critic defined as its "color playfulness."[34] In this respect, *The Child in Search of the Sun* moves well beyond the concerns of Albert Lamorisse's *The Red Balloon* (*Le ballon rouge*, 1956), its main precursor in the genre of children's film, and one that was hugely influential in the Soviet Union during the Thaw era.

The idea of poetic metamorphosis is a persistent strategy in Soviet experiments with color during the 1960s and 1970s; at times, indeed, it verges on a form of spiritual emancipation, even a mode of escapism, which heralds a reluctance, if not refusal, to engage with modern Soviet reality. This is very much part of the aesthetic program of the so-called archaic school. Conceptually speaking, films like Parajanov's *Shadows* and *The Color of Pomegranates* constitute a mode of time travel, one in which the Soviet viewer is transported to historical epochs very much removed from the present day. Both films are immersive experiences, sensory tapestries woven from the fabric of shapes, lines, textures, colors, and acoustic environments. *Shadows* is a screen adaptation of a novella published in 1911 by the Ukrainian writer Mykhailo Kotsiubyns'kyi: this draws upon themes and motifs that belong to the folk-religious culture of Hutsul communities living in the eastern Carpathian Mountains. *The Color of Pomegranates* seeks to resurrect the world of Sayat-Nova, an eighteenth-century troubadour (*ashugh*) celebrated as Armenia's national poet. Although this film essentially constitutes an exploration of Sayat Nova's inner consciousness and the landscapes of his poetic imagination, the outer kernel of his world—as represented by the seminary in which he is educated as a child and adolescent; the sacred manuscripts that he reads as part of his religious instruction; the carpets woven by his parents; the Turkish-style bathhouse in which he first encounters the naked human body; the palace rooms in which he conducts his courtship of Anna, the sister of King Erekle II; and the monastery to which he withdraws after this romance is exposed—is a vital part of the immersive experience.

Iurii Illienko, the Ukrainian camera operator who photographed *Shadows*, has spoken of the "symphonic" orchestration of color in the film—that is, the ways in which individual colors or combinations of colors were exploited as instruments in the creation of a larger poetic and symbolic whole.[35] The film is structured according to a number of discrete episodes, each possessing its own color dominant, depending on setting and theme. One section within this "orchestra" operates within the realm of ethnographic authenticity; it is thus imbued with the "naive," "primitive," and vivid colors associated with Hutsul folk-religious art. A second section is concerned to communicate the shapes, textures, and chromatic plenitude of the natural world: mountains, valleys, fast-flowing rivers, flora and fauna, seasonal shifts, and light conditions at different altitudes and at different times of day. The third section operates within the zone of dramaturgical or psychological-emotional imperative: subdued color tones, even monochrome, are employed for episodes in a minor key; vibrant, exuberant, and intense color is reserved for those in a major key. The most remarkable scene in the film, one of the pinnacles of 1960s color cinematography in the Soviet Union, is the exterior sequence showing the wedding procession of Ivan, the male protagonist, and his wife, Palahna: shot with a handheld camera through autumnal leaves, the rapid panning and abrupt montage are so head-spinning that the colors and shapes of these leaves at times verge on the abstract. Even allowing for the significance of certain interior scenes, for example, the service in the chapel during the opening moments of the film, with its icons and ritual objects, and the postwedding "harnessing" ritual inside Palahna's home, *Shadows* is a film photographed very much *en plein air*.

Symphonic color orchestration is also present in *The Color of Pomegranates*, although here the absence of spoken dialogue, the static and largely axial position of the camera, and the structural organization of the narrative into episodes invite more explicit identification with the early-medieval fresco and the traditions of the Armenian and Persian miniature. Authenticity of location and artifact, including costume, is very much part of the poetic fabric of Parajanov's world in this film. The artifacts and costumes function primarily on the level of ethnographic and decorative detail. Nevertheless, like color, they also perform realistic and pictorial-symbolic functions. The film is a patchwork quilt of leitmotifs, tropes, and symbols that, when taken together, communicate Parajanov's interest in exploring the tension between sensuous embrace of the material world and ascetic withdrawal. As the title of the film insinuates, color is exploited to draw attention to a series of poetic associations or alignments. The blood-red juice of the pomegranate in the prologue, for example, subsequently becomes associated with the red dyes of woven carpets and the fiery-red tunic worn by Princess

Anna at the height of her passion. The virginal, white lace that she sews in her bedchamber (presumably an intended trousseau) is aligned chromatically and in terms of its flowing forms with the milk that trickles gently around the contours of the female breast in the bathhouse. The ascetic world, by contrast, is represented by stone-gray flagstones, charcoal-gray roof tiles, faded manuscript pages, copper-red earthenware jars, and the black cassocks of fellow monks.

Although neither *Shadows* nor *The Color of Pomegranates* can be defined as fabular in the strict sense, their innovative visual aesthetics proved influential as far as genres of the fantastic were concerned. Screen adaptations of folktales and magical tales, as well as classic tales for children, belong squarely within this category. This genre was treated seriously as an art form in the Soviet Union due to the importance attributed to folk culture on the part of the Russian intelligentsia during the nineteenth and twentieth centuries. This had given rise to an astonishingly rich tradition of theatrical and balletic stagings of folkloric texts, as well as musical interpretations, visual reimaginings in the realms of figurative painting and book illustration, and cinematic adaptations, both "live-action" and animated. Given that the authorities treated the genre as a relatively innocuous one from an ideological perspective, it also served at times as a vehicle for quite daring formal experiment. A particularly interesting example is Irina Povolotskaia's *The Little Scarlet Flower* (*Alen'kii tsvetochek*, 1976), a screen adaptation of a short story by Sergei Aksakov that first appeared in 1858 and constituted a Russianized version of Leprince de Beaumont's *La Belle et la Bête* (1756). As photographed by Aleksandr Antipenko, who had worked with Parajanov on the ill-fated (because halted) *Kyiv Frescoes* (*Kyivs'ki freski*, 1966), the enchanting palace of the Beast is faux-Gothic in style, and thus vaguely reminiscent of Jean Cocteau's more famous *La Belle et la Bête* (1946), but the chromatic orchestration (unlike Aksakov's source text) accentuates decay rather than luxuriousness: tarnished silver ornament, faded gilt picture frames, darkly stained (at times mahogany-black) furniture, and a profusion of crimson-red, orange, and straw-yellow, very possibly dried, autumnal flowers. One Soviet film historian describes the effect as akin to an etching or medieval drawing with red chalk.[36]

Painterly explorations of theatricalized ornamental interiors were not the sole preserve of the "archaic" or "fabular" school in Soviet cinematography of the 1960s and 1970s. The experience of otherworldly immersion was also generated by a number of screen adaptations of prerevolutionary literary classics. This procedure was another discreet mechanism with which to resurrect the antiquated modes of being swept away by the October Revolution. Even if the source texts themselves often critiqued the moral lassitude, self-indulgence, and arrogance of the nobility and intelligentsia before 1917, and in so doing were thus rendered palatable from the official point of view, their repackaging or re-presentation during the Brezhnevite era (1964–1982) was frequently suffused with a sense of nostalgia. Much in the manner of the historical costume drama, and drawing their inspiration from the traditions of the theater, both prerevolutionary and postrevolutionary, such productions derive a quasi-fetishistic pleasure from the opulence and elegance, albeit at times faded, of the nobility's town residences and country estates before October 1917. The antique objects and furnishings, the fashionable period costumes, the sumptuous interior decor, and the extensive gardens and grounds, with their ubiquitous gazebos and ponds, are treated as active chromatic agents rather than neutral observers. The most intelligent of these adaptations, *A Nest of Gentlefolk* and *Uncle Vania*, the former adapted from Ivan Turgenev's novel (first published in 1859), and the latter a cinematic restaging of Anton Chekhov's play (first performed in 1898), were shot by Georgii Rerberg, a cameraman of considerable distinction. Rerberg's subtle explorations of light, texture, and tone, and his technique of bouncing natural light off reflecting surfaces rather than resorting to artificial lighting, distinguish him markedly from his contemporaries. His stylistic "signature" is located in the avoidance of dramatic contrast and preference for understatement, which reflects the complexity of human interactions on the emotional and psychological plane. The emphasis on filtered and diffuse light, and chromatic valences that are desaturated and nuanced, for example, during rainfall, or the so-called magic hour, meant that the transitions between color and monochrome in his films, an artistic choice very often born of necessity (i.e., inconstant supplies of Kodak), do not overtly draw attention to themselves. *Uncle Vania* is an excellent illustration of these strategies. After the sepia-tinted monochrome of the prologue, which involves a long, slow tracking shot into the depths of the summer residence in which the dramatic action takes place, and an extensive montage sequence consisting of sepia-tinted photographs that date from the period in which the play is set, the rest of the film is shot within a relatively restricted and muted chromatic range: off-white planks of wood, sage-green plastered walls, sandy-brown jackets, light-gray waistcoats, cream-white shawls, and the dull, gleaming brass of samovars (figure 4.2). Moments of dramatic intensity, when they occur, for example, the anguished moment of parting between Astrov and Elena Serebriakova, are accompanied by the introduction of a melancholic, gently tinted, grayish blue. The restriction of the palette, even if tasteful, parallels the suffocation experienced by the protagonists.

A chapter of this length cannot possibly convey the full range and sophistication of Soviet color cinematography during the 1960s and 1970s. Some of the works that have gained a place among the classics of world cinema, for example, Tarkovsky's *Mirror*, could alone withstand detailed scrutiny in terms of their visual aesthetic. This period witnesses two extraordinary works in color by Sergei Urusevskii, a camera operator who turned to direction in the late 1960s: *The Flight of the Pacer* (*Beg inokhodtsa*, 1968), a screen adaptation of a novella by the Kyrgyz writer Chyngyz Aitmatov; and *Sing, Poet, Sing* (*Poi pesniu, poet*, 1971), a mesmeric evocation of the life of the early twentieth-century peasant poet Sergei Esenin. Biographical films about painters which are themselves stylized visually in accordance with the aesthetics of their paintings—see, for

FIGURE 4.2 Innokentii Smoktunovskii in the role of Uncle Vania in Andrei Konchalovsky's 1970 film adaptation of Anton Chekhov's play.

example, Giorgi Shengelaia's *Pirosmani* (1969)—would also merit detailed attention. The fact that several of the directors discussed in this essay were themselves practicing artists beyond the realms of cinema—Urusevskii was a painter whose works had been publicly exhibited, Parajanov specialized in innovative collage design, and Tarkovsky experimented with Polaroids—further underlines the symbiotic relationship between the fine-arts and decorative-arts traditions and Soviet color cinematography during the Khrushchev and Brezhnevite eras.[37] Their films, and those of other directors, offer visual confirmation of the idea that imperfections in the available medium (color film stock) did not necessarily negate the possibility of creative self-expression. Ultimately, therefore, it could be argued that the imperative of risk was still very much alive and well.

Notes

1   For a study of the early history of Soviet color film, see Philip Cavendish, "Ideology, Technology, Aesthetics: Early Experiments in Soviet Color Film, 1931–45," in *A Companion to Russian Cinema*, ed. Birgit Beumers (Oxford: Wiley-Blackwell, 2016), 270–291.

2   Vadim Iusov, "Vadim Iusov o s"emkakh fil'ma *Andrei Rublev*," accessed July 4, 2021, https://www.youtube.com/watch?v=_A2kK_3pzNs.

3   Svema was a monopack system modeled on the Agfacolor patents that had been acquired by the Red Army as a "trophy of war" in early 1945. Outside the Soviet Union this film stock was referred to as "Sovcolor," and occasionally even "Magicolor," but within the Soviet film industry itself from 1947 onward it was known as DS-1 and LN-1. The two different types referred to the versions sensitized for

shooting in conditions of natural daylight (*dnevnoi svet*) and those sensitized for shooting with tungsten-filament lights (*lampy nakalivaniia*) in studio interiors. Subsequent generations of the respective stocks were indicated by the numbers after the acronyms.

4 *Hakob Hovnatanyan* and *Arabesques* were restored in 2018 as part of the Hamo-Bek-Nazarov Project. My very great thanks to the curator of this project, the writer and filmmaker Daniel Bird, for granting me access to these versions of the films.

5 Sergei Sychev, "'Mosfil'm' pokazal v Kannakh otrestavrirovannuiu *Voinu i mir* Bondarchuka," *Kinopoisk*, May 12, 2018, https://www.kinopoisk.ru/media/article /3171864.

6 V. G. Komar et al., "Obzor rabot po kinotekhnike za 1969 g.," *Tekhnika kino i televideniia* (1970.5): 26.

7 Tamara Sergeeva, ed., "Vsego odna zhizn': Rerberg v vospominaniiakh kinemato-grafistov," *Iskusstvo kino* (2000.8): 70.

8 M. Goldovskaia, "Snimat'—kak chuvstvovat'," *Iskusstvo kino* (1979.7): 82–100.

9 Ia. L. Butovskii, "Kak snimalsia kinofil'm *Premiia*," interview with V. G. Chumak, *Tekhnika kino i televideniia* (1975.9): 34–39.

10 V. Egorov, "Risk protiv standarta: Zametki operatora," *Iskusstvo kino* (1975.7): 120–127.

11 M. Turovskaia, "Interv'iu s Iusovym V. I.," in *Sem s polovinoi, ili Fil'my Andreia Tarkovskogo* (Moscow: Iskusstvo, 1991), 42–51. For Tarkovsky's diary, see the entry for July 11, 1973, in Andrei Tarkovski, *Journal 1970–1986*, trans. Anne Kichilov and Charles H. de Brantes (Paris: Cahiers du cinéma, 1993), 86.

12 Andrei Konchalovskii, *Vozvyshaiushchii obman* (Moscow: Kollektsiia "Sovershenno sekretno," 1999), 111; Sergeeva, "Vsego odna zhizn'," 70.

13 Parajanov's complaint is cited in James Steffen, *The Cinema of Sergei Parajanov* (Madison: University of Wisconsin Press, 2013), 130. The use of Eastman Color has been confirmed in an email to the author dated July 9, 2021, by Daniel Bird, one of the consultants on the restoration project.

14 James Steffen, "What Color Is the Color of Pomegranates? A Critique of the 2014 World Cinema Project/L'Immagine Ritrovata Restoration of Parajanov's Film," April 10, 2018, http://www.jamesmsteffen.net/2018/04/what-color-is-the-color-of -pomegranates-a-critique-of-the-2014-world-cinema-projectlimmagine-ritrovata -restoration-of-parajanovs-film/.

15 Andrei Shemiakin, "Chuzhaia rodnia," in *Kinematograf ottepeli: Kniga pervaia*, ed. V. Troianovskii (Moscow: Materik, 1996), 238–261; Tamara Sergeeva, ed., "'Novaia vol'na'—sorok let spustia," *Iskusstvo kino* (1999.5): 100–125.

16 Ia. L. Butovskii, *Andrei Moskvin, kinooperator* (St. Petersburg: Dmitrii Bulanin, 2000), 216–222.

17 For the stenogram of this conference, see I. G. Germanova, ed., "Konferentsiia po tsvetnomu kino: 17 sentiabria-4 oktiabria 1945: Materialy," *Kinovedcheskie zapiski* 12 (1991): 122–160.

18 The films named by successive participants are *Coney Island* (Walter Lang, Twentieth Century-Fox, 1943); *Münchhausen* (Josef von Báky, UFA, 1943); *The Phantom of the Opera* (Rupert Julian, Universal Pictures, 1925); *The Thief of Bagdad* (Michael Powell, United Artists, 1940); *Bambi* (David Hand, Disney, 1942); *My Friend Flicka* (Harold D. Schuster, Twentieth Century-Fox, 1943); *Memphis Belle* (William Wyler, Paramount, 1943); *Jungle Book* (Alexander Korda, United Artists, 1942); *Woman of My Dreams* (*Die Frau meiner Traüme*, Georg Jacoby, UFA, 1944); *Desperadoes* (Charles [King] Vidor, Columbia Pictures, 1943); *The Women* (George Cukor, 1939); and *The Wizard of Oz* (Victor Fleming, MGM, 1939).

19 Dudley Andrew, "The Postwar Struggle for Color," *Cinema Journal* 18 (Spring 1979): 46.
20 Germanova, "Konferentsiia po tsvetnomu kino," 150–152.
21 Germanova, 135–138.
22 Germanova, 123–125.
23 Maiia Merkel', *Vkliuchit' polnyi tsvet* (Moscow: Iskusstvo, 1962), 54.
24 L. Pustinskaia, "Iz istorii tsvetnogo kino: 1900-1950-e gody," in *Iz istorii kino: Dokumenty i materialy*, vol. 11, ed. N. B. Volkova et al. (Moscow: Iskusstvo, 1985), 194.
25 Cited in Butovskii, *Andrei Moskvin, kinooperator*, 279.
26 Sergei Eizenshtein, "Wie sag'ich's meinem kind?!—Tsvet," in Sergei Eizenshtein, *Izbrannye proizvedeniia*, ed. S. I. Iutkievich, 6 vols. (Moscow: Iskusstvo, 1964–1971), 1: 533.
27 L. Kozlov, "Beseda o tsvete," interview with Andrei Tarkovsky, *Kinovedcheskie zapiski* 1 (1988): 153.
28 F. Provorov, "Pochemu my nedovol'ny kinoplenkoi," *Iskusstvo kino* (1972.7): 133–134.
29 Ionas Gritsius, "Problema bez nomera (zametki operatora)," *Tekhnika kino i televideniia* (1973.6): 55–56.
30 Pustinskaia, "Iz istorii tsvetnogo kino," 194.
31 Egorov, "Risk protiv standarta," 124.
32 Egorov, 127.
33 Mikhail Bleiman, "Chto segodnia? Chto zavtra? 1967–71," in *O kino—svidetel'skie pokazaniia, 1924–1971* (Moscow: Iskusstvo, 1973), 477–569.
34 Merkel', *Vliuchit' polnyi svet*, 135.
35 Ia. L. Butovskii, "Izobrazitel'noe reshenie i tekhnika s"emki kinofil'ma *Belaia ptitsa s chernoi otmetinoi*," *Tekhnika kino i televideniia* (1971.10): 6.
36 T. I. Lotis, *Iskusstvo operatora* (Moscow: Znanie, 1979), 27.
37 A. I. Lipkov and I. S. Urusevskaia, *Sergei Urusevskii: S kinokameroi i za mol'bertom* (Moscow: Algoritm, 2002); Iurii Mechitov, *Sergei Paradzhanov: Khronika dialoga* (Tbilisi: GAMS-print, 2009); and Giovanni Chiaramonte and Andrey A. Tarkovsky, *Instant Light: Tarkovsky Polaroids* (London: Thames and Hudson, 2004).

5

Eastman Color
in 1960s India

RANJANI MAZUMDAR

Ram Mukherjee's *Hum Hindustani* (*We Are Indian*, 1960) is India's first East-man Color film, followed very soon by *Junglee* (*The Untamed*, Subodh Mukher-jee, 1961). *Hum Hindustani* is a film about unemployment, class differences, and everyday struggles in the city of Bombay. The commercial failure of the film has driven it to virtual oblivion. The result is that director Subodh Mukherjee's com-mercially successful *Junglee* is often referred to and remembered as the first Indian Eastman Color film. *Junglee* is an ordinary tale about a grumpy male protagonist's transformation after he meets a beautiful woman in the valley of Kashmir. *Junglee*'s striking quality is its obsessive play with mountain terrain, sunlight, rivers, clouds, and snow. This translation of Kashmir into the pictur-esque in color has its origins in *Pamposh* (Ezra Mir, 1954), a documentary pro-duced by Ambalal Patel, the owner of India's first color film laboratory.[1] Shot on 35mm Gevacolor, *Pamposh* was produced, processed, and printed entirely in India. In his review of *Pamposh* in *American Cinematographer*, Frederick Fos-ter referred to the way a "riotous profusion of colors in the world's most beauti-ful springtime combines with ideal sunlight to provide the perfect testing ground for any color film."[2] In the avalanche of cinematic images of Kashmir that fol-lowed *Junglee*, a timeless imaginary was generated for an audience in the 1960s with limited exposure to India's vast physical terrain. *Junglee* was an experiment that paid off, and the film's phenomenal success at the box office made the region a prime destination for shooting. The presence of film songs in popular cinema was now available for the colorful capture and orchestration of visually lush scenic sites from across the country.[3]

In what follows, I discuss a series of transnational negotiations that redefined the visual culture of popular cinema in the 1960s. Approaching Eastman Color's arrival in Bombay as a machinic force making its way through a heterogeneous assemblage of social and technical spheres can help to foreground a relational and fluid account of change. Assemblage is one of Gilles Deleuze and Felix Guattari's influential concepts where diverse and disparate elements appear to intersect within an imagined spatial configuration.[4] Assemblages are useful in challenging temporal and physical boundaries and invite us to pay attention to an unstable material reality. I draw on this formulation to identify the 1960s as a concrete yet open-ended film context in which creative individuals dealing with color forged links with existing systems of production, geographies, bodies, objects, and the environment. This methodological approach is also consistent with Thomas Elsaesser's assertion that film must be viewed as part of a "culture of experiences and an economy of spectacle" in which "neither individual authors nor individual films are placed at the center."[5] In this chapter, I shift my focus away from genres and directors to chart the transnational context of technological, cultural, and aesthetic exchange that impacted and shaped Eastman Color's imagination of space in 1960s Bombay cinema.

The frenetic production of India's physical geography in popular cinema cannot be viewed in isolation from the acute economic and political crisis of the 1960s. India's first prime minister, Jawaharlal Nehru, set in motion large-scale industrialization and development soon after independence from colonial rule in 1947. These were carried out through five-year plans inspired by Soviet experiments with state planning. In the early 1960s, however, the country plunged headlong into an era of social and economic crisis marked by wars, a steady decline in foreign currency reserves, and food shortages. For the Bombay film industry, the prevailing economic crisis was felt acutely through government regulation over the movement of raw film stock. All negative and positive film at this time was imported from the United Kingdom's Kodak manufacturing facility, which proved to be extremely difficult amid a severe shortage of foreign currency. Thus, issues related to the import of film stock and complications with licenses and quotas kept appearing in newspapers and magazines.[6] Despite these difficulties, however, color was already in the air, urging a new kind of relationship with space. It was wild and uncontrollable—associated with fantasy, spectacle, and obfuscation, on the one hand, and overwhelmingly "real" and "authentic," on the other. As I will show, the cinematic environment during a period of economic strife emerged from the way Eastman Color intersected with prevailing "national anxieties," an expanding tourism economy, production infrastructures, and transnational cultural networks.

Tourism, Heat, and Desire

Between 1937 and 1960, color was rare, difficult to mount, and a luxury available to only a few filmmakers. Prior to Eastman Color's arrival in 1960, only sixteen films had been produced in color. In 1956, a list of fifteen films was released in a publication of the Film Federation of India.[7] Subsequently, in 1957, Mehboob Khan's *Mother India* was released. Color films were usually big-budget productions, and the format used was either Kodachrome or Gevacolor with prints by Technicolor. Eastman Color's monopack process was cheaper and made it easier to use lighter cameras. With the success of *Junglee*, Eastman Color became associated with a sense of lightness, frenetic movement, and tourism.

The expansion of industrialized tourism in the 1960s culminated in the formation of the Indian Tourism Development Corporation in 1966 under the aegis of the Ministry of Tourism with an aim to address travelers within India, as well as international tourists. One of the most persistent campaigns mounted by the ministry carried the byline "To know India, see India."[8] It was at this time that a significant advertising campaign for color still photography was conducted in India by ORWO and Agfa. It is interesting that the focus of these Agfa/ORWO campaigns was not the chronicling of everyday life but the encounter with vistas, iconic monuments, and heritage sites from different parts of the country. The production of space in these campaigns created maps of iconic India, with its temples, forts, sculptures, mountains, forests, and rivers. The imagination of these spaces in color was aided by a reinvention of the Indian railways in the 1960s as it aggressively entered the sphere of domestic tourism.[9]

If the still photograph was suffused with the magic of landscapes and sites in color, the advertisements for celluloid published in both trade and popular film magazines like *Filmfare* seemed to focus entirely on the material base of the film stock. Some of these celluloid advertisements generated lists of key color films.[10] One advertisement for celluloid with an eye at the center states, "Color films are just about our best goodwill ambassadors and foreign exchange earners. That's why the investment in time, talent, and fine materials is so important. . . . For color, Film Centre is the best."[11] Color became associated with financial success, and the advertisements drew attention to the processing prowess of film laboratories. The reference to foreign exchange was a response to a policy of the government whereby foreign currency for the import of color stock was released to filmmakers only on the condition that they would earn three times the amount spent through their international exhibition.[12] The obsessive focus on the material base of celluloid also led to constant discussion on issues related to makeup, light sources, the color of costumes, art direction, cinematography, and other specific techniques.[13] We can see an interesting visual assembling here—the stillness of touristic space in the ORWO and Agfa campaign, the materiality of celluloid and processing in the advertisements for color stock, the reference to the currency crisis, the entry of motion in the cinematic exploration of outdoor locations in film after film, and the industry's decision to recognize color cinematography through the institution of a dedicated award.[14] Color emerges here as an aesthetic force, a material object, a vehicle for unusual economic and cultural transactions, a trigger for the acceleration of a touristic imagination, and a force that could deliver a sensuous charge.

This desire for visual extravaganza, however, coexisted alongside an obsessive focus on the climate conditions affecting the infrastructure of color film. Newspapers, magazines, and the trade press highlighted issues related to processing centers, shortage of equipment for shooting, and hot and humid weather conditions.[15] There were regular news reports on the pressures faced by processing labs, shortage of raw stock, and problems with color correction procedures. In a candid conversation about these issues, Billimoria, a film-processing wizard who was responsible for the equipment at Film Centre, once famously said, "Well a color lab is no less temperamental than the stars. As you can work only in a suitable emotional climate, the color lab also requires a certain temperature."[16] Billimoria played a major role in altering the machines to adapt them to the temperatures in India. Similar problems were faced by the production crew in studio spaces that had no air-conditioning at that time. Heat and dust, combined with the use of blazing lights manned by an army of technicians, were always an issue in Bombay. With color, the use of lights increased, and the infrastructure had to contend with this.[17] The daily experience of Bombay's humid weather, interrupted electricity supply, and heat-related equipment breakdowns placed tremendous pressure on productions, especially in the handling of the stars who had to sit with an additional layer of makeup for color stock. As Nicole Starosielski has suggested, it is important to "attune ourselves to temperatures political operations."[18] Starosielski identifies "thermoceptive" regimes as those that emerge from the way heat reconfigures space, constructing and dismantling environments. She makes a compelling argument about the exchange of heat across bodies as a mode of communication that can often trigger some form of collective action. Human bodies, animals, objects, and infrastructures respond to heat and cold through transactions that lead to adjustments and new strategies for existence. Changes in the temperatures of any building can affect bodies and their skin surfaces; the invisible waves of heat can trigger responses "that escape conscious perception."[19]

The use of color film stock, as already mentioned, increased the heat quotient in studio spaces considerably and created a new context for accidents. Asha Parekh, a leading actress of the 1960s, recalls that during the shooting of *Hum Hindustani*, "the outdoor location visuals were beautiful. Indoors, however, in Bombay, heavy lights were required. These lights were so strong that during an over-the-shoulder shot, my arm started burning. A first aid kit was rushed in by the technicians."[20] On the sets of Guru Dutt's *Chaudhavi Ka Chand* to reshoot the title song in color, Waheeda Rehman recalls, "I had to dip chamois leather in an ice bucket and apply it to my face because the lights burned my skin."[21] It is not surprising that Eastman Color's arrival in a tropical environment instilled a desire to escape from the chaos and heat emanating from studio spaces. Locations were selected accordingly, and within the industry, the "outdoor" became a recurring term to manage and plan shooting schedules. This is evident from the way the trade press began to describe the progress made by various films under production. A prerelease poster for *Aye din Bahar Ke* (Ragunath Jhalani, 1966) carried the tagline "A riot of color blooming in a field of love." At the bottom of the poster is the announcement "Location shooting at Darjeeling, Kalimpong, and Teesta Valley ends today."[22] Landscape, as many have argued, is different from nature's ability to exist independently of humans. Landscapes are unstable, heterogeneous, and volatile imaginations that have emerged from the "relational assemblage of multispecies entanglements."[23] With the camera now armed with Eastman Color stock encountering India's geographic terrain, Kashmir and other scenic sites like Darjeeling, Mussoorie, Nainital, Shimla, and Ooty entered the visual field of filmmakers, making spatial navigation an intrinsic part of the language of color films.

The new relationship to travel was recognized by film journalists: "The Movie camera is on the move, exploring the land for novelty and variety in backdrops, holding the promise of exciting pushback chair travelogues."[24] For an audience that had still not had the opportunity to see India on-screen (since most films were shot in studio spaces or, at best, some locations in Bombay), the mountain terrain was a huge draw, and a new map of the country began to take material form via cinema. The cartographic claim on picturesque locations, especially Kashmir, therefore needs to be placed as an "unintentional" consequence of the assemblage where technological, economic, political, touristic, and climate considerations intersected. Multiple collisions and jostling within the assemblage can erupt into lines of flight that can congeal or assemble into a new formation.[25] The art historian Natasha Eaton, writing about India, identifies color as a line of flight beyond narrative confinement and a device to think afresh about questions related to cultural exchange.[26] While Eaton's focus is on visual culture and art in the charged context of colonialism, I find this turn of phrase useful to suggest that the imagination of Kashmir and other scenic locations was a consequence of such lines of flight—visual inscriptions that emerged from the movement of color across architectural spaces, technology, heat, and desire. The critic Kobita Sarkar noted the use of tourist backgrounds in films of the 1960s, with Kashmir emerging as the most popular site, competing equally with the stars: "Most filmgoers are rarely likely to be able to travel to the lovely mountains of Kashmir or Darjeeling or the beautiful seascapes of the West Coast. The Hampi, Taj Mahal, and Jaipur backgrounds are a once in a lifetime experience for most of the luckier ones, and seeing them again on film evokes some of the personal memories attached to a particular personal visit, while the addition of color brings a dimension of unbelievable vividness to it."[27] Sergei Eisenstein had identified landscape in cinema as free and unburdened from narrative considerations and therefore most open to the depiction of spectacle, moods, emotional states, and spiritual encounters.[28] This approach to spectacle over narrative pull played the decisive role in Bombay cinema's negotiation of color to showcase India as "filmed space."[29] Eastman Color's offer of a transient sensory pleasure, the encounter with unboundedness, and the promise of distinctly new experiences enabled several films of the 1960s to command a presence despite thin storylines and weak performances. Thus, a heterogeneous assemblage of both human and nonhuman actors lodged Kashmir, like many other sites, in the cartographic imagination of India.

The Transformation of Indoor Space

The gradual spread of color in a climate of economic crisis caused a division between large and small production houses. The established stars and music directors became associated with color productions and began to distance themselves from black-and-white films.[30] Film producers recognized that hiring major stars and music directors required an additional financial investment to ensure success at the box office. The new arrangements slowly turned color into a reigning standard for filmmaking in Bombay. This led to an increase in the cost of other branches of filmmaking, and the budgets escalated, not just because of the costs involved in the import of raw stock but also because of the gradual transformation of the material texture of the mise-en-scène. The exploration of outdoor locations was combined with a growing awareness of the expanded role of furniture, fabric, wallpaper, and paint in the crafting of indoor images in color. These changes were evident in the accounts of various unnamed film critics for the *Times of India*, who started to respond specifically to cinematography, art direction, and costume in their reviews of color films. In a short period of a few years, skilled professions, usually subservient to the director, came to the fore.[31]

The review of *Mother India* referred to "the recording, the sets, decor and costumes" positively and made a point about the high standards maintained by Mehboob Productions.[32] *Sehra*'s review in 1963 specifically mentioned the presence of Eastman Color blood. The film was lambasted for being dull and trite, but there was a good word for camera technique and the "ornate quality of the set."[33] Nanabhai Bhatt's film *Cobra Girl* was introduced with the headline "'Cobra Girl' Has Magic Color and Nonsense." The review went on to state, "An adventure piece in Eastman Color, the sets look comparatively respectable, and color receives a modicum of aesthetic consciousness."[34] *Mere Mehboob*, a Muslim social (the term for a Bombay film genre) with elaborate sets to evoke Islamic architecture and culture, was introduced as "Mere Mehboob: A Pleasant, Rainbow Hued Romance." After waxing eloquent on the freshness of the film, the reviewer added, "Making a major contribution to the film's appealing quality is art director Sudendu Roy whose sets, color schemes, and general decor (despite some touches of anachronism) lend the picture great visual charm.

And G. Singh's photography looks like a job lovingly done."[35] These fragments of spectatorial pleasures channeled via the accounts of critics show how in their move from black and white to color, art directors, armed with a new awareness, responded with innovative design strategies.

It is worth reflecting on the practice of a prolific art director, Shanti Das, who was first noticed for his work in *Junglee*. Das was one of the most sought-after set designers in the 1960s and 1970s who worked initially in black-and-white films but was poised at a historical juncture that allowed him to transition from one format to the other. It is hard to find anything significant written about him even though he was a winner of the Filmfare Award for art direction thrice and received a Dada Saheb lifetime award for his work in 2000. Das was born in Dhaka (Bangladesh) and studied art in Kolkata before he ventured into art direction. As a resident of Calcutta, he worked initially in Bengali cinema and after moving to Bombay began working in Hindi films. He was recognized instantly for his craft and ability to create sets for color after the success of *Junglee*. While a long discussion about his work is beyond the purview of this chapter, I will focus on a few key moments to highlight Das's creative ability to draw on internationally circulating currents in art and design. For *Junglee*, Das assembled a set for a popular song and dance number that drew inspiration from Vincent van Gogh's brushstroke style captured in arguably his most well-known painting, *The Starry Night*, which depicts a view from the artist's window when he was in an asylum. The actress Helen, along with several other dancers and Shammi Kapoor, performs a flamenco-style dance onstage to the popular song "Suku Suku." We see giant-sized paintbrushes placed on the right of the stage in front of large frames of abstract paintings (figure 5.1). The stage background is a dramatically painted surface with swirling brushstrokes, and the performance in the foreground is crafted to highlight a diversity of colors using fabric, wall texture, and a range of props. The background is the most dramatic and is an easily recognizable painted surface inspired by *The Starry Night*.

The 1950s and 1960s witnessed van Gogh's gradual entry into popular culture as a major figure via printed colored posters, postcards, film, and music. His rediscovery in the 1950s was also linked to the rise of existentialism in France, which saw the painter's turbulent psychic life accommodated within this philosophical upsurge. He fit the romantic myth of the tormented and tragic artist who went unrecognized during his lifetime.[36] If the recirculation of van Gogh in the 1950s with color photography and existentialist thought brought the artist renewed glory, Hollywood entered the scene with a big-budget spectacular, *Lust for Life* (1956), starring Kirk Douglas in the lead. The overwhelming presence of color was clearly noticed by all, since it brought van Gogh's paintings to a wide public. It is interesting how Shanti Das, unknown to the world but working as a set designer in Bombay, decided to use this painting as inspiration for his stage design. *Lust for Life* was released in Bombay in 1957 at the Metro Theatre and was reviewed by the *Times of India* critic.[37] We also have a morning show

FIGURE 5.1 *Junglee* (Subodh Mukherjee, 1961).

advertisement for the film dated 1959.[38] Although we do not know if Shanti Das saw the film, we know for sure that it screened in Bombay and that van Gogh was very popular in the 1950s and 1960s.[39]

Set design is crucial for the construction of any mise-en-scène, even as audiences tend to take it for granted as "unconsciously registered background."[40] Cinema from around the world, however, has innumerable examples of elaborate expressionist and impressionist sets that were created during the black-and-white era, especially in films dealing with suspense, fantasy, historical subjects, and dream sequences. Yet the issue of "blending" with the story without any overt desire for hypervisibility was generally considered the benchmark of good design.[41] In Bombay's storytelling form, however, visual effects could coexist with the unfolding of the story world, mediated via song sequences. With the introduction of Eastman Color, the visual obsession with effects was no longer contained within song sequences alone but began to influence the overall narrative's spatial texture of designed spaces.

When Shanti Das made his transition as an art director from black and white to color, he consciously flooded interior spaces with objects and wall decor. There is a fascination for plasticity and industrialized forms of color. These objects had little to do with the narrative and yet are highlighted using close-ups. An example of this is the way a wall clock is deployed in *Junglee*. We see a long shot of a blue wall with a clock, cut to a close-up that draws the spectator's attention to its mustard-colored dial. A news item titled "Ultra-modern bedroom set backdrop" referred to Shanti Das's work for *Jhuk Gaya Aasman* and how "a costly carpet on the set attracted attention."[42] This self-conscious play with objects, the texture of walls, floor decoration, fabric, and furniture continued through the 1960s, highlighting the flexible relationship that developed between the cinematographer and the art director.

If the global circuits provided one set of references, the 1960s also saw forms of cultural coding pushed through by the art directors. There are many examples of such coding. *Junglee* includes another sequence, also planned by Shanti Das, in which we see the two protagonists caught in a storm in the mountains. This is the moment when Shammi Kapoor first experiences his attraction for Saira Banu in a log cabin surrounded by snow. A red blanket is used here to convey passion. The use of ruffled hair and crumpled clothing is meant to convey the morning after the first wedding night (*suhaag raat*)—a recurring image in India's popular imagination, captured in many films. Although there is no direct sexual encounter, the bright red blanket placed against a functional space with muted brown logs of the cabin walls and grey stones stacked in one corner heightens the erotic charge of the attraction; the encounter here is designed almost like a form of colorized foreplay. In several films, temple iconography, Islamic imaginations, and ostentatious feudal structures too began to transform as pillars, engravings, sculptures, antique objects, and taxidermy props acquired an expressive force with color (*Ram Aur Shyam, Dil Diya Dard Liya, Neel Kamal, Mere Meboob*). Das himself was involved with a variety of films, even as his eye for a contemporary aesthetic trumped his other work.[43]

The Sway of Colored Light

The privileging of white light under Technicolor's regime in Hollywood has been widely established.[44] With white light it was possible to create frames of high visibility where color would enter as surface (as opposed to light) and strengthen a transparent notion of realism. This was managed through a control over light sources that had to be kept hidden to replicate the perceived "naturalness" of the world. The presence of white light on-screen was the result of significant decisions taken behind the camera. For Technicolor, the production and management of white light emerged as a default template, a "law of emphasis" that did not encourage the use of colored light except in situations where its need could be clearly established, such as the presence of lights in a stage show within the narrative.[45] Technicolor wanted to establish color as the industry norm and not just as a template for stylized use in particular genres like westerns or historical films. Hollywood's orchestration of the "reality effect," established through norms that were consolidated over time, was threatened by the use of colored light. While ambient white light remained invisible on-screen, ambient

FIGURE 5.2 The actress Vyjayanthimala in *Sangam* (Raj Kapoor, 1964).

colored light was hypervisible. A discussion of two sequences where colored light was used quite deliberately and evocatively reveals how norms linked to realism were negotiated; the first is from a Technicolor film, *Sangam* (Raj Kapoor, 1964), while the second, *Jewel Thief* (Vijay Anand, 1967), is in Eastman Color.

Sangam was released in 1964 to tremendous success at the box office. The cinematographer, Radhu Karmakar, had built an impeccable reputation for himself since 1945 with several iconic black-and-white films.[46] He was the favored cinematographer of filmmaker Raj Kapoor, who sent him to train with Technicolor under the tutelage of the British cinematographer Jack Cardiff.[47] *Sangam* was Karmakar's first color film, shot and processed in Technicolor. The film maintains a strong color template with a conscious emphasis on solid surface texture, the color of costumes, and the use of natural light in outdoor spaces. In a sequence set indoors, Radha (played by the actress Vyjantimala) is shown in a white sari, expectantly waiting for her lover, Gopal (Rajendra Kumar), to come and speak to her parents about their future. Radha's face is captured in a close-up; the mother's voice on the soundtrack suggests she must not intrude on the discussion with Gopal (figure 5.2). The camera lingers over Radha's face, expressively communicating her romantic desire, which is emphasized by a reddish flickering color. This creation of colored light is generated with red liquid that is poured into a glass placed in the right foreground. The frame identifies the red liquid as the source through which light penetrates to create the red hue, thus working within Technicolor's mandate of identifying the source of artificial color and adhering to the "law of emphasis." The flicker on Radha's face is also clearly influenced by the glamorous close-ups of female stars associated with the black-and-white era. Karmakar experimented with light in this sequence and moved beyond surface texture but adhered to Technicolor's rulebound structure. No other scene in *Sangam* captures the dramatic use of high-contrast imagery associated with Karmakar's earlier work.

It was with Eastman Color that colored light began to explode wildly on-screen. In a popular cinematic form not wedded to realism, color acquired an unruly, miasmic force, releasing a whole host of sensuous forces. As color expanded to become the predominant form, the play with colored light became even more pronounced. In Vijay Anand's highly successful *Jewel Thief*, the art director T. K. Desai created a modern interior space to showcase the performance of a popular erotic song. The sequence introduces us to a space with different floor levels, textured walls, and large glass doors. Tanuja opens the door to let the protagonist (Dev Anand) enter the living room interior. Through their movements inside this space, we see a combination of sheer curtains, midcentury modern furniture, decorative objects placed against open wall shelves, a white refrigerator, and olive-green carpeting, upholstery, and wall paint. There is an emphasis here on style, contemporaneity, a harmonious approach to color combinations, and the desire for a "tasteful" ambience. Tanuja disappears for a few seconds, and Dev Anand sits down to leaf through a magazine. Suddenly, the lights dim and dramatic colored light, namely, bright yellow and red, envelops the sheer curtains against the glass doors (figure 5.3). We see another set of white curtains layered with blue and purple light move as if on their own volition. Dev Anand walks in the direction of the sheer curtains drenched in red light, looking for Tanuja, who begins to seductively perform to an erotic song voiced by Asha Bhosle. With the song, the living room turns into a colored extravaganza, puncturing its muted surface texture to showcase Tanuja's overtly romantic interest in Dev Anand.

This fascination with an intensely artificial regime of color was a global rage in the 1960s, inspired primarily by dynamism in the fields of textiles, wallpaper, fashion, and design. Virginia Postrel has referred to the 1960s as a polyester decade with a fluorescent touch.[48] In this milieu, color acquired a quality of sonic loudness. The need to respond to color made art directors draw on a referential world of internationally circulating home décor magazines, fashion spreads, photographs, films, and advertisements. What is interesting here is the explicit embracing of colored light to generate chromatic excess. There is no desire or motivation to adhere to the codes of realism so critical to Hollywood's negotiation of color. Unlike the sequence in *Sangam* where the source of the colored light is identified on-screen, in *Jewel Thief* the use of colored light is neither justified nor explained. Colored light exists to propel the movement of situations and songs.

FIGURE 5.3 *Jewel Thief* (Vijay Anand, 1967).

V. K. Murthy, another major cinematographer who created some of the most memorable images for Guru Dutt's black-and-white films, was sent to observe the shooting of *Guns of Naverone* in Britain in 1960. When Murthy returned, Dutt approached him with a plan to reshoot a song sequence of his black-and-white production *Chaudhavi Ka Chand* (1960) after it became a box office success. Dutt decided to reshoot the film's most popular and elaborately staged romantic sequence, believing that the inclusion of the song in color would add novelty to the experience and attract audiences back to the theater. In a conversation with Nasreen Munni Kabir about this sequence, the actress Waheeda Rehman recalled: "The Censor Board wanted the song re-censored and asked us to remove a close-up where I am seen turning my face towards the camera. They said my eyes looked too red and sensual. Guru Duttji said my eyes were red because of the strong lighting and explained the characters were husband and wife, and so where was the problem? If the Censor Board members of that era saw the films of today, I wonder what they would say."[49] This is the unregulated, almost rhizomatic movement of color as it erupts through connections with artificial light, the female body, film stock, and camera movement. The trace of this moment then encountered institutions for the regulation of public morality. The mere surface rearrangement of the song with color could trigger a sensuous charge and anxiety. Color was clearly a force to reckon with.

One of the most significant developments of the decade was the way Helen, a marginal star but a major dancing sensation, reinvented her screen persona. Helen was born in 1938 to a French father and a half-Spanish, half-Burmese mother. She acted in films made in several Indian languages, and her filmic career remains a collage of roles that range from Arabian fantasy films to family and crime melodramas. It was in the 1960s that Helen became a sensation, and her mix of Spanish, French, and Burmese blood resulted in an appearance that seemed more white than Asian. Although she made her initial appearance in the black-and-white era, the performance of her whiteness took shape only after the transition to color. Whiteness was a construction in which she, and her costume designers, actively participated. Thus, the blond wigs, exaggerated eye makeup, and colored lenses became a systematic pattern in her cinematic appearances. Her image tapped into postcolonial racial anxieties, with her foreigner status deployed to position her as westernized. It was the transition to color that spearheaded the psychedelic, colorful, and kitschy appearance of the nightclubs constructed by art directors of that time to house the vamp. Again, in this aggressive use of colored psychedelic light, the codes of realism seemed to have no place. Colored light was in fact embraced in these imagined nightclubs for its ability to showcase sexual excess. Just as Tanuja transformed the living room with colored light to perform her seductive number in *Jewel Thief*, the use of colored light was a recurring element in Helen's screen imagination.

Afterthoughts

There exists a popular perception among cinematographers about the dominance of high-contrast imagery in Bombay cinema's black-and-white period.[50] Almost all the films mentioned by cinematographers who straddled the black-and-white and color phases referred to the use of high-contrast lighting in their black-and-white work. The films included *Citizen Kane* (1941), *How Green Was My Valley* (1941), *Mildred Pierce* (1945), *Great Expectations* (1946), and *The Picture of Dorian Gray* (1945). *American Cinematographer* was read regularly in Bombay in the 1950s and 1960s, and interviews published in the journal with still images became significant for the analysis and understanding of technique. There was virtually no access to practical training whether in institutions or through apprenticeship. When these cinematographers made the shift to color, they saw a reduction of contrast in favor of natural light conditions. This is where the outdoor landscape of mountain areas like Kashmir entered the picture. The experiments with light identified with the studio years were possible because the studios owned equipment. Once the move to locations began, time was critical, since equipment was now being hired and budgets had to be kept under control.

Hollywood's introduction of Eastman Color in the mid-1950s saw the production of adventure and fantasy films, with an eye toward audiences hooked on black-and-white television.[51] The lavish color extravaganzas did bring back audiences to the theaters, but by the mid-1960s, color television had arrived in the United States, and the availability of news and current affairs in color made fantasy less attractive.[52] When the novelty of color began to wear off, there was a desire to rein in the excess associated with color production. This is a different history from India, where domestic television became a presence only in the 1970s. Through the 1960s, elaborately staged Muslim socials, adventure stories, and period and fantasy films coexisted alongside a parallel and much larger thread of lighthearted and breezy films with travel and consumption at the center. These films remained overwhelmingly in sway, linked to expansion in the fields of aviation, railways, and highways. The expansion of these transport forms cannot be separated from the international force of tourism and its sensory charge expressed via the visual technologies of photography and film. The Bombay screen in the 1960s became abuzz with automobiles traveling across mountain terrain, trains winding their way through landscapes, the sites and attractions of European cities, and interior spaces with several kinds of objects and surface texture. These aesthetic constellations, as I have shown, emerged from a network of global culture and technology with no particular desire to control or regulate the excess associated with color. In making its way through a transnational assemblage, Eastman Color unknowingly triggered the cartographic unfolding of a new cinematic map of 1960s India.

Notes

1   Ambalal Patel was a pioneer in the trade of photographic and film equipment. See Sanjit Narwekar, "How One Man's Efforts Made Colour Popular in Indian Cinema," *The Wire*, March 8, 2017, https://thewire.in/film/how-one-man-efforts -made-colour-popular-in-indian-cinema-ambalal-patel.

2   Frederick Foster, review of *Pamposh*, *American Cinematographer*, August 1954, 390, 414–415, 416.

3   *Junglee* was shot using a Mitchel camera for its indoor studio sequences, but the German Arriflex was used for the outdoor sequences, which allowed greater mobility to face the natural and sharp light of the mountains. This information was sourced by the writer and critic Nasreen Munni Kabir.

4   Gilles Deleuze and Felix Guattari, *A Thousand Plateaus: Capitalism and Schizophrenia*, trans. Brian Massumi (Minneapolis: University of Minnesota Press, 1987).

5   Thomas Elsaesser, "The New Film History as Media Archaeology," *Cinémas: Journal of Film Studies* 14, no. 2–3 (2004): 91.

6   See Swarnavel Eswaran's account of Krishnan Hariharan, vice president of the Kodak office during the first two decades of Eastman Color in India. Eswaran refers to issues related to customs duty. Swarnavel Eswaran, "Meet Kodak Krishnan, Eastman's Man from the East," *Scroll.in*, accessed December 30, 2022, https://scroll .in/reel/994501/meet-kodak-krishnan-eastmans-man-from-the-east.

7   See *Indian Talkie 1931–56: Silver Jubilee Souvenir* (Film Federation of India, 1956). 213; *Mother India* aspired for a combination of realism and visual splendor.

8   For a sample of these advertisements, see *Times of India Annual* (1959): 12; *Times of India Annual* (1963): 75; *Times of India Annual* (1965): 91. Bombay: Times of India Press, https://www.ideasofindia.org/project/indian-annual/.

9 Jagjit Singh, "The Railways and Tourism," *Illustrated Weekly of India*, July 16, 1967, 48–49; D.P.S. Ahuja "The Romance of the Frontier Mail," *Illustrated Weekly of India*, July 30, 1967, 46–47.

10 *Filmfare*, December 27, 1963, 36; *Filmfare*, December 25, 1964, 36.

11 *Filmfare*, December 22, 1967, 56.

12 In his autobiography, the cinematographer Radhu Karmakar recalls how Raj Kapoor had to provide one lakh pounds to the Central Government as foreign currency for the shooting of *Sangam* (1964) in Europe. This was paid by the Hindujas in return for the film's foreign distribution returns. The film's success helped to build the Hinduja fortunes. See Radhu Karmakar, *The Painter of Lights* (Orissa: Prafulla, 2005), 105.

13 "The History and Practice of Cinematography in India," *Raqs Media Collective Interviews with Cinematographers*, accessed December 30, 2022, https://works .raqsmediacollective.net/index.php/2001/11/17/the-history-practice-of -cinematography-in-india/.

14 In 1964, a special award for the best color cinematographer was instituted in memory of Ambalal Patel, a pioneer in the trade of film and photographic equipment. See *Filmfare*, December 11, 1964, 12.

15 The following constitute a tiny sample of some of the headlines that appeared during the 1960s: "Raw Film Imports Cut by Half Again," *Screen*, Bombay, July 2, 1965; "Import of Raw Film: Government Should Help Industry," *Movieland*, Madras, March 17, 1967; "Crisis in Color," editorial in *Filmfare*, August 20, 1965, 5; "Raw Stock for Films in Color: New Approach Needed," *Movieland*, Madras, December 30, 1966.

16 *Filmfare*, October 2, 1964, 45.

17 Interview with Ujjwal Nirgudkar, an engineer who worked at the Film Centre laboratory for many years. The early color stock, according to Nirgudkar, was slow because of its ASA rating. The cinematographer Jal Mistry describes how slow color film required a number of lights and how, during one of his color shoots at Filmistan Studios, virtually everything else had to be stopped to ensure there were enough lights for him. Mistry also refers to a flattening of the image with color (in "History and Practice of Cinematography in India").

18 Nicole Starosielski, *Media Hot and Cold* (Durham, NC: Duke University Press, 2022), 3.

19 Starosielski, 4.

20 Asha Parekh, *The Hit Girl* (Uttar Pradesh: Om Books International, 2017), 67.

21 Nasreen Munni Kabir, *Conversations with Waheeda Rehman* (Gurgaon, Haryana, India: Penguin, 2015), 1.

22 *Screen*, Bombay, September 3, 1965, 1.

23 Debashree Mukherjee, "The Aesthetic and Material Force of Landscape in Cinema: Mediating Meaning from the Scene of Production," *Representations* 157, no. 1 (February 1, 2022): 116.

24 *Filmfare*, December 25, 1964, 43.

25 Deleuze and Guattari, *Thousand Plateaus*, 9.

26 Natasha Eaton, *Colour, Art and Empire Visual Culture and the Nomadism of Representation* (London: I. B. Tauris, 2013).

27 Kobita Sarkar, "Background to the Film," *Star and Style*, June 13, 1969, 11.

28 Sergei Eisenstein, *Nonindifferent Nature: Film and the Structure of Things*, trans. Herbert Marshall (Cambridge: Cambridge University Press, 1988).

29 Priya Jaikumar, *Where Histories Reside: India as Filmed Space* (Durham, NC: Duke University Press, 2019).

30 See V. P. Sathe, "Color Comes to Stay in Bombay: Gap between Rich and Poor Deepens," *Movieland*, Madras, April 25, 1969.

31 See "Lighting: Same for Color or Black and White, Says Varshide," *Screen*, Bombay, September 3, 1965, 11.

32 "*Mother India*: An Emotional Drama of Classic Proportions," *Times of India*, October 27, 1957, 3.

33 "*Mother India*," 3.

34 "'Cobra Girl' Has Magic Color and Nonsense," *Times of India*, May 26, 1963, 3.

35 "*Mere Mehboob*: A Pleasant Rainbow Hued Romance," *Times of India*, November 3, 1963, 3.

36 Steven Jacobs, *Framing Pictures: Film and the Visual Arts* (Edinburgh: Edinburgh University Press, 2012).

37 "Lust for Life at the Metro Theatre Today," *Times of India*, April 4, 1957, 5.

38 *Times of India*, January 4, 1959.

39 Lynnette Porter, *Van Gogh in Popular Culture* (Jefferson, NC: McFarland, 2015), 5–12. Shanti Das's daughter, Sharbani, confirmed he was an admirer of the painter (interview with the author, Bombay, December 2023).

40 Tim Bergfelder, Sue Harris, and Sarah Street, *Film Architecture and the Transnational Imagination: Set Design in 1930s European Cinema* (Amsterdam: Amsterdam University Press, 2007), 13.

41 Bergfelder, Harris, and Street, 14.

42 "Ultra-modern bedroom set backdrop," *Screen*, Bombay, January 28, 1966, 12.

43 Sharmishtha Roy recalls Das's work as modern and influenced by design manuals that circulated during the 1960s. He was a contemporary of her father, Sudendhu Roy. Sharmishtha Roy, interview with the author, Bombay, March, 2020.

44 See, for example, Richard Misek, *Chromatic Cinema: A History of Screen Color* (Oxford: John Wiley, 2010); Scott Higgins, *Harnessing the Technicolor Rainbow: Color Design in the 1930s* (Austin: University of Texas Press, 2007).

45 Natalie M. Kalmus, "Color Consciousness," *Journal of the Society of Motion Picture Engineers* 25, no. 2 (August 1935): 146.

46 See the tribute to Karmakar, "Cinematographer Radhu Karmakar: A Distinguished Technician with Many Successes and Thirty Years of Hard Work behind Him," *Filmfare*, April 30, 1965, 13.

47 Karmakar, *Painter of Lights*, 97.

48 Virginia Postrel, "How Polyester Bounced Back," *Works in Progress*, April 21, 2022, https://www.worksinprogress.co/issue/how-polyester-bounced-back/.

49 Kabir, *Conversations with Waheeda Rehman*, 69.

50 See "History and Practice of Cinematography in India."

51 Steve Neale, *Cinema and Technology: Image, Sound, Colour* (London: Macmillan Education, 1985), 145–158.

52 Neale, 145–158.

6

Coloring the Coastline

Italian Beachside Comedies and the Color Film Transition

ELENA GIPPONI

The Beach in Italian Visual Culture

In the summer of 1959, between June and August, Pier Paolo Pasolini embarked on a road trip in his Fiat 1100, covering the entirety of the Italian coastline beginning at Ventimiglia, on the Italian-French border, all the way around the peninsula to Trieste. While Pasolini jotted down his impressions of the trip, Paolo Di Paolo, the photographer accompanying him, assembled a black-and-white photographic reportage. The resulting travel narrative and photo spread were published in three separate installments in the monthly magazine *Successo*, edited by Aldo Palazzi, under the title *The Long Road of Sand*.[1]

It was no coincidence that Pasolini was directing his attention toward the beachside, a site that would also play a key role in his 1965 documentary *Comizi d'Amore* (*Love Encounters*), which was largely shot on the crowded beaches of the Italian Riviera. Pasolini was interested in the liminal space between the temporalities of the no-longer and the not-yet, a central notion in his depiction of Italy's rapid postwar transition from a largely rural society into one of mass industrialization. For Pasolini, the beachside served as a strategic vantage point from which to observe the transformation of Italy in the middle of the boom years (1958–1963), when the nation experienced a period of vertiginous economic growth.

One of the telltale signs of social transformations underway in Italy was the phenomenon of summer beach vacations, which were quickly entering the mainstream, evidence of which Pasolini encountered during his trip. It was at this historical moment that the beach vacation, which had been developing as a social activity from the end of the nineteenth century, went from being a small, aristocratic practice to becoming increasingly accessible to large swaths of the Italian public.[2]

In response to Italy's implementation of paid vacation days, its modernization of the national road and highway network, and the increasing ubiquity of private cars, the number of Italians who went on summer vacation doubled between 1959 and 1965 from 5.5 million to 11 million vacationers; ten years later, in 1975, there would be as many as 20 million.[3] The symbolic connotation of going on vacation was likewise changing: formerly thought of as a place for the regeneration of both the body and the spirit, vacationing was transitioning into a massive experience, into what Christian Uva calls in his study of the beach in Italian cinema a "horizon where a particular carnivalesque condition is acted out" and an "*arena* naturally predisposed to theatricality."[4]

Among the elements that make the beach a particularly carnivalesque place is color, present both, as we will see, on the objects and the bodies collected there and in the many images that have come to document and promote the beach experience. This chapter aims to analyze a specific form of color representation of the beach: the beachside comedy, a subgenre of the *commedia all'italiana*, that comprised approximately fifty films released between the mid-1950s and the mid-1960s.[5] The beachside comedy sometimes overlaps with the film-revue, the film-musical, or the *musicarello*, and is at the same time a hybrid of the tourist comedy, characterized by an explicit promotion of beachside towns as tourist spaces. These films revolve around the summer vacations of their protagonists and were known both for their box office success and for their scathing critical reception. The most frequently recurring structure for these films deploys different episodes and subplots that intertwine in both calculated and fortuitous moments, with the beach serving as a shared stage. The main dramatic impetuses in the beachside comedy are twofold: first, as is the case in most Italian comedy films, the formation of a couple (or several couples); and, second, manifestations of both class anxiety and desires for social mobility. But beachside comedies play a negotiating role not only because they stage the social-anthropological transformation taking place in contemporary Italy but also because they convey the technological and aesthetic transition to a new chromatic regime. The beachside comedy is in fact one of the popular genres of Italian cinema—like the sword-and-sandal (peplum) film, the thriller, the horror film, and the film-revue—through which Italian audiences first presided over the large-scale transition into color.[6] This corpus of films therefore offers a privileged view for reconstructing the mutations in visual modes of perception that occurred as Italy moved into the multicolor era of its postwar economic boom.

The cultural values that were attached to the technological innovation of color film stocks demonstrate how the beachside comedies documented and negotiated the nation's transition into modernity.

Color Technology in Beachside Comedies

Representations of the beach environment in Italian cinema date to the years of postwar reconstruction: *Domenica d'Agosto* (*Sunday in August*, Luciano Emmer, 1950), *Bellezze a Capri* (*Beauties in Capri*, Luigi Capuano and Adelchi Bianchi, 1951), and *La Famiglia Passaguai* (*The Passaguai Family*, Aldo Fabrizi, 1951) are the prototypes of the beachside comedy and were shot in black and white. Color film in Italian cinema arrived only after these films, with the release of *Totò a colori* (*Toto in Color*, Steno, 1952), a film-revue in Ferraniacolor that features a beachside episode set in a villa in Capri and starring Franca Valeri as the "snobbish miss." Even after the arrival of color film in Italy, about fifteen beachside comedies were still shot in black and white, for example, *Frenesia dell'estate* (*Summer Frenzy*, Luigi Zampa, 1963), *Canzoni in bikini* (Giuseppe Vari, 1963), *Follie d'estate* (Carlo Infascelli and Edoardo Anton, 1963), *Desideri d'estate* (Silvio Amadio, 1964), *Veneri al sole* (Marino Girolami, 1965), and *Spiaggia libera* (Marino Girolami, 1965).

Nevertheless, the vast majority of the beachside comedies—more than thirty, about two-thirds of the total, and their most representative iterations—were filmed in color.[7] A small group of these were shot in Ferraniacolor, the Italian monopack technology launched in 1952 and later perfected in sensitivity with Ferraniacolor Type 54: *La spiaggia* (*The Beach*, aka *Riviera*, aka *The Border*, Alberto Lattuada, 1954), *Vacanze d'amore* (*Le village magique*, aka *Magic Village*, Francesco Alliata and Jean-Paul Le Chanois, 1955), *Le vacanze del sor Clemente* (1954, dir. Camillo Mastrocinque), and *Tipi da spiaggia* (Mario Mattoli, 1959). Ferrania, the film stock plant near Savona in Liguria, had been active in film stock production since 1924. Ferraniacolor, based in part on the Agfacolor system, was developed by the manufacturer's research lab thanks to the knowledge shared by some former IG Farbenindustrie technicians and researchers after the patents lapsed. The production of Ferraniacolor, however, lasted less than a decade: in 1959 it was retired from the market because the Italian chemical industry was not able to switch from nitrocellulose to the more efficient triacetate support.[8] Ferrania, on the other hand, remained competitive in the production of small-gauge film stocks and in the black-and-white field with the P30 film (the film stock chosen by Pasolini and other well-known Italian directors in the 1960s).

Another small group of beachside films are printed on Technicolor No. V, the high-quality dye-transfer system from Eastman Color monopack negatives: *Souvenir d'Italie* (*It Happened in Rome*, Antonio Pietrangeli, 1957), *Tempi duri per i vampiri* (*Uncle Was a Vampire*, Steno, 1957), *Leoni al sole* (Vittorio Caprioli,

1961), *Copacabana Palace* (1962, dir. Steno), *I dongiovanni della Costa Azzurra* (*Beach Casanova*, Vittorio Sala, 1962), and *Ischia Operazione Amore* (Vittorio Sala, 1966).[9] The choice of this system seemed linked to the spectacular nature of the productions, which tended to be richer and more authorial, as with *Leoni al sole*, which marked the directorial debut of Vittorio Caprioli, with a screenplay by the celebrated author and screenwriter Raffaele La Capria.

The vast majority of beachside comedies were shot and printed in Eastman Color, the American monopack technology that most major Italian film labs began to process starting in 1954, and which quickly established itself as the industry standard for color film in Italy.[10] They include titles such as *Vacanze a Ischia* (*Holiday Island*, Mario Camerini, 1957), *Racconti d'estate* (*Girls for the Summer*, aka *Love on the Riviera*, Gianni Franciolini, 1958), *Costa Azzurra* (*Wild Cats on the Beach*, Vittorio Sala, 1959), *Avventura a Capri* (Giuseppe Lipartiti, 1959), *Brevi amori a Palma di Majorca* (*Vacations in Majorca*, Giorgio Bianchi, 1959), *Appuntamento a Ischia* (Mario Mattoli, 1960), *Ferragosto in bikini* (Marino Girolami, 1960), *Appuntamento in Riviera* (Mario Mattoli, 1962), *Diciottenni al sole* (*Eighteen in the Sun*, Camillo Mastrocinque, 1962), *L'ombrellone* (*Weekend, Italian Style*, Dino Risi, 1965), *Stasera mi butto* (Ettore Maria Fizzarotti, 1967), *Vacanze sulla Costa Smeralda* (Ruggero Deodato, 1968), and *Colpo di sole* (Mino Guerrini, 1968). As can be argued from the names of the directors, some are more polished or well-thought-out films, such as those by Pietrangeli, Franciolini, or Risi, while most of these titles are rough B movies, especially the copious filmography by Marino Girolami. Regarding the film stocks used, based on these films' credits and posters, it is evident that from the two-year period 1958 and 1959, in conjunction with the withdrawal of Ferraniacolor, Italian cinema was progressively monopolized by Eastman Color, which established itself as the most efficient and economical solution.[11]

Beachside Color Aesthetics

The beachside film genre burgeons when color in Italian cinema—at least in the most popular Italian cinema—is no longer an absolute novelty, but is in its normalization phase, an increasingly common trait of the viewing experience. Despite this, an inevitable attraction is generated in color beachside films, since the teeming beach is a site for a true *explosion* of color.

Studies of the *commedia all'italiana* note the violence and force of impact with which the beach erupts onto the film screen in this period, even in black-and-white films. The beach seemingly serves as a visual manifestation of the momentum of the Italian economic miracle, as Enrico Giacovelli argues: "At the start of the 1960s a visual and aural bomb erupted onto Italy's beaches: the boom. The fact that it was a sudden explosion and not a slow burn is evidenced by the brusque, unbridled, destructive way in which beachside scenes are introduced into films: [they demonstrate] a break in the film's form, brutally opposed to the rest, like futurist machines pitted against the quietude of the moon-light."[12] This is even more true for color beachside films. After their cursory preambles and introductory sequences of varying length, the films often drama-tize the arrival at the beach with both a visual and an auditory "pop": a close-up of a loudspeaker playing a song at full blast (*Ferragosto in bikini*) and a shot of a woman wearing a bright red bikini against the backdrop of a row of multicolor beach umbrellas (*Scandali al mare*) are just two examples of the audiovisual rup-ture brought about by beach scenes.

In terms of sound, the beachside comedies served indeed as loudspeakers for the latest musical trends, recording and boisterously replaying all the hits of the moment, whose lyrics would often describe colorful scenes and objects. For example, in "Pinne, Fucile e Occhiali", one of the most recognizable Italian pop summer anthems, released by Edoardo Vianello in 1962, rhapsodizes: "With our swimming fins, harpoon and goggles / the sea a table-like blue surface / under a sky *of a thousand colors* / we jump in headfirst" ("Con le pinne, fucile ed occhiali / quando il mare è una tavola blu / *sotto un cielo di mille colori* / ci tuffiamo con la testa all'ingiù" [emphasis added]). With regard to the spectacle accompanying these sounds, the beach scenes euphorically exhibit a whole rep-ertoire of colorful objects, as if these films are only truly "in color" after crossing the threshold into the beachside milieu: beach umbrellas, beach lounge chairs, beach cabins, swimsuits and bikinis, clothes, hats and caps with rubber floral patterns, beach robes and bathrobes, swimming fins and beachballs and a whole assortment of inflatable toys, and even new foods and drinks.

An effective summa of this chromatic audiovisual explosion is present in *L'ombrellone*, which in fact marks the apex—and the epitaph, too—of the sea-son of the holiday genre also for the highly conscious use of color film stock. The protagonist of the film is the mild-mannered engineer Marletti (Enrico Maria Salerno), who with his pipe and hat clearly recalls Jacques Tati's Mon-sieur Hulot. He wakes up in his Roman apartment on the eve of the August 15 bank holiday (*ferragosto*) and gets ready to join his wife, Giuliana (Sandra Milo), who is vacationing at the Baltic hotel on the Riviera Romagnola (even the choice of the hotel's name, Baltic, is ironically devoid of any relevant geo-graphic connection with the surrounding landscape). The opening of the film, accompanied by a jazzy instrumental music, is a montage of long shots of Mar-letti driving his white cabriolet through the deserted and silent streets of Rome (here Risi is clearly citing himself, referring to his *Il sorpasso* [*The Easy Life*, 1962]). Suddenly, after an ellipsis, we find the protagonist thrown into a thun-derous and dazzling world: he is stuck in the traffic of Riccione, amidst the sounds of car horns and hordes of bathers. The opening credits are a montage of colorful aerial views of the Romagna coast, a small army of umbrellas and bodies in bathing suits, arranged in colorful rows as far as the eye can see, while the soundtrack is "Sulla spiaggia c'era lei," a hit by the female band Sonia e le sorelle.

FIGURE 6.1 The name of the very crowded beachfront resort of *L'ombrellone* (*Weekend, Italian Style*, Dino Risi, 1965) is, ironically, Solitude.

This opening of *L'ombrellone* could be the audiovisual materialization of what Pasolini writes regarding the new seaside civilization, which according to him begins on the Adriatic Sea, around the town of Francavilla, on the coast of Abruzzo: "a river of establishments called 'Nettuno,' with the season's first bathers; boarding houses with multilingual signs—*Zimmer, Zimmer*, and *Zimmer*; gluttonously licked ice creams; cars with Xs and Js on the license plates, already more than three thousand a day at the border; blaring radios; babies and nannies; tunes continuously playing on jukeboxes and radios."[13] This new mode of vacationing, which Pasolini describes literally as a "multicolor river" (*fiume variopinto*), presents itself as the ideal site not only for reconstructing the social-anthropological changes underway but also for documenting a change in modes of perception, more specifically a resignification of the use of color. To celebrate the acme of the mass holiday culture, Risi aims to stun his protagonist, and with him the spectator: the soundtrack is a nonstop hit parade of pop songs, and the chromatic range is stretched and amplified toward aggressive hues, such as the acid and fluorescent tones of the clothes or the browns and oranges of exaggerated tans. It is no coincidence that the title of the film itself is no longer dedicated to a place but to an object, the beach umbrella, the rainbow banner of this new holiday culture (figure 6.1). Whereas in earlier, nascent stages of beachside tourism, the experience of a seaside stay was promoted as a site for the silent contemplation of the scenery and the activation of all the senses in order to adequately apprehend the surrounding nature, beachside comedies create an audiovisual representation of the beach as a site mediated and contaminated by the audiovisual presence of modern life, which tends to overwhelm and cancel out all the "underlying" natural elements.

Between the Postcard and the Shop Window

Color has always been congenial to the seaside environment. It is enough to glance at any one of the countless images that depict the beachside milieu of the mid-nineteenth century to recognize that the beach, with its omnipresent tutti-frutti-patterned beach umbrellas, was metonymically the site for multicolor spectacle, as Robert Ritchie notes: "Hotels moved quickly to take over the sand in front of their buildings and cover it with *umbrellas of their colors*, the new deck chairs to lounge on, small tables to rest drinks on, and towels, all the better to meet every need of the bather. Beaches soon took on *a patterned array of colors* as each hotel or beach club set out its own equipment" (emphasis added).[14]

More broadly, color adapts very well to shooting the Italian landscape, as described by Gabor Pogany, a Hungarian-born director of photography who had been active in Italian cinema since the 1940s:

> I have been preaching since 1937, in Italy and abroad, that Italian landscapes are ideal for shooting in color, with any system, from Technicolor to Cinecolor to Agfacolor. Every time I went to the mountains, to Tuscany, to Rome, to Naples, along the Ligurian or Amalfi coast, to Sicily, I always repeated this slogan, until it became monotonous. But I could not resist repeating it, seeing a sunset on the Matterhorn, or in Venice; admiring the green Tuscan valleys; the waters of Clitunno; the Sorrento gulf; the paradise of Taormina; the caves of Capri; and I could go on and on. . . . Whoever has the courage to solve the problem of color in Italy . . . will have accomplished the biggest commercial deal imaginable.[15]

Pogany's words echo those of Pasolini, when, at the start of his travel diary, his prose is littered with adjectives that denote the color of the natural elements that surround him, with a particular recurrence not so much of blue hues as green ones, which he attributes both to lush greenery and to the colors of the sea's water. In one passage, Pasolini explicitly alludes to the aesthetic of the postcard, in other words, the representation of the landscape in which the human figure is excluded: "At Sestri, which is like the postcards, I die for a few hours, having entered a postcard."[16] But, as Pasolini moves on to true beachfront towns, these natural tones fade, becoming desaturated and muted. "The Adriatic, in summer, has the same color as a raincoat," he writes, borrowing the phrase from a painter he meets in Venice.[17]

It seems that there is no longer a natural and unitary color palette that defines the beachside landscapes. It is instead replaced by a cacophony of colors, distinctly *artificial* in appearance, in which all colors are equally present and contribute to a sense of saturated vision. With considerable delay, in fact, the so-called color revolution had arrived in Italy, after having already occurred in the United States between the 1920s and 1930s. This chromatic revolution was rendered possible by a radical transformation in the industrial production of color: beginning at the end of the nineteenth century, in tandem with the second industrial revolution, tints and pigments were no longer extracted from organic materials of varying degrees of rarity, since they could now be produced synthetically in a lab. At the core of the extensive "naturalization" of color in the public's mode of perception was, therefore, a fully *artificial* operation.[18]

It is precisely this tension between natural and artificial that dominates the use of color throughout the beachside comedy subgenre and that tightens the visual references between the postcard and the shop window: at the dawn of mass consumerism, color beachside films function not only as postcards of the Italian landscape but also as shop windows for the exhibition of the new color commodities.[19] This shop-window effect in beachside comedies is actually accentuated by another technological advancement adopted by the Italian film industry in the same period, especially in color films: the panoramic wide screen (especially Totalscope and Dyaliscope), which lengthens the film frame, thereby multiplying the "exhibition space" for new colored objects.[20] Out of the total number of color beachside comedies, two out of three are in widescreen.

Take, for example, the opening scenes of *Diciottenni al sole* (Eastman Color and panoramic wide screen): at the pier, while the ferry for Ischia is departing and has already left its moorings, three young men fall out precipitously from a taxicab and board the ferry at the last minute. From the boarding bridge a young woman overlooks the scene; we quickly notice her due to her red hat, which stands out in this visual field—her outfit is black and white. In the following, closer shot, the red of her hat becomes the true catalyst for the scene: one of the three young men, in his rush to board the ferry, knocks the woman off-balance, inadvertently causing her hat to fall into the water. The young woman is none other than Catherine Spaak, who accepts the apologies of the young man (Gianni Garko) without losing her composure and wastes no time in pulling out another hat from her bag, this time a straw hat in green. The green hat will also soon experience a premature end, as it will be inadvertently crushed by the same bungling young man, and will once again be substituted shortly thereafter, serving as a pretext for a romantic plotline with a happy ending for both characters. It is in fact these objects (the young woman's hats) that obtrude in the frame, jutting out from the picturesque landscapes. Further evidence of this visual trope is found just before the film's opening credit sequence: the captain of the ferry heading to Ischia uses a few whistles in Morse code to send a romantic message to a chambermaid facing the boat from the terrace of a skyscraper (the captain will use exactly the same coded message for another woman once he has left Ischia; he has a lover at every port). The chambermaid, in the throes of her romantic idyll, distractedly drops the basket full of clothes she meant to hang to dry, so that the clothes flutter down from the top floor of the building as a shower of multicolored fabrics raining down *above* and *in front of* the postcard images of the Gulf of Naples. This is just one of the many similar examples that could be tended. Another, likewise, centers around bizarre beach hats: the comical head coverings of Sandra Mondaini in *Caccia al marito* (Marino Girolami, 1960), halfway between a shower cap and a wig.

As Maggie Günsberg notes in her study of *commedia all'italiana*, the shop window is a metaphor suitable also for gender issues: "The basic characteristics of the cinematic image as surface, and of the screen as mirror and at times also shop window, bring into play gender-related issues of spectatorial identification involving dynamics of desire, voyeurism and fetishism."[21] Among the "commodities" of consumer culture to be displayed near the beach, we should also include the female body, as several recent feminist analyses of beachside culture have argued: the bikini-clad woman becomes an erotic spectacle for voyeuristic male gazes, especially in B movies such as those directed by Girolami, Veo, or Sala.[22] Beauty contests and fashion shows are indeed recurring elements in beachside comedies, featuring a parade of female characters who sport sophisticated summer outfits and ever-novel styles of swimsuits and bikinis. The bodies on-screen serve partly as mannequins for items of clothing, hairstyles, and accessories. They are so recurring in beachside comedies that they become part of the new seaside landscape boom. This overlap between merchandise and landscape through the female body is made explicit in a scene from *Avventura a Capri*: a group of aristocrats and snobs watch a poolside parade of creations by the stylist Antoine (expressly characterized as homosexual through stereotyping). At the end of the evening, six creations (dress and hairstyle) parade, which have been given the name of the main tourist attractions of Capri (e.g., "Monte Solaro," "Arco Naturale," "Marina Piccola"). The place of honor is reserved for "Grotta Azzurra," a green (and not blue) dress with matching hair, sported by Sandra (Alessandra Panaro), the protagonist of one of the subplots of the film (figure 6.2). In the sign of color, the female body therefore functions as a double attraction: mannequin in the shop window, to

FIGURE 6.2 Alessandra Panaro (Sandra) in *Avventura a Capri* (Giuseppe Lipartiti, 1959) parades with a green dress and matching hair: the outfit is presented as "Grotta Azzurra," one of the main natural attractions of Capri.

promote the dress, and living postcard, to promote the landscape.[23] As Pogany had wished, "the biggest commercial deal imaginable."[24]

Old and New Media

The boom years for Italian cinema are not only the period of mass transition from black and white to color but also a season of expanded intermediality. If the beach is a stage for new products, among the colorful objects that are exhibited is the *image* itself, due in part to the vertiginous increase in the production of images— public and private, as well as professional and amateur—evident in the years of the economic boom. Characters in these films, for example, might distractedly leaf through illustrated color magazines such as *Epoca* and *Tempo*, or grab small-gauge movie cameras to shoot holiday home movies, whereas another recurring genre figure across these films is the photographer, the creator and salesman of images, who roves through the beach in search of photographic subjects to capture for pay. In *Intrigo a Taormina/Femmine di lusso* (*Love, the Italian Way*, Giorgio Bianchi, 1960), for example, Walter Chiari is a photographer who boards the yacht of the commendatore Gino Cervi in order to produce a photographic service for an advertising campaign.

Among the images of *other images*, framed, "accidentally" or on purpose, in the profilmic space, there are also black-and-white photographs, which clearly still occupy an important part of the panorama of the national visual culture (Paolo Di Paolo himself shoots mainly in black and white when traveling alongside Pasolini). It is precisely through the language of black-and-white images that beachside comedies engage in an additional form of mediation with cinema's main rival at the time: television, which launched in Italy in 1954, was by then starting to eclipse cinema audiences.

Beachside comedies are shot through with an intermediality that manifests itself most of all in a dialogue with the world of the mass cultural television show, especially with the appearances of several mainstays of the fledging television variety show, such as the husband-and-wife duo Raimondo Vianello and Sandra Mondaini, as well as the actors Walter Chiari and Ugo Tognazzi, not to mention the many celebrities who appeared in films playing themselves. The television variety show, nevertheless, was still shot in black and white at the time, and would continue to be until February 1, 1977, when the national broadcaster RAI finally introduced color transmissions, years after the United States and most major European countries had made the transition to color. This means that every time a television appears in a color film from this period, its images are in black and white by default, resulting in a small, colorless rectangle in a much larger multicolor frame. *Appuntamento in Riviera*, for example, includes a scene where a talent scout spectates the vocal performance of Tony Renis at the Sanremo Festival. Despite being at the site of the festival, the scout chooses not to watch the show live from the stage but instead in an adjacent small room, sitting in front of a little black-and-white television. Although several people invite him to sit among the audience members, where "one can see better," the music producer insists on staying glued in front of the television because what really matters, according to him, is to be able to "see that which eight million people are seeing." What this scene seems to be communicating is that whereas television is attracting an ever-growing number of spectators, cinema nevertheless allows us to "see better."

The hierarchical relationship between film and television is also asserted in *Appuntamento a Ischia*. In a scene that takes place outdoors on the coastline of Ischia, the arrival of a TV crew attracts the attention of many curious spectators in swimsuits who act as a spectating public. The crew shoots a segment for the popular RAI television advertising show *Carosello* in which the pop sensation Mina plays herself and sings "La nonna Magdalena". *Carosello* is well known for having been shot in black and white for the entirety of its run (from 1957 to 1977); nevertheless, the scene in this film features a smattering of color, starting with the blaring presence of Mina's rainbow-colored outfit. The attractive power of color is so strong as to purport an incursion into the Real. We can therefore include color beachside comedies in the category of media fantasy films, those films, according to Paul Young, in which cinema represents rival media as a defense strategy: "In media fantasy films . . . the film industry articulates most plainly its definitions of film at these critical moments of intermedia rivalry. . . . media fantasy films offer their audiences at once an apologia for social hierarchies in general and a glimmer of resistance to those hierarchies, dialectically folded into the same narrative spectacle."[25]

Positioned squarely at the center of the Italian media landscape in this period, cinema manages to hold together and incorporate all other media forms, from the revue and the *avanspettacolo* play (from which many film iterations, such as Dorian Gray and Mario Carotenuto, derive) to radio (the film *Pesci d'oro e bikini d'argento*, Carlo Veo, 1961, centers around a radio competition), from the photonovel to the *canzonetta*, as well as the various forms of black-and-white media still circulating, such as photography and television. The nodal role that Italian cinema plays between the mid-1950s and the mid-1960s measures itself by its ability to absorb and re-elaborate all the manifestations of audiovisual culture of the time, in which the *new* color visual mode coexists alongside the *old* black-and-white one. Even if the golden decade of the Italian beachside comedy coincides with the first decade of Italian television, mainstream cinema and the beachside comedy in particular rely on the ability to exaggerate color to emphasize that cinema is the definitive modern screen through which one can *see more* and *see better*.

Notes

1   Republished as Pier Paolo Pasolini, *The Long Road of Sand*, trans. Stephen Sartarelli (Rome: Contrasto, 2015).

2 For cultural histories of the beachside vacation, see Robert C. Ritchie, *The Lure of the Beach: A Global History* (Oakland: University of California Press, 2021); A. Corbin, *The Lure of the Sea: The Discovery of the Seaside in the Western World 1750–1840*, trans. Jocelyn Phelps (Berkeley: University of California Press, 1994); and F. Inglis, *The Delicious History of the Holiday* (London: Routledge, 2000).

3 Asterio Savelli, *Sociologia del turismo balneare* (Milan: Franco Angeli, 2009).

4 Christian Uva, *L'ultima spiaggia. Rive e derive del cinema italiano* (Venice: Marsilio, 2021), 11, 118; specifically for the era of the Italian beachside comedy, see 80–102. Unless otherwise noted, all translations are my own.

5 To be more precise, the corpus of the Italian beachside comedy includes "around forty [films] if we take into consideration just the years comprising 1957 to 1965, and more than 60 if we expand our frame of analysis to include all the films since 1949 which somehow discussed Italians vacationing"; Maurizio Zinni, "Rappresentare il benessere. Gli italiani e le vacanze nel cinema del 'miracolo,'" in *Penso che un sogno così non ritorni mai più. L'Italia del miracolo tra storia, cinema, musica e televisione*, ed. Pietro Cavallo and Pasquale Iaccio (Naples: Liguori, 2016), 218. It is also worth noting that the beach movie was a broader, international genre of the era, often produced by American International Pictures; see Pamela Robertson Wojcik, *Gidget: Origins of a Teen Girl Transmedia Franchise* (New York: Routledge 2021); Terry Rowan, *Bikini, Surfing and Beach Party Movies* (Morrisville, NC: Lulu, 2014).

6 Orsola Silvestrini, "Tu vuò fà l'americano. La couleur dans le cinéma populaire italien," *1895. Mille huit cent quatre-vingt-quinze*, no. 55 (June 2008): 25–51.

7 Ruggero Eugeni proposes a set of criteria on why directors would choose to shoot their film in black and white or in color: generally, films set in one place with a set of intertwined vignettes were shot in color, whereas the more reflective travel narrative vacation films were shot in black and white; see "Vacanza," in *Lessico del cinema italiano. Forme di rappresentazione e forme di vita*, ed. Roberto De Gaetano, vol. 3 (Milan: Mimesis, 2016), 359–404.

8 See Federico Pierotti, *Un'archeologia del colore nel cinema italiano. Dal Technicolor ad Antonioni* (Pisa: ETS, 2016); Luca Giuliani, "Una volta si scriveva così: ferrania," in *La materia dei sogni: L'impresa cinematografica in Italia*, ed. Vincenzo Buccheri and Luca Malavasi (Rome: Carocci, 2005), 60–80. According to Giuliani's count, the Italian feature films in Ferraniacolor (1952–1959) number just over a hundred; the copious production of short films and the incalculable quantity of small-gauge films are excluded from the count. On the acquisition of Ferrania by 3M in 1964, see Elena Past, "The Ferrania Acquisition, the Cinematic Archive and the Anthropocene: Celluloid Materialities," *La Valle dell'Eden*, no. 37 (2021): 147–158.

9 As Pierotti emphasizes, when Technicolor opened its Rome offices in 1958, it inaugurated its Italian operations with *Vacanze d'inverno* (Camillo Mastrocinque, 1959), another vacation-themed film but in this case depicting winter vacations instead of summer ones. This was the first Italian film to be printed in Technicolor No. V and was a notable antecedent to the *cinepanettone* holiday comedy films of later years; Pierotti, *Un'archeologia del colore*, 139–141.

10 Pierotti, 133–135.

11 According to Pierotti, the dominance of Eastman Color had already occurred in the 1958–1959 season, coinciding with the beachside films' boom; Pierotti, 136.

12 Enrico Giacovelli, *La commedia all'italiana* (Rome: Gremese, 1995), 161.

13 Pasolini, *Long Road of Sand* (e-book).

14 Ritchie, *Lure of the Beach* (e-book). As Ritchie further points out, among the first sectors to offer color images of the beach at the end of the nineteenth century was

the world of advertising: "This was also the era in which advertising started to push products and services on a national scale. The emergence of national magazines and regional newspapers, of new technologies in printing that created colorful posters, and of national brands all contributed to the emergence of robust advertising campaigns" (159 [e-book]).

15   Gabor Pogany, "Il cinema italiano e il Technicolor," *Cinespettacolo*, no. 3–4 (1948): 5.

16   Pasolini, *Long Road of Sand* (e-book).

17   Pasolini (e-book).

18   For this same reason, the introduction of synthetic dyes, cheap and readily available—Sean Cubitt calls it the "democratization of color"—caused a reversal in the connotations associated with color; color was no longer a sign of wealth and privilege but instead became a vulgar attribute, more readily associated with subaltern subjects (women, children, the uneducated, homosexuals, and poor immigrants presumed to have a "primitive" sensibility); Sean Cubitt, *The Practice of Light. A Genealogy of Visual Technologies from Prints to Pixels* (Cambridge, MA: MIT Press, 2014), 131.

19   It is worth noting that both the shop window and the postcard are modern visual devices, born almost simultaneously in the mid-nineteenth century (about the 1840s for the shop window and twenty years later for the postcard), and both involved in processes of commodification: the postcard mediated and commodified nature, though in a romanticized way (the longing for an unsullied nature), at the dawn of mass tourism; the shop window, thanks to the production of giant glasses, aimed to properly display products in order to push customers to buy. Both devices leveraged the attractive appeal of color.

20   Federico Vitella, *L'età dello schermo panoramico. Il cinema italiano e la rivoluzione widescreen* (Pisa: ETS, 2018).

21   Maggie Günsberg, *Italian Cinema: Gender and Genre* (Basingstoke: Palgrave Macmillan, 2005), 12. More broadly, Günsberg writes: "There is a longstanding link between the screen and the shop window, enhanced by press-books and posters, with the construction of the spectating self mirroring the appearance and lifestyle of the stars in materialist terms of buying clothes, cosmetics, cars and furnishings. . . . The socioeconomic context of the boom resulted in a sharp focus in *commedia all'italiana* on the relationship between people and goods, and also, in particular, on the way goods mediate in relations of gender and class" (61).

22   Natalie Fullwood, *Cinema, Gender and Everyday Space: Comedy, Italian Style* (New York: Palgrave MacMillan, 2015), esp. 65–94.

23   Speaking further of colored items on the female body, the most scandalous color is that of the skin, as demonstrated by one of the subplots of *Vacanze a Ischia* in which Caterina (Isabel Corey) bathes naked in the sea at night. Colonel Manfredi, who was spying on her, is forced by his wife to report her for insulting public decency. The two lawyers charged with defending her—one of them is Peppino De Filippo— will then sew a flesh-colored (*carnicino*) swimsuit, the exact shade of the woman's skin, to demonstrate that actually her body was not naked but modestly covered. The gag could only have worked in a color film.

24   Pogany, "Il cinema italiano e il Technicolor," 5.

25   Paul Young, *The Cinema Dreams Its Rivals: Media Fantasy Films from Radio to the Internet* (Minneapolis: University of Minnesota Press, 2006), xxix.

7

Technological and Athletic Splendor

The Formation of Color in the Socialist Sports Film in China

LINDA C. ZHANG

In June 2021, the Shanghai International Film Festival screened a 4K digital restoration of the classic 1957 film *Woman Basketball Player No. 5* (*Nülan Wuhao* 女蓝5号), directed by Xie Jin (谢晋). The screening of the restoration was part of a forum and large media event that also included a panel of archivists, film festival organizers, and software engineers, as well as a screening of a seven-minute documentary, *Bluer Than Indigo* (*Qingchu yulan* 青出于蓝).[1] Both the panel and the documentary celebrated the collaboration between the China Film Archive and MiGu (a subsidiary of China Mobile), which provided the artificial intelligence (AI) technology used for the restoration. Panelists praised MiGu's AI technology for its ability to reduce the labor and time put into addressing issues such as image, sound, and color degradation. In media reports of this restoration, AI was linked to a greater effort to modernize China's network to 5G technology.[2] The Shanghai film festival event was not just a screening of a restoration but also a celebration of what allowed that restoration to happen. The event's rhetoric celebrated both the 1957 film as a national classic and its digital restoration as the future of China's AI technological capabilities.

During the forum, representatives such as Shi Chuan, assistant chair of the Shanghai Film Association, asserted that one of the major concerns regarding the process was not just how to transfer and maintain the quality of the original celluloid but also how to maintain a sense of the materiality of the film, its date of production, and its broader historical context. In particular, the China Film Archive representatives sought to avoid making the film resemble a high-definition live sporting event while also maintaining the film's color scheme in the digital restoration: the director Xie Jin's use of colder colors to film the pre-1949 world of China, and a warmer set of colors for the post-1949 liberation world of the People's Republic of China (PRC).[3]

The digital restoration, in celebrating both the past and the future of film history together through AI technology, is in fact just the latest iteration of how color, film technology, and *Woman Basketball Player No. 5* (hereafter referred to as *No. 5*) have been discussed together as a symbolic film representing the frontiers of PRC cinema. This chapter considers how color, through technological change, has in fact long been a part of a contested and fraught narrative behind *No. 5*, starting from its original release in 1957. Additionally, with color as an aesthetic and a technology, my analysis also considers how the film has become symptomatic of broader, national claims for technological progress.

In the early years of the PRC, color film was a powerful tool to promote the newly formed socialist nation across cinematic genres. Each purportedly "first" color film of each genre in those years—such as sports, animation, documentary, and even opera film—was heavily promoted by news and media. *No. 5*, filmed with variations of Agfacolor technology, was no exception. One of the most anticipated movies of that year—for both its romantic and youth themes—the film was released in the late summer of 1957. Many reviewers commented on its refreshing portrayal of an energetic and vivacious athletic culture against the backdrop of a new, healthier China during the early years of the PRC. Scholars such as Mao Jian have examined the film's reception, and how the film garnered both praise and controversy for its depictions of urban affluence as well as its portrayal of the athletic female body.[4] Lu and Shuman have focused on the ideological bent of the film, writing about *No. 5*'s significance in creating a victorious narrative of healthy, athletic bodies, associating the visual spectacle of athletic performance with urban modernity, and rewriting the iconography of physical culture with that of the New Physical Culture Movement (*xin tiyu*).[5]

But these studies, while focusing on *No. 5* as a fresh vision of gender, urban modernity, and physical culture under the new regime of the PRC, have not considered how *color*—as a material process, technology, and visual spectacle—complicated both the vision and the narrative about the health of the PRC that it signified. The most comprehensive work on color in Chinese cinemas thus far has been the special edition of the *Journal of Chinese Cinemas* edited by Margaret Hillenbrand in 2012 and focusing on color in PRC film during the 1960s and 1970s. Since then, more work on color film and technology during the Cultural

Revolution in the PRC has been published by Kirsty Sinclair Dootson and Zhaoyu Zhu.[6] Even so, the focus on the period of the Cultural Revolution has overshadowed the earlier socialist period in the 1950s—during which *No. 5* was produced—when color film technology was still being harnessed in the PRC, and when color's potential as a visual tool to portray socialist realist worlds was still being debated, defined, and shaped.

Studies of color film outside of China, conversely, have focused on how different technologies have been formative toward ideological imaginations of nation after the Second World War or how they have been contingently associated with particular film genres, such as musicals, realist films, or documentaries.[7] Jennifer Kapczynski has examined Agfacolor as a cinematic technology together with the broader trajectory of German national cinema and political history, arguing that Agfa has been tied closely to several different "national self-imaginings" of the German state throughout the twentieth century.[8] Through its particular aesthetic and palette, Kapczynski argues, Agfacolor even now evokes nostalgia for "the emotional and visual textures of a bygone era" in recent and contemporary German historical film.

Early PRC films such as *No. 5* present a national self-imagining that lacks a strong tie to any national film stock during a transitional period in national technology. Considering that the film was most likely filmed on Agfacolor- or Sovcolor-related stock, the film manages to construct a colorful filmic world that conveys a sense of the bright future of the PRC, while also borrowing international technology that, in fact, points to exchanges and flows that move outside of that self-contained, national world represented within the film. This chapter examines 1950s film reviews and records from the domestic film industry, including greater exchange of specialist knowledge in color film, increasing amounts of imported color film stock, and eventually the development of the domestic production of color film stock. My analysis covers how within this context, *No. 5* flirted with competing associations—between physical vitality and decadence, and between utility and spectacle—not just in its vision of national health and physical prowess but also in its utilization of new cinematic technology during 1950s China. In focusing on color in *No. 5*, the debate between utility and spectacle in cinematic color aesthetics was also precisely the question that was posed to the technology of color film earlier in the 1950s. I argue that the materialization of color in environment, costume, and mise-en-scène creates a sunny, optimistic, and even healthy vision of the socialist present in 1950s China.

The Development of Color Film Technology during the Early PRC

The fanfare surrounding the restoration of *No. 5* for the Shanghai International Film Festival suggested that the original film was a national triumph, both as a narrative celebrating the PRC's place in international sports and as a forerunner in cinematic spectacle and technology, particularly as the purportedly first color sports film in the nation. At the same time, many of the film festival events glossed over the historical context surrounding *No. 5* when it was released in 1950s, particularly eliding how unevenly the film industry and color film technology developed during the first decade of the PRC. Even now, the histories of the origins of color stock for early PRC color films are often conflicting and still uncertain. Broadly, German color film technology by way of the Soviet Union was seemingly predominant in China, as many of the first color films in China were supported by Soviet training and Sovcolor processes (based on Agfacolor). Different accounts suggest that *No. 5* originally may have been filmed using Agfacolor and imported through Hong Kong, but that film copies may have also been later distributed using Chinese domestically produced stock that was based on Sovcolor or Agfacolor.[9]

During most of the 1950s, color film technology—in the form of information and material—was still being imported predominantly from the Soviet Union and the Eastern Bloc, and much of the newest information and specialized knowledge surrounding film technology was obtained through significant exchange beyond PRC borders. Tony Rayns and Scott Meek found that during these early years, most color films produced in the 1950s were made using the Sovcolor process.[10] Zhong Jingyou and Xu Jin corroborate this trend of both imported technology and expertise, noting that in 1952 many of the Shanghai film studios initiated foreign exchanges and invited film technology experts mostly from the Soviet Union to work in film labs with Chinese film specialists, as a response to a general sense that the domestic industry lacked resources as well as general knowledge and technique.[11] Prior to the 1960s, specialized knowledge, skills, processing techniques, and procedures were still performed in the Soviet Union or the German Democratic Republic.[12] Manuals on color film stock, printers, and development processes were imported and translated into Chinese from the Soviet Union, such as *The Art of Color Film Development*, published by the China Film Press in Beijing in 1957.[13]

For much of the early decades of the PRC, the lack of high-quality, domestic color film stock meant that most studios and directors sought imported stock. Even after the 1950s, monochrome and color film stock were still usually imported from foreign sources—Agfa and Eastman Color through Hong Kong, Ilford from England, Gevacolor from Belgium, Ferrania from Italy, and Fuji from Japan.[14] According to interview anecdotes from the director Xie Jin, the color films he directed prior to *Two Stage Sisters* (1964)—including *No. 5*—mostly used Agfacolor, while *Two Stage Sisters* was shot using Eastman Color.[15] Dootson and Zhu have noted that the PRC bought film stock from Kodak and 3M until at least the mid-1960s and in 1962 also installed Soviet dye-transfer technology (Mosfilm's Pavel Mershin's Soviet system) that was largely based on Technicolor.[16]

Beginning in 1964 and through the Cultural Revolution, entities such as the Shanghai Science Education Film Studio and the Shanghai city cultural committee often ordered Eastman Color and other foreign film stock through Hong Kong due to their consistent quality.[17] Dootson and Zhu and Laikwan Pang have noted Jiang Qing's (Madame Mao) particular preference for Eastman Color stock and the increase in its use during Cultural Revolution–era films of the 1960s and 1970s.[18] Pang's work has characterized this period as one of painful growth for the developing color film industry and the central government in China—caught between balancing its reliance on foreign forms of support and a desire to develop self-sustaining manufacturing for cinema.[19]

The historiography of PRC domestic film stock production, not to mention color film stock, is also not easily clarified and is quite fraught, perhaps due in part to implications in destabilizing the sense of steady progress in the national film industry. Rhetorically, the PRC's film industry has long been part of a broader modernization narrative. For example, from the early 1950s to the early 1960s, the central government sought to cultivate its own domestic film stock production; that effort was also marked by a rhetoric that combined the goals of scientific standardization and cinematic, artistic practice.[20] Dootson and Zhu, as well as Pang, note that the Baoding Film Stock Factory was the first domestic entity in the PRC that was able to produce color film stock on its own.[21]

Domestic film stock production was a massive and often fragmented endeavor. Before the completion of the Baoding factory, there were still other scattered and decentralized efforts to produce domestic color film stock and color photography. City records in Shanghai also show that the Shanghai Institute of Chemical Technology ordered equipment for processing color film in 1955.[22] Zhong and Xu mark 1957 as a key year when the Shanghai Film Technology Plant was formed, centralizing the development of film stock for various Shanghai-based studios. This included the Tianma Studio, which produced both *No. 5* and Xie Jin's later film *Two Stage Sisters*, released in 1964.[23] In 1958, the Shanghai Film Bureau organized a conference among six key Shanghai studios, including Tianma, on the topic of color film techniques and technology.[24] From 1959 to 1960, the Shanghai Photographic Film Factory sought to expand its budget and production plans to include a fully functional lab with the capacity and equipment to process color film.[25] And in 1959, according to Li Nianlu, Li Ming, and Zhang Ming (and contradicting the history on the Baoding factory), the Shanghai Photographic Film Factory was successful in using color film processes and worked together with the Shanghai Film Technology Plant to produce and distribute color film copies of *No. 5*, making it the first film to be distributed in the PRC using domestically processed color film stock; it is unclear whether they used imported negatives.[26]

Just as film stock and technical knowledge were imported into the PRC, Chinese specialists were also sent to train in the Soviet Union. Huang Shaofen (黄绍芬), one of the PRC's leading color specialists involved in *No. 5* and a cinematographer in the Shanghai film industry since 1925, trained in Moscow specifically in color cinematography during 1950.[27] He was best known for his work on color films such as *No. 5* and the opera film *Liang Shanbo and Zhuyingtai* (1953; hereafter referred to as *The Butterfly Lovers*). Filmed in Sovcolor and hailed as the first color film from the PRC, *The Butterfly Lovers* established both a model for adapting stage opera and dance dramas to film and Huang Shaofen's reputation as a color specialist.[28]

As various cultural institutions sought to obtain the expertise and technology to produce color films, a growing debate regarding color's relationship with realism emerged among PRC directors and cinematographers. Rayns and Meek note that Huang Shaofen's work in the later 1956 film *Fifteen Strings of Cash*, directed by Tao Jin, marks a departure from the filmic conventions established by *The Butterfly Lovers*. Tao Jin and cinematographer Huang both sought an increased sense of realism by experimenting with light and color, moving between song and speech freely in the narrative, and using more "orthodox narrative cinema devices" such as wide-angle sequence shots, point-of-view shots, and parallel montage.[29] According to Jay Leyda, *Fifteen Strings of Cash* was a remarkable adaptation of an original Kunqu opera into a color film version that combined a "modern, naturalistic style" with the familiar conventions of traditional opera.[30] In this particular film, a palette that conveyed realism was achieved through a combination of low-key lighting and darker tones and accents. Leyda found that compared with the bright palettes used in *Liang Shanbo*, for *Fifteen Strings* Tao Jin employed "a darker, harsher palette for this macabre comedy: no shining surfaces and plenty of shadow." Tao Jin himself noted disagreements between himself and Huang Shao-fen regarding how to break away from what he called "stylized" opera conventions in favor of a more "realistic method."[31] Pitted against an older heritage of stylized opera forms, darker and harsher palettes combined with low-key and dramatic lighting seemed to offer a greater depth of realism to Tao Jin.

Shen Xilin (沈西林), the cinematographer and primary color specialist who collaborated with Huang Shaofen on *No. 5* and who was also known for his work on *Red Detachment of Women* (1961), directed by Xie Jin, also sought to avoid a distracting, cinematic spectacle in his desire to strengthen the realism in color films. Shen's approach was to seek balance and restraint in the use of color: "Dealing with bright, garish colors is merely just giving films a layer of multicolored clothing. It can only give rise to a superficial mood. Furthermore, too many bright colors distract the audience and detract from their power of attention toward the plot. But it also would be wrong to excessively avoid the vividness and liveliness of color—the color that is the target of the frame—and to not dare to use the power of color. That would greatly impoverish the transformation from color and lose its utility."[32] Shen used the metaphor of bright, garish clothing to illustrate his desire to keep color film technology useful while avoiding its tendencies to overstate or distract. He elaborated further that the goal of using color as well as any other film technology should be to allow the film's already present qualities to emerge with greater clarity, with a focus on setting, theme, and mood:

"Using too much or too little color would inadequately portray the intention of the work. Our films should sufficiently and boldly make every effort to correctly use color to reinforce the infectiousness of the film's mood, highlight the atmosphere of the scene, and give prominence to the personalities of the characters as well as to the theme of the film."[33]

This treatment of color—as a double-edged sword that could either create a greater sense of realism or create a distracting spectacle—resonates with much discourse of color film, particularly Technicolor, in the Western context.[34] As Dudley Andrew notes, Technicolor was perceived in postwar France in terms of its ideological association with Hollywood and use in genres such as musicals. It was interpreted as "purer than reality, needing strong artificial light, aggressive, almost whorish," which processes such as Agfacolor seemed less capable of delivering.[35] Steve Neale also notes how color was perceived as distracting and overwhelmingly associated with fantasy and spectacle.[36] Dootson and Zhu have pointed to the internal contradictions of the use of Technicolor in China, where "Chinese officials wished to enjoy the lush, chromatic design of Technicolor cinema while simultaneously denouncing its corrupting influence."[37]

Shen Xilin expressed similar concerns about vivid color's capacity to distract audiences from acting and facial expressions, diegesis, and narrative action. As a result, color was seen as a threat to a particular form of realist cinema—one that perhaps emulated the lighting and tones of monochrome cinema in the Western context, or perhaps the various literary and visual idioms associated with realism in China prior to 1949.[38] It is important to note, however, that as a mode of expression, realism was contingent on variable contexts and forms, ranging from spectacular realism and magical realism to the revolutionary realism of the Mao era for which color was seen as highly appropriate. While creating new idioms and also sparring with previous formulations of realism, color provided visual pleasure, signified luxury or spectacle, and operated as a celebration of technology. Considering color as a force that has "escaped" conventions of both genre and realism, then, in the next section I consider color's overt application as both sumptuous spectacle and national narrative in the sports film *No. 5*.

Color as National Splendor in *Woman Basketball Player No. 5*

Woman Basketball Player No. 5 visually presents a dazzling and glamorous world, despite the claims made by filmmakers such as Tao Jin and Shen Xilin that the film tried to achieve a realist aesthetic. The film was directed by Xie Jin, with Huang Shaofen and Shen Xilin as the color specialists and cinematographers. I argue that in *No. 5*, color becomes a force that celebrates the splendor of both the young, athletic spirit of the new nation and its technological apparatus.

The world of *No. 5* centers around the concept of teamwork and harmony in the New China through the example of athletics. The protagonist, Lin Xiaojie (played by Cao Qiwei), is No. 5 on the women's basketball team in Shanghai. In the context of the New China as portrayed through the film, Xiaojie learns the importance of teamwork, after suffering setbacks such as injuries, interpersonal conflicts with her teammates, and her own insecurities about her importance to the team. Unbeknownst to her, her mentor, Coach Tian Zhenhua (Liu Qiong), shares a tragic romantic past and a broken engagement with her mother, Lin Jie (played by Qin Yi), who was also a basketball player. Misled by tragedy and miscommunication into canceling their engagement, the two adults still remember each other through the memento of an orchid plant. They meet again and reestablish their connection, and Xiaojie eventually learns the importance of teamwork and comes to terms with her teammates and the past between her mother and Coach Tian.

No. 5 was celebrated for its relatively innovative camerawork in filming the basketball games. Zheng Guoen and Gong Rumei note that unlike other movies produced in that period, the film used a wider range of camera angles to portray the competitive atmosphere on the basketball court, such as low angles for basketball players entering the court, vertical crane shots during the game play to show players reaching for the basket, as well as high angles of elevation to shoot the basketball entering the basket.[39] Moreover, the film was considered innovative in its use of montage and parallel editing to create a greater sense of tension and excitement for the feeling of a live spectator event.[40] At the same time, the cinematography purportedly contained some weaknesses, particularly related to color. According to Zheng and Gong, the cinematographers were not unlike their colleagues throughout the 1950s in that they faced technical difficulties in maintaining consistent color and lighting throughout the different scenes.[41]

Similar issues may have persisted not just in the filming and editing but also in the preservation and restoration of extant copies of the film. In the restored version of the film prior to the 4K version in 2021, during one scene within the film when Coach Tian has a conversation with Xiaojie in his office, the shades of the curtains and their uniforms both switch back and forth between different shots from an initial green shade to a bluer hue.

Even in its unstable expression, in *No. 5* color creates an atmosphere of optimism, in the material objects, the environmental surroundings, and the characters themselves. It celebrates the technology of color film in part by visually depicting a sense of revolutionary optimism in which both the trauma prior to the PRC liberation and interpersonal conflicts are resolved in a bright, colorful, and forward-looking world. Leyda remarks that *No. 5* was one of many films during the late 1950s that dealt with teenagers in contemporary settings, and that it was distinguished by a "sense of ease" unusual to those types of films about youth. Rayns and Meeks comment that the film's narrative was typical in that it juxtaposed "the healing of a pre-Liberation wound with a forward-looking emphasis on the need for both individual effort and teamwork."[42]

Reviewers of the film were especially invested in the "bright" and "youthful" air of the post-liberation world in contrast to the sorrows of the past. For example, Shen Fuwei found that Lin Xiaojie and her teammates portrayed the new opportunities and "the happy life of the youth in the Mao era."[43] In contrast, the melodramatic arc of Coach Tian Zhenhua was especially moving due to the bitterness and pain he experienced as an athlete in the corrupt pre-liberation age, deepened by the romantic tragedy between him and Lin Jie. Thus, for Shen, Tian Zhenhua's role as a coach in the New China was all the more meaningful because he was not just "coaching the younger generation in the art of the sport, but also educating them in their thinking." The reviewer Ke Ling also found that *No. 5* gave a "fresh, youthful air" with its cast, many of whom were actual athletes or first-time actors, as well as the young director, Xie Jin, who was still relatively unestablished in the film industry at the time.[44] Xie Jin himself reported that he wanted to combine the love story in the film with the drama of the changing athletic culture between the "old" and "new" society.[45]

In *No. 5*, color marks the world of a youthful socialist nation. It is environmental, material, and also temporal, marking the *present* of socialism and of its athletic youth. *No. 5* features many exterior shots of naturally lit, bright and sunny weather, in addition to pillow shots of hallways and streets. For example, scenes focusing on Xiaojie and the team are set outdoors and use natural lighting, seemingly exploiting the particular strengths of Agfacolor technology. The natural lighting in *No. 5* emphasizes the cheerful and saturated shades of the characters' makeup and costumes (basketball and practice uniforms). For instance, we see this in one location scene when the members of the women's basketball team stand in a line in the sunny practice court and meet their new coach while wearing alternating colors and whites and with makeup highlighting their flushed faces (figure 7.1).[46] Combined with their cheerful countenances, the color of such scenes conveys their youth and vitality as athletes of the New China.

In *No. 5*, not only the environmental surroundings—clear skies, buildings, and dormitories—but also the objects in the mise-en-scène are clearly lit to allow for a full range of colors.[47] Clark notes how the cheerfulness of *No. 5* is suffused throughout the film in the characters as well as in the luxuriously colorful interiors of the set.[48] Interior objects, sets, and their accompanying materials are well lit and appear well saturated, including the orchid plant, the deep blue-green of dormitory furniture and door frames, and the brilliant red of the pillars in the dormitory common space. Since the typical palette associated with Agfacolor has been characterized as "graying greens, darkly saturated reds, and wan blues," we may even surmise that some of the interior shots featuring saturated hues, particularly the deep greens and blues, were a result of an earlier restoration in this film's history.

Color is just as much of a spectacle even in depictions of the prerevolutionary past. As opposed to the bright and sunny present, the film uses darker,

FIGURE 7.1 The members of the women's basketball team formally meet Coach Tian in their first practice, in *Woman Basketball Player No. 5* (Xie Jin, 1957).

shadowy lighting and deeper tones for flashbacks of the pre-liberation Shanghai. Many of these scenes are set during the winter and focus on the past relationship between Coach Tian and No. 5's mother, Lin Jie. Even then, however, the colors are just as saturated, and the film luxuriates in the deep burgundy of Lin Jie's coat (figure 7.2) and the red satin of Tian's basketball uniform. The outstanding difference between the use of color in the scenes of the past and those of the present lies mostly in the physical surroundings. Both Tian and Lin Jie are surrounded by the corruption and gambling of pre-liberation Shanghai. Tian is asked to throw the game against the foreign team. When he refuses to do so, he is cornered and beaten up by hired thugs in a dark alley outside the court and hospitalized thereafter, unable to pursue his basketball ambitions for the rest of the season.

Tian and Lin are captured by these concerns, set in a shadowy, wintry version of Shanghai. The past is marked by darker lighting, cold weather, and trauma—in direct contrast to the optimistic, post-liberation summery present that Xiaojie and her new generation grow up in. The pre-liberation scenes of Tian's recovery from his attack in the hospital, for example, use dramatic low-key lighting that washes out the hospital scenes to mostly grays, whites, and browns, while also drawing focus to the supine patients in the crowded

FIGURE 7.2 An original lobby card rendering a scene in which Tian and Lin Jie meet in his pre-liberation basketball dorm, in *Woman Basketball Player No. 5*. Courtesy of the C. V. Starr East Asian Library, University of California, Berkeley.

hospital wing. Together with close-ups of Tian's and Lin's pained expressions, these shots emphasize the tragic misunderstandings leading to their breakup as they face indifferent parents, doctors, pawnbrokers, and corrupt team managers. In contrast, the post-liberation scene during which Xiaojie recovers from her injuries (in a different hospital) uses ample natural lighting. The scene is set during a summery day, and the many open windows of the hospital wing draw attention to the surrounding space, light, and air. As a result, the whites of the hospital sheets and uniforms appear softer and warmer together with the pale blushes of the basketball players' cheeks and the red and orange shades of the flowers on Xiaojie's bedside table. Surrounded by concerned doctors, teammates, coach, boyfriend, and mother, Xiaojie is the focus of a scene that conveys the warmth of a community living in New China.

Color is tied to certain material objects just as it is temporally marked. The objects in Xiaojie's world are particularly vivid, such as the small puppets from Xiaojie's home, the Russian stacking dolls that Tian uses to show game strategy, Xiaojie's turquoise thermos and blue radio set, as well as Tian's well-tended orchid plant. Of particular interest is the accordion that belongs to

女籃 5 号

FIGURE 7.3 An original lobby card rendering the bunkbed and accordion argument scene, reproduced in black and white in *Woman Basketball Player No. 5*. Courtesy of the C. V. Starr East Asian Library, University of California, Berkeley.

Xiaojie's bunkmate and teammate. The instrument serves as the center of initial discord among the women's basketball team, but later, near the end of the film, it mediates the reconciliation between the team members.

The accordion first appears toward the beginning of the film when Xiaojie moves into the dormitory later than the rest of her teammates. She selects the lower bunk while asking her boyfriend to move an accordion already placed on the bunk. As he lowers the accordion, the discordant sound of a few keys sounds out, and the red lacquer and pearly white of the instrument reflect the lighting, flashing briefly. Moments later, the original bunk owner—Xiaojie's teammate Wang Aizhu—returns. In an eyeline match, the film shows Aizhu's discovery of the moved accordion, and a tense argument between the two teammates regarding the bunkbed ensues (figure 7.3).[49]

The tension between the two teammates continues when the still-resentful Aizhu hides Xiaojie's explanatory note to the team about missing the first half of an important game. The two women eventually reconcile after Xiaojie's recovery from a leg injury. Upon Xiaojie's healthy return, the camera uses a point-of-view tilt shot to show Aizhu's accordion now residing on the top bunk. The guilty Aizhu surprises Xiaojie with the switched bunks as a gesture of

FIGURE 7.4   A harmonious scene on the train to Beijing, in *Woman Basketball Player No. 5.*

welcome and reconciliation, and the film shows her weeping next to Xiaojie later that night, suggesting Aizhu's admission of wrongdoing. Finally, when the team travels to their national ceremony, the camera focuses on Xiaojie and Aizhu sitting side by side at a train window. The entire team sings a harmonious and optimistic song, with Aizhu accompanying them on the shimmering red and white accordion—colors that recall the color scheme of the team's athletic uniforms (figure 7.4). Here, color's materialization in the accordion draws attention to the texture and weight of certain material objects, while also celebrating the visual pleasure that coincides with the narrative's harmonious resolution. Furthermore, the mediation through the colorful instrument suggests a parable for the collective good: while too much emphasis on the individual leads to conflict, teamwork and open communication can lead to a much happier, collective resolution.

On a larger narrative scale, the drama of the accordion plays an indirect role in resolving the melodrama of the broken careers and truncated romance of the pre-liberation generation. It is only because of Xiaojie's injuries that Tian and Lin Jie are finally reunited in a quietly emotional scene at the hospital. The reconciliation between past and present is continued and played out the most dramatically, perhaps, in the scene where Lin Jie arrives at the ceremony where Xiaojie's team is nationally recognized—standing in rows with the PRC insignia brightly printed on their vivid red uniforms. Using an eyeline match, the film switches between a close-up of Lin's face and a close-up of Coach Tian's visage with flags of various colors as the backdrop. In this moment of heightened emotion, with the national anthem playing, a montage sequence of the two characters' tumultuous past is superimposed on Lin's expression. The darker tones of the past have now become more translucent, until the superimposition ends and returns us to the full-bodied, brighter colors—and opportunities—of the present. After the conclusion of the ceremony, a crane shot transitioning into a medium frontal shot shows Tian and Lin sharing a romantic moment on the empty bleachers. Almost as if he were summarizing the resolution of the temporal disconnect of pre- and post-liberation China, Tian asserts firmly, "The past is the past. No matter what happened, it is time for us to start our new life."

Conclusion

In the summer of 1957, the film critic Tian Lan updated readers of *Popular Movies* on *No. 5*—already advertised as the "first color sports film" in China—to be released later that year in the late summer and early fall. The crew and actors had just gone to Beijing that May to film several key scenes on location, drawing curious crowds whenever they went to key landmarks, such as Tiananmen Square, the Sino-Soviet Friendship Hospital, and the Beijing stadium. Tian mentioned that the film crew chose to shoot a few outdoor training scenes at a university campus—"exceptionally beautiful, and very suitable for filming a color film"—specifically for the gorgeous combination of the red palette of the buildings and the surrounding, lush green environment of the campus trees.[50]

In the middle of the update, Tian Lan noted an incident at the Beijing airport where filming and reality converged. The crew had just finished filming the scene during which the members of the National women's basketball team board a plane. At the conclusion of the filming, however, officials from the actual Chinese National Sports Association, also at the airport at the time, invited the actors to join them in greeting a sports delegation from Japan that had just landed in Beijing. Marveling at this coincidence, Tian Lan writes, "Because actors for color films do not have to wear as thick make-up as they do for black and white films, the [Japanese] guests really thought that the young women greeting them . . . were the actual [National] women's basketball team players. They had no idea that they were actors from a movie!" Tian Lan's narration is remarkable in its commentary, focusing on how the material conditions of producing a color film led to a happy conflation of actual events and the filmic representation of a nation and its athletes.

The power of color, according to filmmakers such as Shen Xilin, needed to be harnessed to both enhance the film's visual style and maintain its ideological sense of realism. Restraint was needed so color would not distract audiences from its realist, ideological intent. However, Shen and his colleagues may have been holding onto a concept of realism that was soon replaced by Mao's revolutionary romanticism and optimistic fantasies of the future. The incident of mistaken identity at the Beijing airport was the very expression of the national aspiration to see Chinese athletic teams recognized on the international stage.

Color film, in these terms, may have been the only acceptable form for portraying the revolutionary direction of the nation. Fully utilizing the aspirational and optimistic qualities of color on the screen, *No. 5* portrayed the healthy athleticism and harmonious teamwork of a forward-looking, spectacularly vivid version of the socialist present. Color—as technology and aesthetic—was still not so easily harnessed or controlled. As the history of its adaptation by PRC film studios reveals, color could be interpreted as a litmus test of the changes to the cultural and aesthetic regime, tied to the goals of modernization of technology and revitalization of physical culture. Color's claim was also, then, a claim in the future of the PRC.

Notes

1 The translation of the idiom could also be interpreted as "Better than the original."
2 See "Classic Film Restoration: The First 4K Restoration of the Premier Sports Color Feature Film," *Shanghai International Film Festival*, June 17, 2009, https://www.siff.com/content?aid=a63317c2-6b13-40c3-b4fe-69397199b792. This source is a film festival report published online after the conclusion of the aforementioned forum on the restoration of *Woman Basketball Player No. 5*. The China Film Archive primarily used AI to help remove noise and scratches from the film. For this purpose, AI was still an experimental process, and technicians had to continually adjust the parameters and continue training the AI technology, since they were particularly concerned with its ability to understand cultural context and emotion; https://k.sina.cn/article_5044281310_12ca99fde02001ew6.html?from=ent&subch=oent, consulted 04.23.2023.
3 Zhang Yi, "*Qinyi Zhuyan, Xiang Mei dianying chunü zuo, Xiejin daoyan Nülanshao 4k xiufu ban shouying," Shanghai Observer*, last modified June 17, 2021, https://export.shobserver.com/baijiahao/html/377384.html.
4 Mao Jian, "Gender Politics and the Crisis of Socialist Aesthetics: The 'Room' in *Woman Basketball Player No. 5*," trans. Zhu Ping, in *Debating the Socialist Legacy and Capitalist Globalization in China*, ed. Xueping Zhong and Ban Wang (New York: Palgrave Macmillan, 2014), 73–84.
5 Xiaoning Lu, *Moulding the Socialist Subject: Cinema and Chinese Modernity (1949–1966)* (Leiden: Brill, 2020), 54; Amanda Shuman, "No Longer 'Sick': Visualizing 'Victorious' Athletes in 1950s Chinese Films," *Historical Social Research Historische Sozialforschung* 43, no. 2 (2018): 225.
6 Margaret Hillenbrand. "Special Issue on the Colour of Chinese Cinemas: Guest Editor's Introduction," *Journal of Chinese Cinemas* 6, no. 3 (2012): 207–210; Kirsty Sinclair Dootson and Zhaoyu Zhu, "Did Madame Mao Dream in Technicolor? Rethinking Cold War Colour Cinema through Technicolor's 'Chinese Copy,'" *Screen* 61, no. 3 (2020): 343–367.
7 Here, I am thinking of the critical work on color film that I reference throughout this chapter, by Dudley Andrew, Joshua Yumibe and Sarah Street, Tom Gunning,

and Steve Neale. Sarah Street and Joshua Yumibe, *Chromatic Modernity: Color, Cinema, and Media of the 1920s* (New York: Columbia University Press, 2019).

8 Jennifer M. Kapczynski, "Imitation of Life: The Aesthetics of Agfacolor in Recent Historical Cinema," in *The Collapse of the Conventional: German Film and Its Politics at the Turn of the Twenty-First Century*, ed. Jaimey Fisher and Brad Prager (Detroit: Wayne State University Press, 2010), 41.

9 In an interview, Xie Jin suggests that films he worked with until 1962 were shot using Agfacolor. Sovcolor, based on Agfacolor technology, however, was noted as being the more prevalent imported stock during the 1950s. Li Nianlu, Li Ming, and Zhang Ming, *Shi ji hui mou Zhongguo dian ying zhuan ye shi yan jiu* (Beijing: China Film Press, 2006), 90; Marco Müller and Tan Xiaohan, "*Yiwei Zhongguo dianying daoyan de kunnan—Xiejin zhuanfang* (1983)," in *Jiubali de dushiren: Dianying Shouce Huayu dianying piping wenxuan*, ed. Tan Xiaohan (Zhengzhou: Henan University Press, 2019), 117.

10 Tony Rayns and Scott Meek, *Electric Shadows: 45 Years of Chinese Cinema Dianying: Zhongguo Dianying Sishiwu Nian* (London: British Film Institute, 1980), E5.

11 Zhong Jingyou and Xu Jin, eds., *Zhonghua Renmin Gongheguo Dianying Shiye Sanshiwu Nian: 1949–1984* (Beijing: Zhongguo Dianying Chubanshe, 1985), 368.

12 Laikwan Pang, "Colour and Utopia: The Filmic Portrayal of Harvest in Late Cultural Revolution Narrative Films," *Journal of Chinese Cinemas* 6, no. 3 (2012): 273.

13 Yue Feisi and Wan Guoqiang, *Caise Yingpian Xiying Gongyi* (Beijing: Zhongguo Dianying Chubanshe, 1957).

14 Zhong and Xu, *Zhonghua Renmin Gongheguo Dianying Shiye Sanshiwu Nian*, 372.

15 Müller and Tan, "*Yiwei Zhongguo dianying daoyan de kunnan*," 117. Distributed copies of *Two Stage Sisters*, according to Xie, were actually developed with Orwocolor.

16 Dootson and Zhu, "Did Madame Mao Dream in Technicolor?," 343, 354.

17 *Shanghai shi dianyingju geming weiyuanhui guanyu "Shijiewuji" shenqing Yisiman caise jiaopian deng de han*," Shanghai Municipal Archives (Shanghai, April 16, 1973), 4; Ma Tianshui, Xu Kingxian, and Wang Xiuzhen, "*Zhonggong shanghai shiwei bangongshi, Shanghai shi geming weiyuanhui bangongshi chao gao dan . . .*," Shanghai Municipal Archives (Shanghai, 1973), 1–3.

18 Dootson and Zhu, "Did Madame Mao Dream in Technicolor?," 357; Pang, "Color and Utopia," 273.

19 Pang, "Color and Utopia," 263–282.

20 Pang, 271.

21 Pang, 271.

22 *Shanghai Huagong xueyuan guanyu caisejiaopian yici tubugong guan ji xu shebei de baogao* (Shanghai Municipal Archives, Shanghai, 1955), 1–2.

23 Zhong and Xu, *Zhonghua Renmin Gongheguo Dianying Shiye Sanshiwu Nian*, 370.

24 "*Shanghai shi dianyingju bangongshi guanyu zhaokai 'Caise dianying zhipian jishu huiyi'*" (Shanghai Municipal Archives, Shanghai, January 29, 1958).

25 Shanghai Light Industry Design Institute, "*Shanghai ganguang jiaopianchang kuoda chubu sheji, di er juan di liu pian*" (Shanghai Municipal Archives, Shanghai, 1959).

26 Li, Li, and Zhang, *Shi ji hui mou Zhongguo dian ying zhuan ye shi yan jiu*, 89–90.

27 Rayns and Meek, *Electric Shadows*, B4; Jay Leyda, *Dianying Electric Shadows: An Account of Films and the Film Audience in China* (Cambridge, MA: MIT Press, 1972), 361.

28 Ho Chak Law, "Restaging Zhu Yingtai in Early Communist China: Shaoxing Opera, Color Film, and the 'New Woman,'" *TDR: The Drama Review* 65, no. 2 (2021): 87.

29 Rayns and Meek, *Electric Shadows*, F35.

30 Leyda, *Dianying Electric Shadows*, 218.

31 Leyda, 218.

32 Zhang Guoen and Gong Rumei, *Zhongguo Dianying Sheying Zhuanye Shiyanjiu, Dianying Sheying juan, shang* (Beijing: China Film Press, 2006), 329.

33 Zheng and Gong, 329.

34 Kapczynski, "Imitation of Life," 44.

35 Dudley Andrew, "The Post-war Struggle for Colour," in *Color: The Film Reader,* ed. Brian Price and Angela Dalle Vacche (New York: Routledge, 2006), 44.

36 Steve Neale, "Technicolor," in *Color: The Film Reader*, ed. Brian Price and Angela Dalle Vacche (New York: Routledge, 2006), 22.

37 Dootson and Zhu, "Did Madame Mao Dream in Technicolor?," 361.

38 Tom Gunning, "Applying Color: Creating Fantasy of Cinema," in *Fantasia of Color in Early Cinema*, by Tom Gunning, Joshua Yumibe, Giovanna Fossati, and Jonathon Rosen (Amsterdam: Amsterdam University Press, 2015), 16.

39 Zheng and Gong, 270.

40 Zheng and Gong, 270.

41 Zheng and Gong, 273.

42 Leyda, *Dianying Electric Shadows*, 230; Rayns and Meeks, *Electric Shadows*, E7–E8.

43 Shen Fuwei, "Yiwei Shenchang *Nvlan Wuhao*," *Dazhong Dianying*, no. 14 (1958): 28.

44 Ke Ling, "Woguo de diyibu caise tiyu gushipian *Nvlan wuhao*," *Dazhong dianying*, no. 16 (August 1957): 10; Liu Li. "Xunzhao *Nvlan Wuhao Ji*," *Dazhong dianying*, no. 5 (1957): 28. Xie Jin and his assistant director, Ding Li, were reported to have specifically scouted young athletes to play the main character, Lin Xiaojie (number 5).

45 Xie Jin, "Chuangzao *Nvlan wuhao* de yixie tihui," *Dazhong dianying*, no. 10 (August 1957): 10.

46 Chen Chan, Lao Zong, and Liu Li, "*Changli Changwai kan 'Nvlan*,'" *Dazhong Dianying*, no. 8 (1957): 27. According to Chen, Lao, and Liu, this scene was difficult to film at first because the young actresses were too stiff until the assistant director surprised them by asking them suddenly to run a few laps.

47 Kapczynski, "Imitation of Life," 41.

48 Paul Clark, *Chinese Cinema: Culture and Politics since 1949* (Cambridge: Cambridge University Press, 1987), 106.

49 Li Ying, "*Nvlan wuhao* Zhong de qingnianren," *Dazhong dianying*, no. 4 (February 1958): 12. A fan reviewer of the film, Li Ying, wrote that this scene and the argument over the bed were especially compelling and relatable to her own experiences as a university student.

50 Tian Lan, "*Nvlan wuhao* zai Beijing," *Dazhong dianying*, no. 12 (1957): 25.

8

The Chinese Film Collection at the University of South Carolina

HEATHER HECKMAN, LAURA MAJOR,

AND LYDIA PAPPAS

The University of South Carolina (USC) acquired its Chinese Film Collection in 2009 when more than 800 titles were transferred to the Moving Image Research Collections (MIRC) from the Washington, DC, embassy of the People's Republic of China. The films span a period of more than fifty years, from the late 1940s to early in the twenty-first century, and are overwhelmingly color productions, with black-and-white films representing less than 1 percent of the total collection (only six titles). Together, they were a project of cultural diplomacy, intended for viewing by American audiences and members of the Chinese diaspora. They cannot be considered either a random or a representative sample of total film production in the PRC over the second half of the twentieth century, but they nevertheless constitute a broad and accessible cache of Chinese mainland productions in diverse genres, with particularly strong representation of documentary works. While due attention has been granted to the nation's filmmaking industry and to analyses of the works themselves, English-language scholarship on technology, and particularly on color, in the Chinese film industry remains thin.[1] In this chapter, we seek both to encourage future scholarly engagement with MIRC's Chinese Film Collection and to generate hypotheses about color film stock adoption in the Chinese industry.[2] We survey MIRC's collection, which is primarily but not exclusively 16mm and includes 181 Agfa-Gevaert prints, 380 Fuji prints, 124 Eastman Color prints, 10 dye imbibition (IB), presumed Technicolor, prints (all 35mm), and three ORWO prints, looking for patterns in film stock choice across producers, genres, periods, and postproduction variables.[3] We also consider the stability of the color processes relative to one another, drawing on preservation metadata gathered by MIRC staff.

Our survey corroborates and refines some lines of scholarship, extends others, and points to some new areas of inquiry. In their excellent history of the Beijing Film Laboratory's adoption of the Technicolor dye imbibition process, Kirsty Sinclair Dootson and Zhaoyu Zhu point to the scale of print runs—which could be very large indeed in the People's Republic, given geography and population size—as the factor that initially drew Chinese interest in the method, as well as the one that triggered its demise.[4] Although MIRC possesses few Technicolor IB prints, careful inspection of our physical holdings supports the idea that this relatively prosaic and short-term consideration was a primary driver of adoption. We find, as well, that the disproportionate use of color film stock for animated productions, noted by Laikwan Pang in the 1950s and 1960s, seems to have persisted into later decades. Pang suggests that live-action color shooting was discouraged to avoid higher import costs; this, too, may be borne out by the physical materials stored at MIRC.[5] We also find evidence of disproportionate fading rates between unmarked stocks that may have been domestically manufactured and imported stocks. Clusters around particular years or periods may offer clues for future scholarship on the Chinese laboratory industry.

With only a handful of films produced before and during the Cultural Revolution (1966–1976),[6] and none produced after 2004, the bulk of MIRC's collection dates to the years between the reopening of the Beijing Film Academy in 1978 and the PRC's mandates to restructure film studios and consolidate theaters into chains.[7] Productions from the middle to late 1980s are most robustly represented, from the 1982 graduation of the Fifth Generation filmmakers from the Beijing Film Academy to the reforms introduced at the end of the decade that reduced production output.[8] While the works of Fifth Generation filmmakers during these years are well known internationally, domestically they circulated weakly, if at all—when as many as 70 million people may have attended films each *day* in China.[9] Relatively few Fifth Generation works are included in MIRC's collection. Zhang Yimou's *Red Sorghum* (1987), the first Fifth Generation film to reach wide audiences both domestically and internationally, is perhaps the best-known exception to this rule.[10]

Most of the titles held by USC were produced during the resurgence of China's centralized studio system after the Cultural Revolution. Dozens of studios are represented in the collection, but one, Central (or Chinese) Newsreel and Documentary Film Studio (Zhong yang xin wen ji lu dian ying zhi pian chang),

Table 8.1
Number of Titles in Collection by Production Company

Producer	Titles
Zhong yang xin wen ji lu dian ying zhi pian chang (Central Newsreel and Documentary Film Studio)	284
Beijing ke xue jiao yu dian ying zhi pian chang (Beijing Science Education Film Studio)	53
Zhu jiang dian ying zhi pian chang	49
Shanghai ke xue jiao yu dian ying zhi pian chang (Shanghai Science Education Film Studio)	45
Shanghai dian ying zhi pian chang (Shanghai Film Studio)	39
Beijing dian ying zhi pian chang (Beijing Film Studio)	38
Shanghai mei shu dian ying zhi pian chang (Shanghai Animation Studio)	28
Changchun dian ying zhi pian chang	27
Ba yi dian ying zhi pian chang	26
Zhongguo nong ye dian ying zhi pian chang	21
Hubei dian ying zhi pian chang	20
Tianjin dian ying zhi pian chang (Tijan Film Studio)	17
Xi'an dian ying zhi pian chang (Xi'an Film Studio)	16
Beijing dian ying xue yuan qing nian dian ying zhi pian chang	7
Emei dian ying zhi pian chang (Emei Film Studio)	7
Gansu sheng dian ying jia xie hui ying shi zhi zuo zhong xin	6
Guangxi dian ying zhi pian chang	6
Nanjing dian ying zhi pian chang	6
Zhongguo er tong dian ying zhi pian chang	5

accounts for more than a third of all titles (table 8.1). This is more than five times as many as the next most represented studio, the Beijing Science and Education Film Studio (Beijing ke xue jiao yu dian ying zhi pian chang)—itself also a nonfiction producer. The Central Newsreel and Documentary Studio was the primary documentary outlet of the government. It derived from the Chinese Communist Party's original film production unit, the Ya'nan Film Group, active during the Civil War. In the 1990s, as theatrical attendance plummeted, it was reorganized under China Central Television. Similar fates befell at least one science studio and Shanghai Animation Film Studio (Shanghai mei shu dian ying zhi pian chang).[11]

As the studio names indicate, MIRC's Chinese Film Collection is predominantly a collection of documentary and nonfiction works. More than two-thirds of the titles were classified as documentaries by the archive's catalogers, and this may represent an undercount, as some of the nearly fifty animated films likely tackle nonfiction subjects. The majority would have been made before the emergence of the New Chinese Documentary Film Movement in the 1990s.[12] Two hundred titles were classified as feature films by catalogers; most of these were produced in mainland China.[13] In a sense, even these feature films can be understood as what Haidee Wasson and Charles Acland have labeled "useful cinema," at least in the way they were repurposed for the American domestic context. Before their donation to USC, these prints would presumably have been distributed in the United States on the educational circuit and to repertory film series at universities and art houses, "in order to satisfy [the embassy's] organizational demands and objectives."[14]

As mentioned earlier, color productions dominate the collection and represent a diverse set of color stock manufacturers: Fuji (47 percent), Agfa-Gevaert (22 percent), Eastman Kodak (15 percent), Technicolor (1 percent), and ORWO (less than 1 percent). The remaining 100-plus titles (approximately 12 percent of the collection) have no edge codes or other indicators of manufacture. Over 90 percent of the titles in the collection are represented by 16mm elements, while 70 titles out of more than 800 titles are on 35mm. The latter include all 10 of the Technicolor titles, 44 of the Kodak titles (approximately 35 percent of the Kodak titles, or 5 percent of the entire collection), 15 unidentified titles, and only 5 of the 380 Fuji titles. Kodak and Technicolor appear to be overrepresented among 35mm prints. Conversely, all 181 of the Agfa-Gevaert films, as well as all three of the ORWO films, are 16mm.

The film *New Year's Sacrifice* (1956) is the earliest color feature in the collection. No identifying markings can be seen along its edges, or rails, and its manufacturer is unknown. There are few productions from the 1960s in the collection, but many of these are, like *New Year's Sacrifice*, printed to stock of unidentified provenance. About the industry at large, Pang writes, "The majority of films made in the mid-1960s were still shot in black-and-white, for the film stock could be produced domestically." Pang dates local manufacturing of color stock to the mid-1960s, when the Baoding Stock Factory "started to operate in full gear."[15] Unidentified stock continued to appear in MIRC's collection after the Cultural Revolution; indeed, most of the films printed to unidentified stock date to 1978–1984. However, its use waned in the mid-1980s, with relatively few films released after 1985 on unmarked stock. It seems plausible, then, that many of the unmarked film stocks were manufactured domestically.

Fuji was adopted by documentary filmmakers in the 1980s, and it rapidly dominated the titles sent to the embassy in Washington, DC. Eastman Kodak and Agfa are represented by earlier releases but are never used at the same rate as Fuji once the latter begins to ship to DC. And while Eastman Kodak stocks were used in productions released as early as 1973 and continue to be used into the new century, Belgium's Agfa-Gevaert products, adopted after 1976, seem to have been marginally favored over their American competition. Technicolor's Chinese installation, which was widely publicized and has achieved almost a cult status among archivists and historians, is not absent from MIRC's collection, but neither is it robustly represented. Technicolor is limited to the immediate post–Cultural Revolution period, with titles released between 1979 and 1983.

Severe fading affects some of the Fuji, Eastman Kodak, and Agfa-Gevaert titles but none of the Technicolor or ORWO titles.[16] (Technicolor famously has colorfast properties, whereas ORWO, which accounts for just three titles, may simply benefit from its small sample size.) Interestingly, the edge codes of the severely faded Fuji materials indicate provenance from two years of raw stock production: 1983 (thirty-eight titles) and 1984 (two). Milder fading is observed in fourteen more Fuji prints from 1983. A single Fuji print from 1977 and another from 1980 also exhibit some fading, but no fading is evident on any Fuji materials dated 1985 or later, and most prints struck on Fuji stock manufactured before 1983 boast colorfast characteristics. With only two titles showing no signs of dye fading, the fade rate for Fuji 1983 stock in the collection is over 95 percent. Fading in the Kodak materials, which more seriously affects 35mm than 16mm prints, is concentrated earlier in the period scope.[17] Kodak prints dated to 1973 (two), 1974 (two), 1976 (one), 1977 (one), 1979 (eight), and 1982 (four) strongly lean pink; those produced later exhibit robust color reproduction. Just as 1983 appears to have been a bad year for Fuji, 1979 was a bad year for Kodak—MIRC's Chinese Film Collection contains no unfaded prints with the double circle (··) edge code that Kodak stamped on material manufactured in 1979.[18] Both Kodak and Fuji materials printed to stock manufactured beginning in the mid-1980s are in very good color condition. For example, the collection holds two copies of the documentary *Shatoujiao—A Little Town between Guangdong and Hong Kong* (1996), one on Fuji stock and one on Eastman Color. Both are unfaded, though the Fuji print is timed warmer. The same cannot be said for Agfa-Gevaert elements, which include faded elements from titles released as late as the 1990s.

Prints from all these manufacturers fare better, though, than prints on unidentified stock(s). Indeed, the majority of the severely faded film in the collection is of unknown provenance (52 percent).[19] And while very few titles on unidentified stocks were released after 1983, there is still fading in titles from the late 1980s and beyond. The disproportionate rates of dye fading in the unidentified materials (which, recall, account for less than 15 percent of the titles in the collection) is intriguing. Further efforts to identify these materials could yield an important contribution to the technological history of film production in the PRC.

Every studio with more than five titles in the collection is represented by prints from multiple manufacturers. Central Newsreel and Documentary Film Studio (which, recall, produced a plurality of titles in the collection) sent prints struck on raw stock from all represented manufacturers, but it seems to have favored Kodak over Agfa, using the former in 23 percent of the titles and the latter in only 9 percent. With the other major producers, there is variability in the rates of use of each manufacturer's raw stock products, with some perhaps showing mild favoritism for one product line over another. For example, Beijing Film Studio and Shanghai Film Studio (two of the most prolific producers of feature films in the PRC, which were established as regional producers in 1949 when the

People's Republic was founded) provided Agfa, Kodak, Fuji, Technicolor, and unidentified stocks but at different rates. Beijing shipped more Agfa, whereas Shanghai shipped more Fuji and unmarked film. Agfa ($n = 15$) stock accounts for 40 percent, a plurality, of the Beijing titles in our vaults (n = 38), but just 13 percent ($n = 5$) of the Shanghai titles ($n = 39$).[20] Conversely, Fuji captures the plurality for Shanghai Film Studio, with 44 percent of titles ($n = 17$) compared with 29 percent ($n = 11$) for Beijing Film Studio. Unmarked film was used for 18 percent of the Beijing titles ($n = 7$) and for 28 percent ($n = 11$) of Shanghai titles, making it proportionally larger than Kodak or Technicolor for both studios.

Potential exceptions to this story are the Beijing Science and Education Film Studio and the Shanghai Animation Film Studio, neither of which is represented on Eastman Kodak elements among films transferred to the embassy. Both are among the more prolific producers in the collection, and, interestingly, they specialized in animation. Unsurprisingly, 100 percent of the titles from the Shanghai Animation Film Studio are animated, but so are more than 25 percent of the films from the Beijing Science and Education Film Studio (fifteen out of fifty-three). In fact, none of the fifty animated films in MIRC's Chinese Film Collection are on Eastman Kodak stock.[21] Writing about the 1950s and 1960s, Pang observes, "animated . . . colour films proliferated," while live-action "narrative film-makers were discouraged from filming in colour due to the high costs of imported film."[22] High rates of color animated film in MIRC's Chinese Film Collection suggest that this bias may have persisted.

Two prints in the collection stand out as anomalies: *Shaolin Temple* (1982) and *The Summer Palace* (1979). These titles have an unmistakable red cast and, on quick inspection, appear to have undergone severe cyan fading. For example, the production tag for the Chung Yuen Motion Picture Company that opens *Shaolin Temple* is reduced from bold green and yellow against a blue background to orange and light yellow against a maroon one. During the title sequence, we see yellow characters over a medieval caravan. One costume retains a wan yellow, but blues and greens are almost entirely absent, as they are throughout the film (figure 8.1). Similarly, in the documentary *The Summer Palace*, a bleached sun appears in a maroon sky over a red pool of water. Subsequent low-angle shots of flowering trees show a sky that leans toward Pantone Plum.

Closer inspection, however, provides clues that these two prints may instead be Technicolor copies of faded chromogenic prints of unidentified origin. Both feature the faint relief image that characterizes Technicolor IB prints. And while *Shaolin Temple* is a very clean print, edges of *The Summer Palace* are splattered with pink dye. (Several of the IB prints in MIRC's collection have similar tell-tale splatters along the sprocket holes.) The look and feel of the physical prints for *Shaolin Temple* and *Summer Palace* are more consistent with an IB copy from a faded original than with a faded copy of an IB original, though the latter would certainly make more sense from an archival perspective.

FIGURE 8.1 *Shaolin Temple* 少林寺 (1982, anamorphic print). Chinese Film Collection, Moving Image Research Collections, University of South Carolina Libraries.

Why print Technicolor when you do not have color information? The answer may have been cost. Dye imbibition was an inexpensive way to generate large print runs. Henry Wilhelm quotes a 1979 delegation from the U.S. Society of Motion Picture and Television Engineers: "With the Beijing and Shanghai laboratories now making release prints to be shown throughout all of China, large numbers of prints are made of each subject. Our Chinese friends told us that the print costs on a dye imbibition process in the single subject quantity in which they are made are considerably less than for conventional color positive materials and that the color quality is comparable for both systems."[23] We might speculate, then, that films were selected for Technicolor printing based on the scope of their release, rather than—or in addition to—aesthetic criteria.[24]

In conclusion, we found diversity in film stock manufacturers across producers, genres, and periods but few indicators of the particular laboratories that struck the prints. We found bad years for Kodak and Fuji stock but stable dyes in stocks for both manufacturers after the early 1980s. Agfa materials, in contrast, exhibited dye fading well into the following decade. Unmarked stocks had the highest rate of fading and were particularly heavily relied on in the years immediately following the Cultural Revolution. What was the provenance of these stocks? Were they manufactured in the PRC or imported? We hypothesize that Technicolor printing correlates with the size of the print run and that Eastman Color was eschewed for prints of animated productions. Do those hypotheses hold? If so, are we broadly correct that cost drove those trends? Did labs and studios have film stock options, or were choices constrained by scarcity? These and other avenues for research into the history of color technology in the People's Republic would require scholars to bring together evidence from multiple sources. For example, we would be fascinated to know more about the Chinese laboratory sector, which, like its U.S. counterpart, is neglected in secondary literature. Was printing of some titles in MIRC's collection outsourced to other nations? If so, what proportion? Comparative work across archival collections could determine whether the diversity of film stocks displayed in our collection is an artifact of its intended audience abroad, or whether that was typical of prints that circulated on the domestic market, as well. Scholars might also compare these holdings with other collections of "useful cinema." In our U.S.-based experience, diverse film stocks are the norm for the nontheatrical market. We are perhaps most eager, though, to learn more about the many Chinese Film Collection titles that already sit in our vaults, awaiting scholarly analysis and contextualization. Many titles in our holdings have never benefited from close description in English-language publications, and, to our knowledge, fundamental questions about the history of color design remain. Our vaults are open.[25]

Notes

1 Works published by Laikwan Pang and by Kirsty Sinclair Dootson and Zhaoyu Zhu stand as notable exceptions to this rule; see Kirsty Sinclair Dootson and Zhaoyu Zhu, "Did Madame Mao Dream in Technicolor? Rethinking Cold War Colour Cinema through Technicolor's 'Chinese Copy,'" *Screen* 61, no. 3 (Autumn 2020): 343–367; Laikwan Pang, "Colour and Utopia: The Filmic Portrayal of Harvest in Late Cultural Revolution Narrative Films," *Journal of Chinese Cinemas* 6, no. 3 (2012): 263–282. More information on the history of moving image technology is available for earlier and later periods, and for Hong Kong and Taiwan rather than mainland China. The collected volume *Early Film Culture in Hong Kong, Taiwan, and Republican China* covers the first decades of the twentieth century; see especially Ting-yan Cheung and Pablo Sze-pang Tsoi, "From an Imported Novelty to an Indigenized Practice: Hong Kong Cinema in the 1920s," in *Early Film Culture in Hong Kong, Taiwan, and Republican China: Kaleidoscopic Histories*, ed. Emilie Yueh-yu Yeh (Ann Arbor: University of Michigan Press, 2018), 71–100; Yoshino Sugawara, "Toward the Opposite Side of 'Vulgarity': The Birth of Cinema as a 'Healthful Entertainment' and the Shanghai YMCA," in *Early Film Culture in Hong Kong, Taiwan, and Republican China: Kaleidoscopic Histories*, ed. Emilie Yueh-yu Yeh (Ann Arbor: University of Michigan Press, 2018), 179–201; Ling Zhang, "Rhythmic Movement, Metaphoric Sound, and Transcultural Transmediality: Liu Na'ou and *The Man Who Has a Camera* (1933)," in *Early Film Culture in Hong Kong, Taiwan, and Republican China: Kaleidoscopic Histories*, ed. Emilie Yueh-yu Yeh (Ann Arbor: University of Michigan Press, 2018), 277–302. Michael Curtin covers the rise of television and video technologies but does not detail the assimilation of mid-twentieth-century innovations; see Michael Curtin, *Playing to the World's Biggest Audience: The Globalization of Chinese Film and TV* (Berkeley: University of California Press, 2007).

2 We were able to identify the laboratory for just one film in the collection: *The Three Swordsmen* (1994). Countdown leader indicates that our copy of this Hong Kong *wuxia* production was struck by Universal Laboratory Limited in Hong Kong. Because only a handful of Hong Kong–based productions were included with the films stored and circulated by the Chinese embassy in Washington, DC, we must be extremely cautious in generalizing from this single example.

3 We were unable to identify the film stock manufacturer for the remaining 115 color films in the collection.

4 Dootson and Zhu, "Did Madame Mao Dream in Technicolor?"

5 Pang, "Colour and Utopia," 271.

6 Notably, all the black-and-white films in the collection predate the Cultural Revolution. Out of twelve titles in the collection released before 1966, six are black-and-white features. We believe Cai Chusheng's epic *A Spring River Flows East* (1947), which won the Zhongzheng Culture Prize named for Chiang-Kai Sek but was nonetheless among a handful of postwar films accepted by the Communist Party, is the oldest film in our holdings. Four more black-and-white features were released in the 1950s: *Marriage of the Fairy Princess* (1955; reportedly the first Huangmai opera to appear on film); *Li Shizhen* (1956; a biopic about the Ming dynasty herbalist); *The Family* (1956; about a bourgeois family in 1910s urban China); and *The Lin Family Shop* (1959; a Maoist production that was banned for several decades). A sixth, *Serf* (1963; an account of serfdom in Tibet that valorizes the People's Liberation Army), is the last black-and-white title. It seems plausible that these titles were distributed in the late 1970s, when many pre–Cultural Revolution films were rereleased. See Yingjin Zhang, *Chinese National Cinema* (New York: Routledge, 2004), 225.

7 Wendy Su, *China's Encounter with Global Hollywood: Cultural Policy and the Film Industry, 1994–2013* (Lexington: University Press of Kentucky, 2016), 81–88. Su includes *Mountain Patrol* (2004), the most recently produced film in the collection, in her chapter titled "Artistic and Critical Cinema under a Triple Threat: Marketization, Hollywoodization, and State Censorship." See also Christopher Berry and Mary Ann Farquhar, "Chronology," in *China on Screen: Cinema and Nation* (New York: Columbia University Press, 2006).

8 Yingjin Zhang explains, "The economic reform of the film industry further disadvantaged the studios. Previously, in the centralized planned economy, studios produced features according to the quotas approved by the Film Bureau and received a flat fee of RMB700,000 per title from China Film Corporation regardless of box office takings. During the late 1980s, however, new reform measures changed this system of guaranteed purchases, and the distributors now either paid RMB9,000 per print or split the revenue by the pre-agreed percentage points." See Zhang, *Chinese National Cinema*, 239. See also Ying Zhu, *Chinese Cinema during the Era of Reform: The Ingenuity of the System* (Westport, CT: Praeger, 2003), 53.

9 Zhang, *Chinese National Cinema*, 228, 236. Zhang points to the works of Tian Zhuangzhuang, noting that just *two* and *seven* prints of *On the Hunting Ground* (Liechang zhasa, 1985) and *The Horse Thief* (Daoma zei, 1986) were sold, respectively.

10 Other works by Fifth Generation filmmakers in the collection include Junzhao Zhang's *The Loner* (1986, 16mm); Tian Zhuangzhuang's *The Drum Singers* (1987, 16mm); Huang Jianxin's *Back to Back, Face to Face* (1994, 16mm) and *Sleepless at Night* (1997, 16mm); and Li Shaolong's *Red Suit* (2000, 35mm).

11 Zhu, *Chinese Cinema during the Era of Reform*, 85.

12 Documentaries from this earlier period are somewhat caricatured by Chris Berry and Lisa Rofel, who write in the introduction to their fascinating volume on New Chinese Documentary, "Before 1990, all documentary was state-produced, and took the form of illustrated lectures." See Chris Berry and Lisa Rofel, "Introduction," in *The New Chinese Documentary Film Movement: For the Public Record*, ed. Chris Berry, Lisa Rofel, and Lu Xinyu (Hong Kong: Hong Kong University Press, 2010), 4. Perhaps unsurprisingly, we have found the films in the collection to be much more diverse in form and content than a series of "illustrated lectures." As just one example, Jie Shen's *Light Cavalry Girl* (1980), produced by the Central Newsreel and Documentary Film Studio, has become a favorite among the Orphan Film Symposium community.

13 Hong Kong, for example, is represented by the coproduction *Shaolin Temple* (1982), starring Beijing's Jet Li and shot in mainland China.

14 The "*something* in particular" these films were trying to "*do*" remains open for scholarly inquiry and debate. Haidee Wasson and Charles R. Acland, "Utility and Cinema," in *Useful Cinema* (Durham, NC: Duke University Press, 2011), 3.

15 Pang, "Colour and Utopia," 271.

16 Two of the ten Technicolor prints are pink, but we do not believe they are faded as we detail later in the chapter.

17 One Kodak 16mm title is severely faded, but sixteen 35mm films from the same manufacturer are severely faded. All the faded Fuji and Agfa films are 16mm.

18 It is tempting, but premature, to draw a causal link between the higher fade rate in 1979 and the interest in the "hot process" noted by members of the April 1979 SMPTE delegation to the PRC. See William D. Hedden, Frederick M. Remley Jr., and Robert M. Smith, "Motion-Picture and Television Technology in the People's Republic of China: A Report," *SMPTE Journal* 88, no. 9 (September 1979): 617. The higher-temperature ECP-2 process afforded shortened total processing times, which may have been particularly appealing given China's reportedly large print runs. Unfortunately, we were unable to tell whether MIRC's prints from that year were struck on hot process–compatible 7383 Eastman positive print film.

19 Among these unidentified, severely faded titles, the ratio of 16mm to 35mm is identical to the 9:1 ratio for the collection overall.

20 There may also have been (forgive the pun) finer grain differences in film stock adoption than these numbers can reveal. The 1979 SMPTE delegation noted that Beijing Film Studio "was the only facility we saw in China using 5247 color camera film." The other studios used less expensive 5254 film, judged to be of inferior quality by the SMPTE engineers. See Hedden, Remley, and Smith, "Motion-Picture and Television Technology in the People's Republic of China," 612.

21 Changchun Film Studio produced three of the seven animated films that were not produced by either the Shanghai Animation Film Studio or the Beijing Science and Education Film Studio. We were unable to identify the production studio for the remaining four. Changchun Film Studio printed to Eastman Color on at least three occasions for its live-action productions but did not deliver any animated films on Eastman Color stock to DC. In addition to looking for correlations between producer and color stock, we also looked for correlations between language and color stock (e.g., whether a print was subtitled, dubbed, or available only in the original Chinese). If any such correlations exist, they were not evident in this sample.

22 Pang, "Colour and Utopia," 270–271.

23 Henry Wilhelm and Carol Brower, *The Permanence and Care of Color Photographs: Traditional and Digital Color Prints, Color Negatives, Slides, and Motion Picture* (Grinnell, IA: Preservation Publishing, 1993), 349.

24 Alternatively, these two prints may have been produced using an IB process with less stable dyes than Technicolor's, or with a chromogenic process that incorporated a strongly tanning bleach.

25 Catalog records for the 800-plus titles in MIRC's Chinese Film Collection are available at https://perma.cc/WJD5-USTD.

9

The Lights That Raised
Up a Storm

Neon and the Nikkatsu Action
Color Film, 1957–1963

WILLIAM CARROLL

Inoue Umetsugu's *The Stormy Man* (*Arashi o yobu otoko*, 1957), sometimes known in English as *The Man Who Raised Up a Storm*), opens with a shot of Ginza's 4-chōme intersection in Tokyo.[1] Filmed in daylight, the area is fairly bland, even if it is bustling with cars and people. The buildings are mostly gray and brown, and the sky is overcast. Though *The Stormy Man* was filmed in Eastman Color, its colors are neutral and decidedly unspectacular. However, a cross-dissolve slowly replaces this image with one from the same vantage point at night. Black covers most of the screen, and the only things visible in the image emanate from diegetically placed light sources: a column of tiny, distant car headlights down the center of the image, but, more important, multicolored neon lights on the sides and tops of buildings of the Ginza district.

Variations on this same opening were used in numerous other youth-oriented action films also made by Nikkatsu Studios shortly thereafter. Noguchi Hiroshi's *Ginza Whirlwind* (*Ginza Senbuji*, 1959) skips the daylight image and just opens with a view of Ginza 4-chōme's neon lights at night. Nakahira Kō's *Mud-Spattered Purity* (*Dorodarake no junjō*, 1963) opens with the daylight image of this intersection and withholds the nighttime image in its full glory until near the end of the film. Many other Nikkatsu films from this era set key scenes in the district at night and emphasize the neon. What is significant is not just the presence of the neon lights but their dominance over other light sources. In these scenes, the vast majority of the image is dark; whatever is visible is illuminated by hues cast by neon lighting.

Nikkatsu Action Cinema, the genre of youth-oriented action films made at Nikkatsu Studios to which *The Stormy Man*, *Ginza Whirlwind*, and *Mud-Spattered Purity* belonged, was ascending during the convergence of three important trends in postwar Japan: the push toward color production in the late 1950s Japanese film industry, the proliferation of neon lighting in the cityscapes of Tokyo and other Japanese metropolises in the postwar era, and the growth of a hedonistic youth culture during the same period that constituted both the subject and the target audience for Nikkatsu Action. As a genre that embraced and appealed to the hedonistic and rebellious youth culture of the period while combining elements of Hollywood film noir and musicals in a postwar Japanese setting, Nikkatsu Action demanded a style that evoked energy and spectacle, and these bright, colorful lights provided a new formal element for filmmakers to develop this sensation.

In addition to these broad cultural trends, Nikkatsu Action filmmakers were cultivating the genre's style just as the broader Japanese film industry was in the early stages of transitioning to color. Like others working in Japan's film industry at the time, Nikkatsu Action filmmakers had made the majority of their films through the middle to late 1950s, taking for granted that the colors in front of their cameras would be reduced to monochrome when printed on film. With the introduction and proliferation of color to their filmmaking process, filmmakers were able to record the Tokyo metropolis's transformation in color. However, while Nikkatsu Action films frequently contained location shooting in newly emerging nightlife districts throughout Japan that could now be documented by the filmmakers in color, the genre was, in many respects, highly artificial and also prominently featured artificial set designs, in addition to the standard commercial filmmaking elements of costume design and lighting that, even in location shooting, were deliberately placed by filmmakers. This introduced a new set of questions and logistical problems for the filmmakers. What were the appropriate colors for sets and costumes? Which color light sources should be used to illuminate the costumes, sets, and performers in the film? And how could, or should, color design try to create spatial continuity between exterior settings shot on locations and interior settings shot in the studio? I argue that the confluence of these phenomena pushed Nikkatsu Action filmmakers to a unique approach to the problem of color that allowed light sources to dominate and shift the color palettes of their images.

Neon Light in Postwar Japan

Neon light was not a new phenomenon to Japan in the postwar era. Neon lighting was prominent in Tokyo's entertainment districts by the 1920s,[2] and Tokyo itself "led the world in neon decoration" in the next decade.[3] Tokyo's transition into a "nightless city" (*fuyajō*, a term used in reference to the prominence of electric lighting that kept the city illuminated when the sun did not) stretches back to its transformation during the Meiji period.[4] As Tokyo looked to European cities in the late nineteenth century to modernize, two ways it did so were by the introduction of electric lighting on a massive scale,[5] and the construction of more open public spaces under the inspiration of European-style plazas.[6] In particular, street corners of major intersections were transformed into open, public spaces, as "faces" of the newly transformed city.[7] One of the earliest such spaces to be transformed in this way was Ginza's 4-chōme crossing,[8] which, after continued transformation through the first half of the twentieth century, would become a prominent site for many Nikkatsu Action films. In this sense, the image of this intersection coming to life with neon light in the opening of *The Stormy Man* was less a novelty than evidence of the district's rebirth in the postwar era.

However, to the young stars and audience members of Nikkatsu Action films, Tokyo's neon lights must have seemed like a novelty as they appeared in the 1950s. Blackouts in major cities were common during World War II because of air raids, and the firebombing of Tokyo had destroyed large swaths of the city; even if Tokyo had been lit by neon in the 1930s, there was little evidence of that by the end of the war. The screenwriter Sasaki Mamoru describes the Ginza district of 1946 as a "burnt field" where the black market thrived.[9] Though buildings were reconstructed and legitimate businesses began to be reopened in the area, it was not until 1949 that new neon lighting began to be used for advertising businesses, and "Ginza's nights got bright for the first time after the war."[10] Construction of neon continued apace with Japan's postwar economic recovery, and in 1953, Tokyo symbolically reclaimed its title as neon capital of the world with the construction of the world's largest neon light: a globe advertising Morinaga sweets, which is featured prominently in the opening titles of *The Stormy Man* as well as in numerous other Nikkatsu Action films.[11]

The Ginza district's retransformation in the postwar era was perhaps symbolic of the nation's recovery in the period of high economic growth. However, the target audiences of these films, who were teenagers and young adults in the late 1950s when the films were released, would have had no memory of the opulence of the Ginza's neon lights in the Taishō and early Shōwa periods. To some, they seemed a way of breaking from the past, as articulated by the filmmaker Ōshima Nagisa: "The dreamlike lines of mercury lamps began to light up here and there. . . . Ah! With this the sensibility of the Japanese will change!"[12] As a novelty, these neon lights became associated with the youth culture, particularly in the many nightclubs advertised in neon lights that were frequented by characters in the films. The reemergence of neon in Tokyo also coincided with the growth of color in Japanese cinema in the 1950s. In these senses, the colors of Ginza's neon lights were also "new" to film audiences of Nikkatsu Action Cinema in the 1950s.

Nikkatsu's Transition to Color

The Japanese film industry began its transition to color in earnest in the 1950s. As with the film industries in many other parts of the world, there had been practices of adding color to black-and-white film during the postproduction process dating back to the silent era.[13] There were, additionally, experiments with color stock in short films in the 1940s.[14] However, the first theatrically released feature film that was both shot and released in full color was Kinoshita Keisuke's *Carmen Comes Home* (*Karumen kokyo ni kaeru*), released in 1951. The other major studios in the industry at the time, which included Tōei, Tōhō, and Daiei, all released their first color films within a few years. The color processes used were largely determined by the studios: Shochiku and Tōhō adopted Fujicolor, Tōei adopted Konishiroku's Sakuracolor process, and Daiei adopted Eastman Color. There was widespread frustration in the industry with the color palettes offered by Fujicolor and Sakuracolor, however: Fujicolor was seen as inadequate for its reds, Sakuracolor for its yellows.[15]

Since Nikkatsu did not resume film production in the postwar era until 1954, its entrance into color production was more belated than these other studios. However, in 1955, Nikkatsu released its first color feature, *The Green Music Box*, using Konicolor, a newer, three-strip color stock from Konishiroku.[16] The film is a children's fantasy that uses color to enhance its elaborate sets and costumes. Although it differed from the action films oriented toward teenagers and young adults that the studio would make in the coming years, its use of color in association with elaborate fantasy dance sequences is demonstrative of the spectacular nature of color in the Japanese cinema of the 1950s more broadly. Subsequently, Nikkatsu switched its color process to Eastman Color and would continue to use the latter for the films discussed here.[17] Eastman Color is often cast as the inexpensive and inferior alternative to Technicolor in histories of color in the Hollywood film industry: it is a monopack process as opposed to Technicolor's three-strip process, meaning that it requires a third of the film stock and does not rely on special cameras; however, the richness of colors is markedly inferior, and the color fades both more rapidly and unevenly. Within the context of the Japanese film industry, Eastman Color was, however, seen as an improvement over Fujicolor and Sakuracolor in the color palette that it offered. As a company, Technicolor was also notorious for the controls it exerted on films that used its film stock, even internationally;[18] using Eastman Color sidestepped this issue. Further, the process was new enough that its tendency to fade or develop "vinegar syndrome" was not yet discovered; in any case, given that most Nikkatsu Action films at the time played for only one to two weeks (at most) in their initial release, Eastman Color's fading problem was not likely to be seen as a pressing concern even if it had been known at the time.

The Nikkatsu Action Color Idiom

In the description of the critic Watanabe Takenobu, Nikkatsu Action Cinema began to take shape in 1956 with the release of two big hit films: *Season of the Sun* (*Taiyō no kisetsu*, Furukawa Takumi) and *Crazed Fruit* (*Kurutta kajitsu*, Nakahira Kō).[19] These films were both focused on rambunctious youths in postwar urban Japan, referred to as the "sun tribe" (*taiyō-zoku*), both based on novels by Ishihara Shintarō, and they both starred Shintarō's younger brother Yūjirō, who came to embody that youth culture. Like the majority of Nikkatsu's films at the time, both films were in black and white. However, both films contain several elements that would ultimately help determine the color design of Nikkatsu Action Films: the prominence of hip nightclub spaces and, in the case of the latter film, music sung by Ishihara. Ishihara's baritone would become a key part of his star persona, and of Nikkatsu's multimedia marketing of the genre by releasing theme songs performed by the star around the same time as the films' release. This, in turn, ensured that musical performances, nightclub interiors, and nightlife districts would become key settings of films starring Ishihara, and in those with stars whose persona was raised in imitation of him, which would contribute to the formation of the Nikkatsu Action color idiom.

Though Ishihara's initial star persona was formed around the *taiyō-zoku* films, the subject matter and generic appeal of the films shifted somewhat as his star power rose in the following years. Combining elements of the earlier *taiyō-zoku* films with American and French crime films while continuing to emphasize Yūjirō's singing, Nikkatsu shaped Yūjirō as, in Michael Raine's words, "a successful balance of tuneful romanticism and tough-guy bravado."[20] Raine cites *I Am Waiting* (*Ore wa matteru ze*, Kurahara Koreyoshi), *The Eagle and the Hawk* (*Washi to taka*, Inoue Umetsugu), and *The Stormy Man* of 1957 as the key films that contributed to this transition.[21] The year 1957 was also when Nikkatsu began using Eastman Color more widely in its film productions, including for both *The Eagle and the Hawk* and *The Stormy Man*, as well as *The Winner* (*Shōri-sha*, Inoue Umetsugu) from earlier the same year. These films often combined film noir narratives with some form of musical and dance performance (particularly, in this case, *The Winner* and *The Stormy Man*). This blend of genres would provide an interesting opening when it came to color design, as the crime films that the filmmakers were imitating were, for the most part, not originally in color.

Watanabe marks the period of 1959–1962 as the height of Nikkatsu Action Cinema's popularity.[22] This time also roughly coincides with the overall peak in theatrical attendance before its decline in the late 1960s. During this period, Nikkatsu expanded its output of action films by promoting other stars in Ishihara Yūjirō's image. Dubbed the "diamond line," this group of male stars resembled Ishihara in their crooning baritone, youthful good looks, and matinee idol qualities, though not necessarily in equal amounts. While the expansion of the genre allowed for a greater variety in the types of films being made, the majority of these films continued to feature both exterior neon lighting in night scenes and interior stage lighting. Further, Nikkatsu greatly expanded the number of films that it released in color after 1959; while through 1958 it had reserved color for only its biggest-budget films with Ishihara, by 1960 many of its films with even lesser "diamond line" stars were in color.

The genre declined somewhat in popularity in the mid-1960s with the rise of *ninkyō* films at Tōei and traveling gambler films at Daiei (both subgenres of the yakuza films set in the early modern era), and with the overall decline of theatrical attendance in Japan.[23] Nikkatsu responded in part by producing its own *ninkyō* films, whose color designs did not follow the idiom described in this chapter. Some individual filmmakers who had worked in Nikkatsu Action Cinema responded by leaving the studio. Most famously, Nikkatsu fired its filmmaker Suzuki Seijun in 1968; numerous others, however, found employment in Hong Kong, making variations (or, in some cases, outright remakes) of the films that they had once made at Nikkatsu for Shaw Brothers Studio. This includes individuals who had been formative filmmakers of Nikkatsu Action Cinema, such as Nakahira Kō and Inoue Umetsugu. However, even as this was taking place, Nikkatsu Action films continued to be made throughout the 1960s, and the genre enjoyed something of a resurgence near the end of the decade.[24]

Following the success of *Crazed Fruit* and *Season of the Sun* in 1956, Nikkatsu focused on promoting Ishihara Yūjirō in a series of starring vehicles the following year, including *The Winner*, *I Am Waiting*, and *The Stormy Man*. Michael Raine has given a detailed account of how Nikkatsu promoted Ishihara's rise to stardom, emphasizing, among other things, the importance of the theme songs of *I Am Waiting* and particularly *The Stormy Man*, each of which was sung by Ishihara and released as a single.[25] This set underway a practice of multimedia stardom for Nikkatsu's Action stars: Ishihara would continue to sing and release theme songs for his films, and Nikkatsu's stars who followed him would do the same. As a result of this practice, Nikkatsu Action films often feature musical performances in a nightclub stage space. The stage spaces of modern Ginza nightclubs would become foundational to other aspects of the genre's aesthetics, including its color designs.

In *The Winner*, Inoue took advantage of the film's exterior nighttime scenes in Tokyo's Ginza district and interior stage spaces in nightclubs as a pretext for intense color designs. In particular, an extended stage ballet sequence featuring Kitahara Mie dancing on an artificial Ginza created on a theatrical stage foreshadows many of the techniques that Inoue would develop in *The Stormy Man* later the same year: neon lights dominate the color design of the scene over the colors of costumes or the set, and their cycling and flickering shift the color scheme throughout the performance. Though the association between musical performance and color would appear to replicate the prominence of color designs in Hollywood musicals, an important difference quickly emerges. Richard Misek makes a useful distinction between *surface color* (the color of objects as they appear in white light) and *optical color* (color created by lighting).[26] Surface color can be understood as an approach using color-by-subtraction: the film's starting point is white, full-spectrum light (or close to it) that illuminates the hues of objects themselves. Optical color, by contrast, can be understood as an approach using color-by-addition: the film's starting point is total darkness, where lights of specific colors enter and shade everything that they illuminate with their own specific hue.

Misek describes the difference between the two as their respective creative starting points: films that play primarily with surface color, using neutral lights to highlight the colors of costumes and set design, use white as their creative starting point, while films that primarily play with optical color, using multicolored lights to cast specific colors over the colors of costumes and set designs, use black as their creative starting point. As a key example, Misek discusses a trend in 1980s Hollywood cinema that used black, rather than white, as its creative zero point, a trend he associates with the work of Ridley Scott, Adrian Lyne, and Michael Mann.[27] This means not just that most of the images are dark, but that the specific hues of diegetically placed light sources dominate the color palettes of the objects they illuminate, in contrast to what had been the norm in classical Hollywood, where neutral light sources ensured that the colors of the surfaces of the objects themselves dominated. Nikkatsu filmmakers working in night scenes in the Ginza and other nightlife districts in the 1950s and 1960s used this approach, twenty-five years or more earlier than in any of the Hollywood films that Misek cites. The preference for optical color seen in Nikkatsu Action films is one feature that distinguishes them from any of the Western films they are allegedly imitating; it is also one that can be found subsequently not only in other Japanese films but also in films made in popular contexts in, for example, Hong Kong, where Nikkatsu Action films were also popular during their heyday in Japan, and where many Nikkatsu Action filmmakers wound up making films in the late 1960s, as the genre's popularity was waning in Japan.

Misek argues that even within musicals, classical Hollywood films tended to use white light and to create their more elaborate color schemes with *surface color*: the props, set designs, and costumes, as spelled out in the guidelines of Hollywood's Society of Motion Picture and Television Engineers.[28] At Nikkatsu, however, Inoue and other filmmakers quickly began using colored light filters in stage spaces, street scenes in the Ginza district (motivated by implicitly off-screen neon lights), and even in interior spaces in the Ginza district (motivated by implicitly off-screen neon lights coming in through windows). Inoue would intensify and play more extensively with optical color filters in his subsequent films: in *The Stormy Man*, he began the practice of cycling rapidly through different light filters over its protagonist during stage performances (figure 9.1).

As stated previously, Nikkatsu Action films could be seen as combining elements of crime dramas from Hollywood and European films with the stage spectacle of musicals. Numerous Nikkatsu Action films, in fact, heavily borrowed elements of specific crime films from abroad, or even their entire premises.[29] Though it may be easy to dismiss the films as simply recombining elements from previously made films, color provided a unique way that imitation could quickly become innovation. In the Hollywood industry, musicals were, by the late 1950s, a genre that was mostly filmed and released in lavish color. The crime film genre, by contrast, was one of the last holdouts in black and white.[30] Thus, even if some film noirish settings resembled those of Hollywood films, the color designs for them were original. The exterior neon-infused lighting that cast uniform colors across characters and objects did not have an obvious antecedent in any of the films that were being imitated. In other cases, Nikkatsu filmmakers gave color to lighting techniques that were common: for example, one lighting technique frequently seen in American film noir is a pulsating exterior light at night that intermittently casts light and shadow over a scene, frequently to heighten tension during suspenseful sequences. The majority of the Hollywood films to use this technique were in black and white, meaning that the shift was a simple back-and-forth between illumination and shadow. Alfred Hitchcock used a color variation on this technique in the climax of *Rope* (1948), his first Technicolor film: alternate green and red neon lights pulsate, first through a background window, and subsequently over the characters themselves, making for an unusual experiment with shifts in optical color. The strength of the light color is nevertheless tempered by the neutral lighting inside the apartment. Nikkatsu Action films would take this technique further: light sources of multiple colors pulsating over sequences, motivated by exterior light sources coming in through windows, but with no neutral interior light source to temper them. As a result, these scenes would produce multiple striking visual transformations of the entire color palette as the light colors cycled throughout a scene; further, because the colored lights were often the sole light sources for these scenes, they would transform the color palette in a more complete way.

Nikkatsu Action films' emphasis of *optical color* over *surface color* distinguished films in the genre not only from Hollywood films but also from other Japanese films made in the same period. Nightclub districts with neon lighting were also frequented by the salarymen of Ozu Yasujirō's films made at Shōchiku, and he transitioned to color in 1958 at roughly the same time that Nikkatsu Action Cinema took off. However, people are hardly ever visible in exterior shots of neon signs of his films, and the lighting within the *izakayas* tends much more toward neutral white light. Thematically closer to the Nikkatsu Action films, Kihachi Okamoto's *The Big Boss* (*Ankokugai no kaoyaku*, 1959), made at Tōhō,

FIGURE 9.1 Cycling stage light filter in Inoue Umetsugu's *The Stormy Man* (1957).

features a plot about a gangster whose younger brother sings at a music club popular with teens, combining the musical and crime film elements common to many Nikkatsu Action films. However, the stage space, nightclub space, and nighttime exterior spaces are illuminated with neutral white light rather than color filters. Two years later, Okamoto's *Blueprint of Murder* (*Ankokugai no dankon*), also for Tōhō, would use filtered light for some interior nightclub sequences much closer to the design used by Nikkatsu Action filmmakers, but only after the techniques had already been in regular use by Nikkatsu filmmakers.

The emphasis on optical color had two important implications for the color designs of Nikkatsu Action films. First, it gave sequences in the Ginza district (and, later, similar nightlife districts in other parts of Japan) a vibrant color scheme, but one unlike those found in Hollywood musicals. Since color-filtered light would function as the key light for an entire frame, the resulting image would appear in subtle variations in hues of the color of the light filter that was illuminating them. As a result, the colorful individual frames in Nikkatsu Action films tend to be either uniform in color design, or else to divide sections of the image into different colors based on multiple colored light sources, or what Misek refers to as "chromatic zoning."[31] Second, it allowed for much more rapid transformations of the color scheme of an individual shot without editing. In *The Stormy Man*, for example, Inoue uses multiple colored light filters cycling over Ishihara during his performance so that he and his surroundings quickly change colors throughout the performance. Filmmakers also frequently used these rapid color transformations to introduce kinetic energy, enhanced by the vibrancy of the colors, into scenes like Ishihara's drum solo. Many scenes incorporated colored lights coming in through windows and alternating or cycling through different colors. A particularly baroque example can be found in *The Volcano's Wind* (*Umi o wataru hatoba no kaze*, Yamazaki Tokujirō, 1960) in which Shishido Jō attempts to break into a safe in a nightclub at night. Alternate pink and green lights shine into the room as the scene's key light, so that the sequence's light scheme in its entirety constantly shifts between pink, no key (black) and green figure 9.2).[32] Thus, optical color, more than surface color, allowed individual colors to dominate sections of the frame, or the frame in its entirety, providing a new way for Nikkatsu filmmakers to create striking and abrupt visual transformations through color.

The Hong Kong Connection

As the Japanese film industry waned in the 1960s, many filmmakers left Japan's studio system that had once dominated the industry. Some filmmakers became independent, and some sought out producers abroad. Few of the Nikkatsu Action filmmakers had enough of a reputation to do either. However, at the same time

FIGURE 9.2 Cycling green and pink light filters in Yamazaki Tokujirō's *The Volcano's Wind* (1960).

Japan's film industry was declining, Hong Kong's popular film industry was growing rapidly. Nikkatsu Action films had been bought and released by Shaw Brothers Studio in Hong Kong and Southeast Asia.[33] Their popularity with audiences when released in these regions prompted Shaw Brothers to recruit Nikkatsu Action filmmakers in an effort to "increase the volume and diversity of its productions."[34] Among the directors, Nakahira Kō, Matsuo Akinori, and Inoue Umetsugu wound up directing films in Hong Kong for Shaw Brothers in the late 1960s, bringing elements of Nikkatsu Action Cinema along with them.

In addition to the talent brought directly from Nikkatsu, the city of Hong Kong itself in the 1960s offered the same pretext of neon lighting for these filmmakers to continue using similar optical color techniques that they had used when working in the Japanese studio system. Christopher Ribbat has characterized the history of neon in Western Europe and the United States as initially peaking in the 1930s, fading during World War II, and reviving only briefly in the immediate postwar period before developing negative associations, after which is was no longer widely used by newer and higher-end businesses.[35] By contrast, it endured and continued to dominate in night landscapes in major cities in Asia such as Tokyo and Hong Kong, especially in those cities' most vibrant commercial districts.[36] The reasons for this are outside the scope of this chapter, but for our purposes it has continued to give filmmakers in Japan and Hong Kong a convincing pretext to experiment with optical color in their films' lighting designs.

Inoue Umetsugu's work in Hong Kong is of particular interest here, as Inoue had directed Nikkatsu's earliest color film, *The Green Music Box*, as well as many of the formative films of the Nikkatsu color idiom such as *The Winner* and *The Stormy Man*. His first three films for Shaw Brothers in 1967 draw heavily both thematically and stylistically from his previous work in Japan: *King Drummer* (*Qing chun gu wang*) is a direct remake of *The Stormy Man* in a Hong Kong context, *Hong Kong Nocturne* (*Xiang jiang hua yue ye*) reconfigures elements of his earlier *The Night We Danced* (*Odoritai yoru*, 1963), and *Operation Lipstick* (*Die wang jiao wa*) combines common settings and character types from Nikkatsu Action films with an outlandish spy plot. Nakahira's *Summer Heat* (*Kuang lian shi*, 1968) likewise remakes *Crazed Fruit* in a Hong Kong setting. In each of these cases, the films' combination of neon-lit exterior night scenes and nightclub stage spaces allows Inoue to play similar games with color and lighting. However, it should be acknowledged that by comparison to the films these filmmakers had made in Japan, their experimentation with color is constrained in their work at Shaw Brothers. Filtered colored lighting and chromatic zoning that had been present in the Nikkatsu Action Color idiom are still present but confined to the background; foreground characters are primarily lit with flat, neutral lighting that prevents more thorough color experimentation and makes foreground characters appear to be detached from their neon-lit environments.

Two decades later, many Hong Kong films of the 1980s and 1990s exhibit experiments with optical color that have close affinities with the Nikkatsu Action color idiom. Perhaps the most famous example internationally is Wong Kar-wai, who likewise uses neon lighting in street scenes and nightclubs of Hong Kong to bathe entire images in the light of a single optical color. In some respects, Wong takes this experimentation further: Misek points out that his films frequently use daylight-balanced color stock during neon-lit night scenes to exaggerate the effects of the colored lighting.[37] Did Wong derive inspiration from the Nikkatsu Action films that had been popular in Hong Kong in his youth? Was this the product of frustration with the Hong Kong remakes that divorced characters from their surroundings through discrepancies in light colors? Or did Wong and other later Hong Kong filmmakers come upon this similarity incidentally, simply as a result of Hong Kong's own transformation into a neon-lit night landscape resembling Tokyo's? Whether the link is the result of conscious inspiration, unconscious inspiration, or a simple coincidental stylistic convergence, Wong and other Hong Kong filmmakers of his generation have continued experimenting with neon-motivated optical color in a framework set by Nikkatsu Action filmmakers in the 1950s and 1960s.

Conclusion

This chapter has presented an overview of a color idiom that emerged out of Nikkatsu Action Cinema in the 1950s and 1960s. Though the genre has often been regarded as being both evidence of postwar Japanese westernization and derivative of Western films in itself, I have argued here that the confluence of the growth of neon lighting in postwar Tokyo, the setting and thematic concerns of the films themselves, and the filmmakers' and studios' willingness to allow light rather than surface to dominate color designs, unlike what was common elsewhere at the time, mean that Nikkatsu Action filmmakers developed an innovative approach to color that was distinct from the films the genre was supposedly derivative of. Further, I have suggested that this idiom had influence beyond Japan thanks to the circulation of Nikkatsu Action films in Hong Kong (as well as farther throughout East and Southeast Asia thanks to the connections of the films' Hong Kong distributors) and the activity of Nikkatsu Action filmmakers within the popular Hong Kong film industry as Japanese popular cinema declined.

Building on Misek's terminology, the Nikkatsu color idiom can be understood broadly as the use of optical color rather than surface color to dominate color design, using black rather than white as the filmmaker's "creative zero point." While Misek identifies this approach to color as beginning decades later, looking back to these Nikkatsu Action films allows us to see that it was in use in Japan much earlier than in Hollywood or Europe. Further, observing the circulation of Nikkatsu films (and filmmakers) in Asia shows that this approach had a long-lasting transnational influence, particularly on Hong Kong cinema. Finally, beyond using color lights to dominate the color schemes of images, Nikkatsu Action filmmakers used this approach for more rapid and striking shifts in the color schemes of images. Growing out of the ascendant postwar Japanese youth culture, the embrace of color by the Japanese film industry, and the spectacular neon-lit rebirth of the Ginza district, these films pointed to new possibilities in color design that subsequently have been explored by filmmakers across the globe.

Notes

1 Streets are not named in Japan, so neighborhoods, blocks, and intersections are numbered within a district. The designation 4-chōme refers to a subregion of Ginza, specifically the one with the highest concentration of neon lighting.
2 Elise K. Tipton, "Faces of New Tokyo: Entertainment Districts and Everyday Life during the Interwar Years," *Japanese Studies* 33, no. 2 (2013): 194.
3 Miya Elise Mizuta, "Luminous Environment: Light, Architecture, and Decoration in Modern Japan," *Japan Forum* 18, no. 3 (2006): 344.
4 Mizuta, 341.
5 Mizuta, 341.
6 Jinnai Hidenobu, *Tokyo: A Spatial Anthropology*, trans. Kimiko Nishimura (Berkeley: University of California Press, 1995), 147.

7 Hidenobu, 147.

8 Hidenobu, 150–151.

9 Sasaki Mamoru, *Neon sain to gekkō kamen: Kobayashi Toshio no Senkōsha* (Tokyo: Chikuma Shobō, 2005), 56.

10 Mamoru, 57.

11 Edward Seidensticker, *A History of Tokyo 1897–1989: From Edo to Showa, the Emergence of the World's Greatest City* (Tokyo: Tuttle Publishing, 2019), 493.

12 Ōshima Nagisa, "Banishing Green," trans. Dawn Lawson, in *Color: The Film Reader*, ed. Angela Dalle Vacche and Brian Price (New York: Routledge, 2006), 118.

13 Hiroshi Komatsu, "From Natural Colour to the Pure Motion Picture Drama: The Meaning of Tenkatsu Company in the 1910s of Japanese Film History," *Film History* 7 (Spring 1995): 70–72.

14 Okajima Hisashi, "Color Film Restoration in Japan: Some Examples," trans. Akiko Mizoguchi, *Journal of Film Preservation* 66 (October 2003): 33–34.

15 Hisashi, 33.

16 Hisashi, 35. Sarah Street explains that Konicolor's "approach was similar to that of Technicolor, but the processing was different, involving a coated emulsion to develop each color." See Sarah Street, "The Monopack Revolution: Global Cinema and *Jigokumon/Gate of Hell* (Kinugasa Teinosuke, 1953)," *Open Screens* 1, no. 1 (2018): 10.

17 Jasper Sharp, "Japanese Widescreen Cinema: Commerce, Technology and Aesthetics" (PhD diss., University of Sheffield, 2013), 213–218.

18 Dudley Andrew has written about Technicolor's practice of sending "color consultants" to productions where Technicolor was being used in France; see Dudley Andrew "The Post-war Struggle for Color," in *Color: The Film Reader*, ed. Angela Dalle Vacche and Brian Price (New York: Routledge, 2006), 42.

19 Watanabe Takenobu, *Nikkatsu no karei na sekai* (Tokyo: Mirai-sha, 2004), 24. Mark Schilling has condensed much of the information contained in Watanabe's book in English, alongside new interviews and Schilling's own critical evaluations. See Mark Schilling, *No Borders, No Limits: Nikkatsu Action Cinema* (Godalming: FAB Press, 2007).

20 Michael Raine, "Ishihara Yūjirō: Youth, Celebrity, and the Male Body in Late 1950s Japan," in *Word and Image in Japanese Cinema*, ed. Dennis Washburn and Carole Cavanaugh (Cambridge: Cambridge University Press, 2010), 212.

21 Raine, 212.

22 Watanabe, *Nikkatsu no karei na sekai*, 24.

23 Watanabe, 25.

24 Watanabe, 25–28.

25 Raine, "Ishihara Yūjirō," 214.

26 Richard Misek, *Chromatic Cinema: A History of Screen Color* (West Sussex: Wiley-Blackwell, 2010), 6.

27 Misek, 135.

28 Misek, 128.

29 For further discussion of this phenomenon, see Ryan Cook, "Transnational Remakes and Adaptations—*Casablanca* Karaoke: The Program Picture as Marginal Art in 1960s Japan," in *The Japanese Cinema Book*, ed. Hideaki Fujiki and Alastair Phillips (London: BFI Publishing, 2020), 1154–1175.

30 Edward Buscombe, "Sound and Color," *Jump Cut*, no. 17 (April 1978): 23.

31 Misek, *Chromatic Cinema*, 143.

32 I would be remiss not to mention the films of Suzuki Seijun here, which feature some of the most striking color transformations of Nikkatsu Action Cinema. I have

argued that while the color transformations in his films derive from these broader color trends in Nikkatsu Action Cinema, his work departs from other Nikkatsu Action films in that he frequently dispenses with any diegetic pretext to justify the striking color transformations, unlike other Nikkatsu Action filmmakers, who more typically continued to rely on pretexts such as exterior neon and stage lighting to justify these shifts. See William Carroll, "The History of a Broken Blue *Fusuma*: Colour in Suzuki Seijun's Nikkatsu Films," in "Cinema and Mid-century Colour Culture," ed. Elena Gipponi and Joshua Yumibe, special issue, *Cinéma&Cie* 32 (Spring 2019): 15–26.

33 Yoshiharu Tezuka, *Japanese Cinema Goes Global: Filmworkers' Journeys* (Hong Kong: Hong Kong University Press, 2012), 65.

34 Kinnia Yau Shuk-ting, *Japanese and Hong Kong Film Industries: Understanding the Origins of East Asian Film Networks* (London: Routledge, 2009), 88.

35 Christopher Ribbat, *Flickering Light: A History of Neon* (London: Reaktion Books, 2011), 11.

36 Ribbat, 120–21.

37 Misek, *Chromatic Cinema*, 145.

10

Color as a Foreign Accent

Brazilian Films and Film Laboratories in the 1950s

RAFAEL DE LUNA FREIRE

Brazil in Foreign Color

Until the late 1940s, Brazilian fiction feature films were often criticized for their low technical quality in comparison to foreign cinema, especially Hollywood productions, which had been prevalent in the local market since the second half of the 1910s. Small and poorly equipped, Brazilian film laboratories processed only black-and-white film, and complaints about flaws resulting from film processing were frequent. Even the few Brazilian studios, for instance, Cinédia (created in 1930) or Atlântida (1941), had their own laboratories that produced irregular, often poor, results.

Color films seen by Brazilian audiences were almost exclusively foreign. A star like Carmen Miranda, who had reached enormous success in Brazilian musical films such as *Alô, Alô, Carnaval* (Adhemar Gonzaga and Wallace Downey, 1936) and *Banana da Terra* (Ruy Costa, 1939), was first seen in color on Brazilian screens in her earliest Hollywood film, *Down Argentine Way* (Irving Cummings, 1940). Brazilian film magazines reported with great interest the presence of foreign filmmakers who occasionally shot and screened documentary footage in the country, especially when using Technicolor.

This chapter provides a detailed historical overview of the slow and stuttering production of color films in postwar Brazil, not only in fiction but particularly in short documentary films. I describe the main challenges and hurdles faced by those who sought to produce color films in Brazil in the 1950s, with special attention to changes in Brazilian film laboratories at that time. The attempt to master color film technology must be understood more broadly in the context of the late 1940s, a period marked by advances in the development of the Brazilian film industry.

In Rio de Janeiro, Atlântida consolidated a successful formula of musical comedies (known as *chanchadas*), which attracted large audiences despite being criticized in the press. At the same time, in São Paulo, the richest city in the country, the wealthy bourgeoisie turned its attention to Brazilian films after years of neglect, mobilizing financial resources on a scale never seen before with the goal of "creating" a world-class Brazilian cinema on a par with the postwar development of the country. The main symbol of this "industry rush" was the Companhia Cinematográfica Vera Cruz, created in São Paulo in 1949.

Although Vera Cruz made unprecedented investments in the construction of studios, purchase of equipment, and hiring of foreign technicians, the changes brought about by this industrializing drive coexisted with restraints of the infrastructure of Brazilian cinema. All of Vera Cruz's films, for instance, were black and white, and laboratory services were provided by the Rex Film laboratory, which was founded twenty years earlier by Hungarians Adalberto Kemeny and Rudolf Rex Lustig.[1]

Another consequence of World War II was an intense European migration, which resulted in the arrival in Brazil of seasoned foreign technicians and artists. In Rio de Janeiro, in 1947 the French engineers Mathieu Adolphe Bonfanti and Paul Alphonse Duvergé created the Companhia Industrial Cinematográfica S.A. (CIC), dedicated to cinema services, including film development and duplication.

The creation of CIC was also related to initiatives that bypassed the current Brazilian studio system in developing independent productions, which involved filmmakers obtaining finance, renting studios and equipment, and hiring services, casts, and technicians. Producers experienced in the *chanchada* musical comedies first used this model, and it was soon after adopted by filmmakers who, inspired by Italian neorealism, pursued an auteur, low-budget cinema with increased aesthetic and political ambitions.[2]

A milestone in this so-called independent cinema was *Rio 40 Graus* (Nelson Pereira dos Santos, 1955), the debut feature film by the young filmmaker then affiliated with the Brazilian Communist Party. Without the support of a studio, Nelson Pereira dos Santos made use of the infrastructure that had been created to provide services to independent productions, such as the CIC laboratory. Films like *Rio 40 Graus* were responses to Vera Cruz, whose films were criticized for allegedly expressing an elitist cosmopolitism that drove them away from an "authentic" national identity. Although the technical improvements enabled by the São Paulo studios were well received, many critics and filmmakers expressed a growing desire for films that critically depicted Brazilian social reality, in tune with the new European and Latin American cinemas. In this sense, Hollywood's lavishness became synonymous with an escapist and alienating cinema that was associated with "the faux brilliance of the Technicolor," in the words of a critic at the time.[3]

In the 1950s, new monopack 35mm negative-positive color film stocks enabled professional color filming without the equipment and high costs associated with Technicolor. Their adoption in Brazil was, however, neither fast nor simple, given, among other reasons, the lack of laboratories in the country able to develop and print color stocks. Thus, the stunning color images of Rio de Janeiro, as seen in *Seven Wonders of the World* (Tay Garnett et al., 1956), a production by Cinerama released in Brazil in 1960, continued to be an attraction offered to Brazilians through foreign productions.[4] This meant that color remained associated with the opulent Hollywood model, which proved unattainable for Brazilian cinema, even with the large investments by Vera Cruz.

Despite its postwar development, Brazilian cinema remained mostly black and white well into the early 1960s. Foreign films remained the main way Brazilians could see themselves and their country in color on cinema screens. An alternative route was, however, created through international co-productions and using overseas laboratories.

Color and Foreign Laboratories

Although Brazilian feature fictional cinema of the 1950s broke several barriers, color remained largely the exception. For instance, neither the first Brazilian animated feature film, the remarkable *Sinfonia Amazônica* (Anélio Latini Filho, 1953), nor the first Brazilian wide-screen films, such as the thriller *Redenção* (Roberto Pires, 1959), were able to overcome the color barrier. Yet between the release of *Sinfonia Amazônica* and *Redenção* and because of the main São Paulo studios' aim of producing Brazilian films of international quality, the first initiatives to produce color feature films took place. Using the recent monopack 35mm color film stocks, the solution found by producers was to develop and process them in laboratories overseas. Thus, the Multifilmes studio, created in São Paulo in the wake of Vera Cruz, in 1953 produced the film *Destino em Apuros*, directed by Italian-Austrian Ernesto Remani and photographed by Hubert Corel using Anscocolor negatives (a U.S.-based Agfacolor derivative). Considered the first Brazilian feature film in color, *Destino em Apuros* was developed in the American laboratory Houston Color. According to Máximo Barro, who worked as production assistant on the film, the production faced many problems and hardships. The production used expired negatives (that should have been discarded) that Remani and Corel had brought from Argentina, from where, according to Barro, the director and the photographer had fled.[5] Color played a part in increasing the cost of the film, and its box office gross did not recover the investment. *Destino em Apuros* was not the only color feature film made in Brazil in the 1950s by foreign filmmakers using questionable methods.

Beyond the difficulties in getting color film stock in Brazil, the additional laboratory costs also hampered the adoption of color by Brazilian film producers, especially in the face of the financial crisis hitting the main São Paulo studios in the mid-1950s. However, color films through international coproductions became increasingly common, as did the use of laboratory services in Argentina, Europe, and the United States. Color was used particularly for documentary feature films that explored the exuberant nature of Brazil through exoticizing hues. Aimed at international audiences, these coproduced films were often directed by foreign filmmakers, including *Magia Verde* (Gian Gaspare Napolitano, 1955), which was filmed with Italian Ferraniacolor, and *Feitiço do Amazonas* (Zygmunt Sulistrowski, 1955) and *Sob o céu da Bahia* (Ernesto Remani, 1956), both filmed with Eastman Color.

The number of foreign productions filmed in Brazil grew in the second half of the 1950s as the country began to stand out internationally, and not only for its exuberant nature. The FIFA World Cup in 1958 featuring a young Pelé, the international success of Bossa Nova by Tom Jobim and João Gilberto, and the construction of Brasília, the country's new bold capital marked by the modernist architecture of Oscar Niemeyer and Lúcio Costa helped Brazil gain greater international visibility. In addition to its natural beauty and artistic and sporting talent, Rio de Janeiro's long-standing reputation as the "Marvelous City" also made it a privileged location for color romances and musicals for export. This tendency was exemplified by the Argentine Agfacolor coproduction *Meus Amores no Rio* (*Mis amores no Rio*, Carlos Hugo Christensen, 1958) and most notably by the huge success of the French Eastman Color coproduction *Orfeu do Carnaval* (*Black Orpheus*, Marcel Camus, 1959), which won the Oscar for Best Foreign Language Film and the Cannes Palme d'Or.

The Modernization of *Cavação*

Although historians have traditionally given greater attention to the feature production of Brazilian fiction films, short documentaries have represented the majority of local production since the silent era and allowed many professionals and film companies to continue their careers in Brazil. From the early twentieth century, the majority of Brazilian filmmakers survived using the practice known as *cavação*, a Brazilian slang for "making ends meet," which designated, for instance, the production of commissioned documentary films, sponsored by politicians, farmers, or businessmen, for promotional or advertising purposes. In

1934, a screen quota law established the mandatory screening of a Brazilian short film to accompany the exhibition of every foreign feature film. However, because the producers of short films were not properly paid for their commercial exhibition, the *cavação* remained the main alternative for financing short films screened under the law, especially newsreels, "through disguised sponsored content."[6]

On the other hand, throughout the 1950s, some companies dedicated to the production of documentary short films also sought to improve their productions technically. The objective was to differentiate themselves from competitors, mainly in Rio de Janeiro and São Paulo, and to attract the largest clients in the government or private sector. This was the case of Isaac Rozemberg, owner of the Organizações Cinematográficas I. Rozemberg. Born into a Romanian Jewish family, Rozemberg (1913–1983) immigrated to Brazil at the age of eighteen to escape compulsory military service, landing in Bahia. He worked as a peddler and a photographer's assistant, but it was in Rio de Janeiro that he managed to get closer to the world of cinema. In the second half of the 1930s, he started working as a film reporter and, like many other film technicians during the Estado Novo dictatorship (1937–1945), transferred to a government agency. In 1940, he worked at the Press and Propaganda Department (DIP), the powerful Estado Novo body for propaganda and censorship. He then began making films through the Bahia State Department of Press and Propaganda (DEIP), producing newsreels and institutional films. Self-taught, Rozemberg was in charge of all stages of the short films he produced, from the script to development and printing. As a sideline he dedicated himself to what he called "sponsored documentary," a more acceptable term than the pejorative slang *cavação*.

After the war, with the end of the dictatorship and the extinction of the DIP and the DEIPs, Rozemberg created the Organizações Cinematográficas I. Rozemberg, in Rio de Janeiro. He continued making newsreels and documentaries, always in black and white. It was the Thirty-Sixth International Eucharistic Congress, in 1955, that motivated him to produce his first film in color. Hosted by one of the largest Catholic nations in the world, the event was widely reported in the Brazilian press and mobilized hundreds of thousands of followers.

Flagrantes do XXXVI Congresso Eucarístico Internacional was shot on 35mm Agfacolor film, with cinematography by the Brazilian-based German Heinz Forthmann (1915–1978), who was responsible for taking the exposed negatives to Hamburg, where the German laboratory Geyer-Werke developed the material.[7] According to the records in the Rozemberg's family collection, by the end of 1955 three reels of 366 meters each (a little over an hour's worth of images) were sent to Germany, returning to Brazil three months later, by air transportation.

However, weeks before the International Eucharistic Congress, Rozemberg wrote to the Alex laboratory in Buenos Aires to obtain information on its color film development and printing services, informing the lab that the Argentine Mario Pagés (1912–198?) would be the cinematographer for his documentary.[8]

The laboratory replied that it had been working with Ferraniacolor for two years and would also have the capability of processing Eastman Color, "but as there has been no import into the country to date, we do not have the necessary chemicals for processing."[9] As Rozemberg revealed in his letters, the availability at that time in Brazil solely of Agfacolor color negatives must have led him to change both cinematographers (from Pagés to Forthmann) and laboratories (from Alex in Argentina to Geyer-Werke in Germany).

First screened in a special session at the Brazilian Press Association on May 21, 1956, a little over a year later, "the color newsfilm" about the Thirty-Sixth International Eucharistic Congress was part of a program that also included two black-and-white documentary short films by Rozemberg that had been finished the previous year. One was about one of the works carried out by the city administration as preparation for the congress (the dismantling of the Morro de Santo Antonio) and the other also contained images of the event. In July 1956, *Flagrantes do XXXVI Congresso Eucarístico Internacional* (figures 10.1 and 10.2) was screened at the luxurious Metro Passeio Theater as a "national complement" to the Tom and Jerry Festival, preceding some Hanna-Barbera animations (also in color) produced by Metro-Goldwyn-Mayer, owner of the theater. The film also competed for the award for Best Short Film of the Year at the Fourth Brazilian Federal District Film Festival.

Amid several competing newsreels that recorded the event, Rozemberg's color film clearly stood out. As a result, the filmmaker made plans to continue filming in color in Brazil in the second half of the 1950s. Documents preserved in his family's collection, however, reveal the great difficulties he faced in obtaining color raw film stock as well as in using foreign laboratories.

FIGURE 10.1 Title card of *Flagrantes do XXXVI Congresso Eucarístico Internacional* (scanned from 16mm print frame).

FIGURE 10.2 Black-and-white postcard of the XXXVI International Eucharistic Congress to be compared with the Rozemberg's color film of the same event (figure 10.3).

Smuggling Color

After the negatives of *Flagrantes do XXXVI Congresso Eucarístico Internacional* were developed in Germany and sent to Brazil, the film was edited and its soundtrack created in Rio de Janeiro. Rozemberg could initially make only 16mm and 35mm positive prints in black and white in Brazilian laboratories, and he needed to send the edited negatives back to Germany for color prints. The 16mm print of the film studied for this chapter has a black-and-white title card: a letter written and signed by Don Helder Câmara, who was the congress organizer, dated September 7, 1956, and read by the narrator. This was a later addition to the final version, filmed and developed in Brazil and, therefore, in black and white, unlike the rest of the color film.[10]

Besides spending more time and money (for shipping and due to currency exchange rates) to use foreign laboratories, Brazilian filmmakers such as Rozemberg also had to navigate the complicated national bureaucracy to gather the paperwork to authorize the shipment of film cans abroad, with all the risks involved in transporting negatives, especially undeveloped ones. A reliable shipping carrier was of the utmost importance but was not easy to obtain. It was also very difficult to legally buy unexposed color negatives in Brazil due to import restrictions, and many producers had to resort to the black market or find alternative sources. In a letter to his friend Nilzeth Neves, a New York–based employee of the Brazilian delegation of the United Nations, Rozemberg reported not having a representative in Germany to purchase color film stock, asking for her help in buying the product in the United States. The letter stated: "The important thing is that you arrange for me to send the material, without the necessary import license, by private or diplomatic means. Do not think that I only want to harm the tax authorities. The thing is that it would create such a bureaucracy that would prevent us from working. Not only that, but also this film will have to be developed and printed there."[11] As an example of such improvised arrangements, in the end Nilzeth's sister, who was returning to Brazil, brought the package personally.

Months later, Rozemberg wrote again to Nilzeth asking her help to take the exposed negatives of the color films he had made in Bahia at the end of 1955, the first after the International Eucharistic Congress, to the Kodak laboratory in New Jersey.[12] These consisted of nearly 1,200 meters of reversal 16mm Kodachrome Commercial film stock and approximately 200 meters of 35mm Eastman Color film stock. In addition to developing and printing the Eastman Color negative, he wanted to make black-and-white positive copies from the reversal material for editing. However, the New Jersey laboratory informed Rozemberg that the duplication from Kodachrome was done only in Rochester. Further, the developing and printing of Eastman Color was completed only in commercial laboratories and not at Kodak, and the Color Service and De Luxe laboratories, both in New York, were suggested.[13]

As a result of a misunderstanding, instead of having the 35mm negatives moved from New Jersey and taken to a commercial laboratory in New York, all the material went to Rochester, where another mistake was made: the Eastman Color exposed negative was developed as if it was Kodachrome reversal film stock, leaving it worthless, which generated a great loss for the Brazilian producer. As compensation, Kodak offered 2,000 meters of Eastman Color raw stock.[14] As for duplicating the reversal material itself, the high cost of the service made Rozemberg give up the idea, and he stated that he would directly edit the original material.[15] In the following years Rozemberg sought out other laboratories, such as Pathé's in New York, facing new difficulties such as misplacements, damage to the negatives, high costs, and considerable bureaucracy.

Whereas Rozemberg was part of the "commercial" trend of Brazilian documentary cinema, the industry basically consisted, at the time, of small companies, generally created around filmmaker-owners and with few employees or collaborators. The main difference in relation to the many competitors was the higher technical quality of the films, especially in terms of cinematography but also in postproduction. Even so, these companies had difficulty coping with the costs, risks, and challenges of shooting, developing, and printing color film in the 1950s. In other words, despite the obvious differences between film companies of different sizes, in general, Brazilian film producers faced common obstacles, as the example of filming in color shows.

Short Film *d'auteur*: Color as an Exception

If *cavação* was still the dominant practice in postwar Brazilian cinema, it also changed at the end of the 1950s. As it was easier to find viable forms of financing for short documentaries, especially through governmental bodies or cultural and research entities, making a documentary short film the first step for many first-time Brazilian filmmakers. As a consequence of this energizing tendency, short documentaries made by young and politicized filmmakers in different parts of the country were able to escape from the conservatism and academicism of current productions that were characterized by the omnipresent narration of a radio-like, didactic, and grandiloquent character, combined with orchestral music used redundantly with the images. Thematic and aesthetically distinct from the traditional Brazilian documentaries screened in theaters through the "screening quota," documentary short films such as *Arraial do Cabo* (Paulo Cezar Saraceni and Mário Carneiro, 1959) and *Aruanda* (Linduarte Noronha, 1960) were forerunners of the world-famous Cinema Novo in the 1960s.

In the wake of the realist and politicized features of the aforementioned "independent cinema," such as *Rio 40 graus*, these short documentaries were also made by small teams, with a low budget and few technical resources, and almost all were in black and white. As the filmmaker Glauber Rocha wrote in 1963, documentary short films were "the best school for training professionals. . . . The documentary facilitates the experience, provides means to dominate the technique and to try the creation without the commercial risk of the feature productions."[16] Although it was part of this trend of new documentaries, one film was an exception to the black-and-whiteness of the others: the short color film *O Grande Rio* (Gerson Tavares, 1959), practically forgotten since the early 1960s.[17]

A painter born in the state of Rio de Janeiro, Gerson Tavares (1928–2021) discovered his passion for cinema while living in Paris on a scholarship, which led him to attend the prestigious Centro Sperimentale di Cinematografia in Rome in 1956. Back in Brazil two years later, he formed a partnership to produce sponsored and commercial films as a way of making a living from cinema. At this time of international interest in Brazil, his friend and Italian cinematographer Giampaolo Santini suggested making three short color films on the country for foreign audiences. Tavares would need to render the production viable, while Santini would pay for the color negatives and film laboratory. Through the producer Ruy Pereira da Silva, in 1959 Tavares directed these three documentary short films with Ferraniacolor stock: *Arte no Brasil de Hoje*, *Brasília, Capital do Século*, and *O Grande Rio*.

The film that is of greatest interest for this discussion, *The Great River* (*O Grande Rio*), gained national recognition when it won the 1959 gold medal for Best Film at the I Certamen Internacional de Cine Documental Ibero-Americano

FIGURE 10.3 Crowd gathered in front of Rio de Janeiro's Guanabara Bay in a faded 16mm color print of the film about the International Eucharistic Congress (1956).

y Filipino de Bilbao, in Spain, at a time when international awards for Brazilian cinema were still rare and much celebrated. In a sensitive and critical way, *O Grande Rio* approaches the São Francisco River through the life and culture of the riverside populations, highlighting the misery that especially devastated the backlands of the Northeast, the future setting for renowned films of Cinema Novo.

Although Tavares's short films also resembled traditional Brazilian documentary film productions, for example, those by Rozemberg—color films on national subjects for international audiences—they introduced important differences in their form and content, especially *O Grande Rio*. If films such as Rozemberg's *Flagrantes do XXXVI Congresso Eucarístico Internacional* were grandiloquent and monumental in how they drew attention to modern and urban Brazil (figure 10.3), in contrast, *O Grande Rio* had a marked poetic character, with songs, voices, and noises recorded on location interspersed with sober narration. No signs of the state were shown, revealing the abandonment of the region by the government. The film's focus was on the contrast between the riches of popular culture and the misery of the population of the interior of the country, ravaged by drought, which brought it closer to documentaries such as those that would be the forerunners of Cinema Novo (figure 10.4).[18] Through these contrasts, it allows us to perceive the differences, but also the various intersections, between what would be called the "old" and the "new" Brazilian documentary, between commercial and auteur cinema.

One element that could bring Tavares's film closer to the traditional documentary and distance it from the films that sought that form's renewal is color, which at the time symbolized, as we have seen, the spectacle of industrial cinema and high production costs. However, this was not the case with *O Grande*

FIGURE 10.4 Funeral of a child in the arid backlands of northeastern Brazil in the film *O Grande Rio* (Gerson Tavares, 1959).

Rio, which was made with minimal crew and a low budget. It was also a short film with no commercial or promotional character, screened mainly in film festivals but not in commercial theaters preceding foreign feature films through the screening quota. According to Tavares, the cinematographer Giampaolo Santini collected unexposed Ferraniacolor negative leftovers from larger European productions he had participated in—a strategy that other Brazilian filmmakers would later repeat. Santini was responsible for taking the exposed negatives to Italy, where they were developed at the laboratory La Microstampa, in Rome. A Brazilian priest living in the Vatican did the voice-over.[19]

As a surviving print attests, *O Grande Rio* also circulated in Brazil in a black-and-white 35mm copy, made at the Rex laboratory. Displaying a title card announcing the gold medal at the Bilbao Film Festival, this later print was certainly made in Brazil following the granting of the award. Possibly, the interest in *O Grande Rio* at that time motivated the printing of a new copy, which, in Brazil, could only be made in black and white.[20]

The popularization of color film production in Brazil could not rely on the complex and often informal strategies of resorting to foreign laboratories used throughout the 1950s. As a matter of fact, it depended on changes in the infrastructure of services in Brazilian cinema.

Brazilian Laboratories

The conquest of color by Brazilian laboratories came about through the initiative of various people. Nonetheless, the work in particular of two Hungarians is worth highlighting: Joseph Illes (aka Josef Illés, ca. 1926–?) and George Jonas (aka Jonas Gyorgy, 1927–2012), who met while still in their teens in a studio and film laboratory in Budapest.[21] Self-taught, inventive, and talented, together they developed and licensed a type of colored film in the early 1940s called Chemicolor, which interested Kodak in Hungary and Ferraniacolor in Italy.[22] They immigrated to Argentina, where Illes had relatives, and ended up employed at the Alex laboratory in Buenos Aires, the largest in South America. In the 1950s, they moved to São Paulo, where they took over as heads of the recently created laboratory of Divulgação Cinematográfica Bandeirante (DCB), a company that produced the newsreel *Bandeirante da Tela*, which aimed at promoting its real owner, the politician Adhemar de Barros.[23]

After leaving DCB, Illes and Jonas created a laboratory that pioneered the printing of color photographs in Brazil. In 1955, Jonas discovered that the department store Mesbla had received a batch of Anscocolor raw film stock. As he later recalled: "They didn't know what to do with that merchandise. There was no laboratory to develop it. It was a shipment sent by mistake."[24] The two bought the stock and decided to make a demonstration of what they called the Illes-Jonas process for developing color films. They borrowed the DCB laboratory facility, Vera Cruz filming equipment, and Paulo Sá Pinto's Marabá theater to hold a special screening. The showcase featured a "pretty girl in colorful clothes" (reusing the set and model of an advertising production) and was widely reported in the press as the first color film developed in Brazil.[25]

With the test film done, Jones and Illes made an agreement to set up a color film department in the CIC laboratory in Rio de Janeiro. While Illes remained in Brazil, Jonas moved to Bolivia, where he managed to buy a large quantity of unexposed Ferraniacolor negative, which he sent back to Illes. In 1956, trade magazines reported a new color test film developed and processed in Brazil by the two, this time using Ferraniacolor stock and the CIC laboratories.[26] The following year, however, the CIC laboratory suffered a fire and closed down.[27]

With the end of the CIC and still owning a large amount of unexposed color film stock, Illes and Jonas decided to set up their own small laboratory in São Paulo. In partnership with producer Mario Audrá Filho, owner of the Maristela studio, and Paulo Sá Pinto, the largest exhibitor in São Paulo, the two bought part of the remaining CIC lab machinery.[28] Thus, in 1958, Illes and Jonas opened the Policrom laboratory, specializing in color films. An article in *Cine Reporter* stated, "The equipment used by Policrom comes from the United States and France, adjusted to meet local conditions."[29] The laboratory advertised its capacity to develop and print Kodak, Ferrania, Ansco, Agfa, and any other color stock.

In the same year, 1958, the competing lab Rex Film also began processing East-man Color film, after having announced it for several months. Between 1954 and 1956, Oswaldo Cruz Kemeny, the son of one of Rex's founders, took a chemistry course at the University of Southern California while also interning at the renowned laboratories of Consolidated Film Industries in Los Angeles.[30] Upon his return to Brazil, he created the infrastructure to develop and print color films at Rex. To compete with Rex and enter the São Paulo market, the Rio de Janeiro laboratory Líder Cinematográfica—the main lab in Rio de Janeiro after the closure of CIC, from which it also bought machinery—acquired Policrom, which was experiencing financial difficulties, although keeping Jonas and Illes as directors.[31]

Therefore, in the transition to the 1960s, there was a movement toward modernization (and concentration) in the industry compared with the previous reality of many small and relatively precarious film laboratories. This development benefited from the quota obligation established in 1954 that specified Brazilian distributors must strike at least half of their foreign black-and-white prints in Brazilian laboratories. Despite complaints from distributors and critics, by the end of the 1950s there were already indications that the quota would soon expand to also encompass color film printing.[32] It was the growing market for film processing that enabled Rex and Líder, the largest and best-equipped Brazilian laboratories that would dominate the market, to process color films, which resulted in a gradual increase in the production of Brazilian color films, now developed domestically.[33]

The Full Turn to Color in Brazil

In his book *À margem do cinema brasileiro* (1963), the researcher Francisco da Silva Nobre included a chapter titled ". . . And We Haven't Yet Conquered Color" in which he explained, "The high cost of production (around three times that of black-and-white film) and the nonexistence of specialized laboratories (almost all the developing continues to be carried out in the United States and Argentina) contribute to the slow evolution that we have been experiencing in this particular area."[34] Yet, if the evolution had been slow throughout the 1950s, it accelerated precisely at the time Nobre was writing his book. In the field of fiction feature films, the adventure film *A Morte Comanda o Cangaço* (Carlos Coimbra, 1960), shot in Eastman Color—a brand that was identified on the film's poster—was one of the first feature productions in color to be developed in Brazil, achieving great commercial success. *A Morte Comanda o Cangaço* was developed at Rex, having Oswaldo Cruz Kemeny as a "color technician," as was the practice in Hollywood Technicolor productions.

Throughout the first half of the 1960s, color was used mainly in genre films, "commercial" productions that would be overshadowed in the history of Brazilian cinema by the growing critical (and eventually commercial) success of auteur, dramatic, and realistic films, initially all in black and white. These films were diverse, including the masterpieces of Cinema Novo, such as *Vidas Secas* (Nelson Pereira dos Santos, 1963) and *Deus e o Diabo na Terra do Sol* (Glauber Rocha, 1964), which achieved international acclaim.

In this sense, color remained associated until the mid-1960s not only with spectacle, in opposition to realism, but also with a supposedly "foreign" look that resonated most proximately with Hollywood. As such, it was evaluated by various critics as the maximum expression of the United States' cultural imperialism, as supposedly "reflected" in national genre cinema.

Color was also associated with the commercialism of private and governmental propaganda films. After all, the better-produced *cavações*, such as the films of George Jonas or Isaac Rozemberg (both foreign-born naturalized Brazilians), more rapidly adopted color at the beginning of the 1960s, accompanied by the development of audiovisual advertising in Brazil.[35] The military dictatorship established in the country after 1964, which was supported by much of the major business sector and sustained by the anticommunism campaign of the United States and the national big media companies, reinforced the investment in nationalist propaganda, with an emphasis on technical quality, of which color was a great emblem.

Cinema Novo, in turn, would only adopt color definitively in the feature films made in the late 1960s, when it sought to reconcile experimentalism with spectacle in a context of fierce censorship, the need for commercial survival, and the influence of Tropicalism: a critical and creative reaction to authoritarian nationalism. The largely forgotten musical romance *The Girl from Ipanema* (*Garota de Ipanema*, Leon Hirszman, 1967), which was inspired by the world-famous Bossa Nova song and shot in Eastman Color, was announced as the first Cinema Novo color film, but the trend would consolidate only in 1969, with the critical success of Joaquim Pedro de Andrade's *Macunaíma* and Glauber Rocha's *Antonio das Mortes* (*O Dragão da Maldade contra o Santo Guerreiro*).[36] In these two films, also shot in Eastman Color, color would no longer be understood as foreign: it too had to be swallowed, in the modernist anthropophagic metaphor taken up by Tropicalism.[37] But color also became an unavoidable commercial necessity as a result of growing competition with foreign and national color films: between 1968 and 1969, the number of Brazilian color comedies, thrillers, and westerns increased significantly.[38] Soon, the competition also came from the beginning of regular colorcasting on Brazilian television. In the early 1970s, the color barrier was definitively overcome by Brazilian cinema.

The mode of production of Brazilian color films in the 1950s, with its dependence on foreign laboratories and the difficult access to scarce and expensive raw color film stock, often smuggled from abroad, reinforced the understanding of filmic color as an imported technology. In this sense, the practical and economic difficulties for color production in Brazil corroborated the understanding of it as something foreign also in the ideological sense. This foreign accent was initially rejected by filmmakers with nationalist and revolutionary intentions, while simultaneously being aspired to by producers who wanted films with "international quality." However, these differences could also be blurred, as we have seen, in the complex reality of postwar Brazilian cinema.

If Brazilian cinema became definitively colorful only in the 1970s, this chapter has investigated some of the first experiences of color films made in Brazil in the 1950s, many of which, unfortunately, are lost or inaccessible. The few works from this period currently preserved, such as *Flagrantes do XXXVI Congresso Eucarístico Internacional* and *O Grande Rio*, are therefore fundamental records for a history yet to be better known.

Acknowledgments

I would like to acknowledge the support of the Fundação Carlos Chagas Filho de Amparo à Pesquisa do Estado do Rio de Janeiro (FAPERJ), through the Jovem Cientista do Nosso Estado grant. I also thank Reizi Rozemberg and Patricia Civelli for granting access to their family's documents.

Notes

1. See Hernani Heffner, "Adalberto Kemeny," in *Enciclopédia do Cinema Brasileiro*, ed. Fernão Ramos and Luiz Felipe Miranda (São Paulo: Senac, 2000), 309.
2. Luís Alberto Rocha Melo, "Cinema Independente: Produção, distribuição e exibição no Rio de Janeiro (1948–1954)" (PhD diss., Fluminense Federal University, 2011).
3. R. Magalhães Júnior, "O progresso do cinema inglês," *A Cena Muda*, no. 39 (1947): 3.
4. On the Brazilian segment of *Seven Wonders of the World*, see João Luiz Vieira, "The Forest and the City: Rio as an Immersive Landscape," *Streetnotes* 26 (Spring 2019): 148–162.
5. Alfredo Sternheim, *Máximo Barro: Talento e altruísmo* (São Paulo: Imprensa Oficial do Estado de São Paulo, 2009), 47–53.
6. Ely Azeredo, "O suplício dos cine-jornais," *Tribuna da Imprensa*, June 27, 1956, 4.
7. On Forthmann, see Marcos de Souza Mendes, "Heinz Forthman e Darcy Ribeiro: cinema documentário no Serviço de Proteção aos Índios, SPI, 1949–1959" (PhD diss., University of Campinas, 2006).
8. On Pagés, see Antonio Leão da Silva Neto, *Dicionário de fotógrafos do cinema brasileiro* (São Paulo: Imprensa Oficial do Estado de São Paulo, 2010), 108.
9. I. Rozemberg, letter to Cannio Santini, June 27, 1955; Cannio Santini, letter to I. Rozemberg, June 30, 1955, Rozemberg family collection.
10. Inspecting this 16mm print, I found that the spliced-in title card was a later addition, printed in Kodak negative manufactured in 1956, while the rest of the print used Agfacolor stock, with German notes in the head leader and the tail of the reel. It is currently the only known print of the film and was in possession of Alberto Ortigão, who inherited it from his father, an engineer at the Rio de Janeiro city administration. It was then donated to the Audiovisual Preservation University Lab (LUPA-UFF).
11. I. Rozemberg, letter to Nilzeth Neves, November 3, 1955, Rozemberg family collection.
12. I. Rozemberg, letter to Nilzeth Neves, March 13, 1956, Rozemberg family collection.

13 Kodak Processing Laboratory, letter to I. Rozemberg, March 1, 1956, Rozemberg family collection. Kodak's representative listed possible difficulties related to transportation and customs clearance of films coming from Brazil, suggesting that such a procedure was not very common. The same observation had been made to Rozemberg by the Argentine Alex laboratory employee the previous year: "The only serious inconvenience is the entry and exit of materials from the country, which is seriously hindered by customs laws and regulations" (Cannio Santini, letter to I. Rozemberg, June 30, 1955, Rozemberg family collection).

14 P. W. Sweeney, letter to I. Rozemberg, April 20, 1956; P. W. Sweeney, letter to I. Rozemberg, May 3, 1956, Rozemberg family collection.

15 The practice of shooting with 16mm reversal color film stock would continue in Brazil. The adventure feature film *Bruma Seca* (Mário Brasini and Mário Civelli, 1961), for instance, was entirely shot with 16mm Ektachrome Commercial stock. It was then developed and blown up to a 35mm negative in a foreign laboratory. The color prints from the 35mm negative, however, were already struck in a Brazilian lab; Rex Film, letter to Banco do Brasil, March 17, 1961, Memória Civelli collection.

16 Glauber Rocha, *Revisão crítica do cinema brasileiro* (Rio de Janeiro: Civilização Brasileira, 1963), 118

17 Rafael de Luna Freire, "A trilogia de curtas-metragens documentários de Gerson Tavares de 1959," *Doc on-line* 20 (September 2016): 5–25. The film was released on DVD through my project Rescue of Gerson Tavares's Films. On the DVD, see Angelica Gasparotto de Oliveira, "Rescue of Gerson Tavares's Cinematographic Work," review of Coleção Gerson Tavares, distributed by Associação Cultural Tela Brasilis, *Moving Image* 19, no. 2 (2016): 145–148.

18 *O Grande Rio* was grouped with these films, even by Glauber Rocha, in two articles written in 1960 and 1961, respectively. Freire, "A trilogia de curtas metragens," 13–15.

19 Freire, 15–17.

20 The black-and-white print is from the Cinemateca Brasileira collection, and its good physical condition suggests that it had not been projected many times, unlike the 16mm and 35mm color prints of the film I examined.

21 The information cited here comes mainly from the autobiography George Jonas, *A cor da vida* (São Paulo: Editora de Cultura, 2009), and Jonas's interview in Paulo B. C. Schettino, *Diálogos sobre a tecnologia do cinema brasileiro* (Cotia: Ateliê Editorial, 2007).

22 The system consisted of "toning various colors on the film," using aniline dyes that also attacked the gelatine and formed "strange colors" that gave the "illusion of color"; Schettino, *Diálogos sobre a tecnologia*, 308. Also see Jonas, *A cor da vida*, 73–4.

23 Rodrigo Archangelo, "Um bandeirante nas telas de São Paulo: O discurso Adhemarista em cinejornais (1947–1956)" (master's thesis, University of São Paulo, 2007), 45–46.

24 Jonas, *A cor da vida*, 165.

25 *Cine Repórter*, June 4, 1955, 1. A few months later, the short documentary *Natureza Carioca* was screened, directed by Homogêneo Rangel and with cinematography by the Ukrainian George Tamarski, another foreigner who immigrated to Brazil in the 1950s. Also filmed with Anscocolor and developed in the DCB laboratory, it was also publicized as the "first color film released and copied in the country"; *Diário de Notícias*, October 23, 1955, 8.

26 *Cine-Repórter*, April 15, 1956, 4.

27 Apparently, the CIC fire was a fabrication, for the sake of collecting insurance, and there was no real damage to the laboratory; Schettino, *Diálogos sobre a tecnologia*, 260.

28 Jonas, *A cor da vida*, 187–188.

29 *Cine Repórter*, January 18, 1958, 4.

30 *Cine Repórter*, August 4, 1956, 12.

31 According to Jonas, "Paulo Sá Pinto sent services to the laboratory and did not pay"; Schettino, *Diálogos sobre a tecnologia*, 314. Also, Mário Audrá Jr. allegedly embezzled from Policrom to pay debts; Jonas, *A cor da vida*, 196.

32 In 1952, the owner of CIC laboratory defended the black-and-white printing quota for foreign prints in Brazil, describing the situation: "Unfortunately, of the 500 foreign films screened on average per year in Brazil, only 15% have their titles or prints made in the country"; see Mathieu Adolphe Bonfati, *Carta ao 1º Congresso Nacional do Cinema Brasileiro*, September 23, 1952, Alex Viany collection, Cinemateca do MAM-Rio.

33 "Revelação de filmes em cores," *Revista do Geicine*, no. 1 (1961): 28.

34 F. Silva Nobre, *À margem do cinema brasileiro* (Rio de Janeiro: Pongetti Editores, 1963), 100.

35 In the wake of the crisis of São Paulo's biggest film studios, production companies specializing in advertising films, such as Jota Filmes and Lynx Filmes, had already emerged in the late 1950s, a development that raised the technical quality level of the expanding television advertising. See Schettino, *Diálogos sobre a tecnologia*, 246; Cybelle Angelique Ribeiro Tedesco, "Lynxfilm: Uma contribuição à memória do audiovisual paulista" (PhD diss., University of Campinas, 2015), 54.

36 Stefan Solomon provides an excellent analysis of the intermedial use of color in Glauber Rocha's first color feature film, *Antonio das Mortes*, while also noting that the director had already made the short documentary *Amazonas, Amazonas* (1965) in color. In fact, *Amazonas, Amazonas* was an obvious *cavação*, having been made by Rocha on commission by the state government. See Stefan Solomon, "'The Cloak of Technicolor': Intermedial Color in *Antônio das Mortes*," *Screen* 60, no. 1 (Spring 2019): 140.

37 Young filmmakers like Rogério Sganzerla and Julio Bressane, front men of the contemporary and more experimental Cinema Marginal, criticized how color was used in those Cinema Novo films, arguing over the very meaning of a supposedly tropicalist cinema in the late 1960s. See Leonardo Esteves, "O processo da cor no cinema brasileiro moderno: Aspectos técnicos e estéticos," *Estudos Históricos* 36, no. 78 (January–April 2023): 114–134.

38 Rodolfo Neder, "O desafio da cor," *Filme Cultura* 2, no. 12 (May–June 1969): 49; José Mário Ortiz Ramos, *Cinema, Estado e lutas culturais: Anos 50, 60, 70* (Rio de Janeiro: Paz e Terra, 1983), 63.

11

British Film Criticism and Global Color

SARAH STREET

British filmmakers' reputation for producing distinctive, "quality" Technicolor films was firmly established in the 1940s. But these works were far from numerous: in 1948, for example, of the 705 feature films (including reissues) released in Britain, 45 were in color and of these only 10 were British.[1] Even though British technicians built up considerable color expertise and Britain had its own laboratory for Technicolor processing, following the introduction of monopack stocks in the early 1950s, color films still were far from the norm. Many filmmakers remained cautious, wishing to avoid charges of the "gaudiness" that critics often associated with American color films. British directors and technicians trod a careful path between wishing to exploit color while at the same time avoiding bold effects that might distract or confuse audiences. The "British School of Technicolor" so admired by French critics for its tasteful, pastel-like appearance, made UK producers and directors relatively more careful in the demonstration phase of both Technicolor and Eastman Color.[2] It was not until the 1960s that British directors and technicians began to experiment quite overtly with color in feature films such as *Tom Jones* (UK, Tony Richardson, 1963), *Modesty Blaise* (UK, Joseph Losey, 1966), and *Don't Look Now* (UK, Nicolas Roeg, 1973), as well as in avant-garde modes associated with filmmakers and artists such as Lindsay Anderson, Don Levy, Peter Watkins, Margaret Tait, and Malcolm Le Grice. By the end of the 1960s, most films were shot in color, coinciding with the decade's association with the vibrant colors of psychedelic art, home décor, and fashions. It became more or less essential for a film to be made in color if it was to be widely distributed at home and abroad, as producers equated color with commercial value, particularly in popular genres such as fantasy, crime and spy thrillers, historical films, pop musical films, and comedies and contemporary drama.[3] Ken Loach shot his realist drama *Kes* (1969) in color somewhat reluctantly, using a monochrome-like, subdued palette, since, as producer Tony Garnett remarked, by that time "colour had become a requirement in feature filmmaking."[4] It was also increasingly recognized that filmmakers could use color creatively to distinguish their films, develop recurring motifs, or work in symbiosis with costume and set designers who responded to the period's vibrant chromatic culture.

British films were not the only color films seen and reviewed by critics in Britain. American films continued to dominate the box office, and films from other countries were regularly reviewed in *Sight and Sound*, the publication that this chapter foregrounds due to its centrality in British film culture at the time. Until the 1970s, *Sight and Sound* and the closely associated *Monthly Film Bulletin* were, as Mattias Frey notes, "traditional bulwarks of national film culture," offering "a functional critique (and promotion) of British cinema with a liberal humanist attitude towards 'world cinema'—attending increasingly to formal shapes."[5] The chapter seeks to understand how British critics discussed color films as an increasing number were seen and attracted comment, especially those considered to be innovative or as demonstrating "quality" values. They contributed to the development of a critical vocabulary that was evolving around color on-screen that arguably had an impact on British color films. It is appropriate to place this foregrounding of critical observation within theoretical perspectives developed by Pierre Bourdieu, particularly relating to his works on taste, distinction, art, and commerce.[6] While other scholars have referenced Bourdieu's theories in relation to the art cinema market in general, this chapter's focus shows how they are also suggestive of how color was understood to function within both art and commercial cinema, particularly in relation to modes of exhibition such as the film festival circuit.[7] The chapter sheds new light on how color films were reported, with close analysis of titles that attracted particularly interesting insights into the cultural understanding of color during a period when, as far as film was concerned, it became more or less ubiquitous.

Critical discussion of color in Britain was overshadowed by the dominance and perceived qualities of realist cinema. The tradition of "quality" identified with realism was deeply entrenched within critical discourses that dominated from the 1940s.[8] Prime examples were the gritty, social realist new wave (1959–1963) of black-and-white British films, including *Room at the Top* (Jack Clayton, 1959), *Saturday Night and Sunday Morning* (Karel Reisz, 1960), and *A Taste of Honey* (Tony Richardson, 1961). These films' reputations for offering "authentic" commentaries on working-class life aligned them with monochrome social realist photography. Color was considered inappropriate for this aesthetic style because of its associations with artificiality, fantasy, and visual excess. As Julian Petley has argued, the many nonrealist, visually sumptuous British films in genres such as horror and melodrama can be thought of as a "lost continent" of films that were largely underappreciated and even dismissed by critics.[9] In France films such as *Peeping Tom* (Michael Powell, 1960) and Hammer Film Productions' color horror films were, however, received more enthusiastically by publications such as *Positif* and *Midi-Minuit fantastique* that applauded their antirealism and their challenge to prevalent boundaries of taste.[10]

Sight and Sound and *Monthly Film Bulletin*, film journals published by the British Film Institute since 1934, reflected contemporary debates around film evaluation in Britain. From the late 1950s, *Sight and Sound* increasingly emphasized the need for films to advocate social change by exhibiting humanist values and engaging with politics.[11] Focusing on its commentaries about color indicates a residual interest in issues and approaches that had been evident in the journal *Sequence*. This publication ran from 1947 to 1952 and involved writers who went on to publish in *Sight and Sound*, including Penelope Houston, Gavin Lambert, and filmmakers Lindsay Anderson and Tony Richardson. An emphasis on style and mise-en-scène surfaced in descriptions of color that kept alive an interest in cinema as an art form with established and emerging aesthetic conventions. British writings about color films in the 1950s and 1960s showed curiosity about how color was being deployed, and *Sight and Sound* also put these discussions in juxtaposition with international interventions in debates on color by reproducing significant writings by filmmakers such as Carl Dreyer and Sergei Eisenstein.[12]

How critics responded to color forms a case study into how a particular aesthetic attribute was seen to influence a film's style and content. Color perceived as stylistic excess divorced from meaning was often derided and associated in the British press with films considered to align with the "lowbrow," commercially driven values that Bourdieu theorized in relation to "higher-brow" works of art that attracted a particular type of critical discourse and were associated with the acquisition of cultural capital. As Guy Austin observes, Bourdieu's distinctions between restricted and large-scale cultural production as part of the "market for symbolic goods" are relevant to the demarcations often drawn between auteur and genre cinema. These distinctions surface in film discourse when, for example, critics elevate art cinema above popular, genre-driven forms.[13] If one considers film criticism to be representative of a field, the struggles within it that Bourdieu identified as central to the dynamics of field theory can be seen to play out not only between different critics but also in the "competences" they demonstrated in their writings. As far as color is concerned, some critics clearly had more knowledge than others, drawing on "the previous knowledge of the strictly artistic principles of division which enable a representation to be located."[14] It is interesting in this regard to chart how critics perceived "excess" differently; while some did not develop a vocabulary toward appreciating how this could be used creatively, others saw chromatic obtrusiveness as a means of elevating a work. Much as Bourdieu writes about the "tools" needed to "decode" texts, the acquisition of knowledge about color can be thought of as bringing it into greater visibility and recognition. Since many of *Sight and Sound*'s reviews of color films were included in the journal's reports on international film festivals, these works began to be associated with and were legitimized by the "world" and "art" cinema categories that such reportage advanced. By comparison, the reviews in *Monthly Film Bulletin*, with their emphasis on plot descriptions of British and American genre films that were currently circulating in Britain, did not allow for extended reflections on color.

As the number and variety of international color films increased, so too did the showcasing of stocks such as Agfa (German) and Ferraniacolor (Italian). Imported films and international stocks demonstrated a variety of "looks," which challenged critics to appreciate their different production contexts. The increasing number of films that were distributed outside their country of origin, particularly through being exhibited at film festivals, raises additional issues relating to variations in cultural understandings of color. These arise, in part, from different speech communities so that, as Siegfried Wyler explains: "English 'brown' does not correspond to French 'brun' or English 'blue' is different from the Italian 'blue' ('blu,' 'azzurro'), or quite drastically, the basic colour terms 'pink' and 'purple' are very specific English colour names which lexicologists find hard to define in bilingual dictionaries."[15] It is therefore feasible that a director's use of color for an intended effect might be perceived somewhat differently, depending on where the film was shown and who was its viewer/reviewer. As Bourdieu would put it, every work is "made twice, by the originator and by the beholder, or rather, by the society to which the beholder belongs."[16] Some languages, for example, have more or fewer color terms, such as Italians using *blu* for dark blue and *azzurro* for light and Hungarians using two basic terms for *red*. Of course, depending only on color terms can be arbitrary, and as Wyler notes, art historians and critics tend to use a rather limited number of generic terms to describe colors because it is surprisingly difficult to do justice to the infinite variety of ways in which artists use tints, shades, and even aberrant color mixtures.[17] In addition to using color names such as red or blue, art critics also show different degrees of sensitivity in making expressions about color such as "dark" or "light" and "warm" and "cold."[18]

In literature, colors can be referred to symbolically, or by using descriptions that in addition to designating an object's color "actively contribute to the creation of a picture in the reader's mind."[19] In this sense the critic can be creative in using language to describe the *effects* of colors, taking advantage of their "propensity for association" and "suggestiveness" so that additional meanings can be attached to standard color designations.[20] At their most narrow, the terms critics used to describe color in films might not even mention the colors but instead refer to them being "tasteful," "subtle," or "lurid," depending on the example.

One reviewer of *Horrors of the Black Museum* (UK, Arthur Crabtree, 1959) commented on its blood effects by likening their redness to ketchup: "The highlights, served with lashings of tomato ketchup, stretch credulity to near breaking point."[21] This is in keeping with the critical dismissal of horror films as antirealist, "lowbrow," and tasteless. By contrast, *painterly* is often used as a positive indicator, demonstrating how some critics related film colors to art historical traditions and thereby investing the film in question with respectable "higherbrow" credentials. When Gavin Lambert reviewed René Clair's first color film, *Les Grandes Manoeuvres* (France, 1955), he described it as "a discreet, tasteful palette that evokes *salon* painters of the era."[22] The film, set in a French provincial garrison town just before the First World War, used muted colors except for red accents on military uniforms. Clair chose this palette so that he could "keep reality at a distance."[23] These two very different strategies for using color in an antirealist way—the horror film's ketchup effect seen to "stretch credulity," and Clair's approach used as a distancing effect—thus elicit responses that reflect each film's very different positioning as a cultural product and the degrees of "quality" with which they were invested.

The discussion of color films in *Sight and Sound* was encouraged by its regular reportage in the 1950s and 1960s of film festivals, particularly Cannes, Venice, and Edinburgh. During this period, festivals became crucial venues for the exhibition of foreign films, and prizewinners were virtually guaranteed international distribution. The impact of U.S. antitrust actions in the late 1940s and early 1950s against the major, vertically integrated Hollywood companies, and a shift in Hollywood's export market away from the United Kingdom and toward Italy, created a greater space for the exhibition of European, Japanese, and Indian foreign-language films in the United Kingdom beyond the festival circuit.[24] In July 1956, the *Kinematograph Weekly* reported that attitudes were changing toward films from abroad: "Today Italian and French offerings are no longer considered freaks.... Continentals have brought real money to the commercial box-office and also given British and American directors a lesson in artistry."[25] At the same time, the circulation of *Sight and Sound* increased as it became "a standard bearer for the new art cinema" with an emphasis on foreign art films.[26] Many of the films discussed were black and white, particularly following the success of *Roma città aperta/Rome, Open City* (Italy, Roberto Rossellini, 1945) and other Italian neorealist films. When color films such as *Il Gattopardo/The Leopard* (Italy, Luchino Visconti, 1963), *Les parapluies de Cherbourg/The Umbrellas of Cherbourg* (France, Jacques Demy, 1963), and *Il deserto rosso/Red Desert* (Italy, Michelangelo Antonioni, 1964) won prestigious festival prizes, attention was drawn to color as an expressive attribute. Penelope Houston, who edited *Sight and Sound* from 1956 to 1990, described the color in *Les parapluies de Cherbourg* as "some of the most carefully elegant colour design ever put on the screen," while the overt color experimentation in *Il deserto rosso* was appreciated as "the major unsettling element in a total landscape of disturbing strangeness," and was seen as being used to "dissolve order and confound expectation, to strike a series of dissonant chords or to construct a momentary visual harmony."[27] Antonioni's deliberate subversion of realistic colors and changing a set's color within the context of a sequence were identified by Houston as subjecting the audience "to a series of greater or lesser visual shocks."[28] The scene she referred to occurred toward the end of *Il deserto rosso* when the impressions of the character Giuliana are conveyed through color following a love scene when the room changes from beige to purple and pink.

When Houston and Gillet interviewed notable directors such as George Cukor, Nicholas Ray, and Joseph Losey, they were asked about color. Ray, for example, was recorded as being "deeply interested in colour, and the cinema's failure to exploit it imaginatively, to know how and what to select."[29] Perhaps inspired by this observation, when Houston saw the "modern romance" *Un homme et une femme/A Man and a Woman* (France, Claude Lelouch, 1966) at Cannes, she was responsive to the film's strategic deployment of a chromatically varied style of color, black-and-white, and sepia-toned shots in delineating the central couple's lifestyle and occupations, namely, a film script supervisor and a racing driver. To this end, Houston appreciated the "commercial" look of sequences that resembled contemporary advertising used for the widow and widower's Sunday trips to the seaside resort Deauville with their children. The embedding of a color "look" within the film's diegetic world was understood as an acceptable presentation of the glossy commercial values so derided in other contexts.[30] Houston's review of François Truffaut's first color film shot at Pinewood Studios, the dystopian *Fahrenheit 451* (UK, 1966), similarly appreciated the choice of an appropriate color style to reflect the film's world in which books are outlawed and adults behave like "docile children."[31] Her description of the film's striking use of "childish" primary colors captured something of their force when used in this context: "A very red, shiny fire-engine rocketing through a countryside of very green grass; the warm, glinting, nursery firerail brass of the firestation; the blocks of yellow, mahogany, pale blue in Montag's home. Outside silver birches soften the regimented landscape."[32] Color is thus integral to the depiction of a totalitarian world and the central character's attempts to resist oppression. While Houston's use of the word *childish* might normally have been taken as criticism, in this instance it was an appropriate way to describe the unusual primary color effect presented in *Fahrenheit 451*.

Taking a less open view of what color could bring to a film, Lindsay Anderson's responses to titles screened at film festivals tended not to highlight cases of overt "color consciousness" in positive terms. His descriptions reinforced his commitment to films that dealt with social and political issues, disliking the use of color "for its own sake," an opinion he expressed stridently in a report on advances in color prompted by his visit to Cannes in 1954, when he viewed no fewer than seven systems: Technicolor (US), Eastman Color, (US) Agfacolor (Germany), Sovcolor (Russia), Gevacolor (Belgium), Ferraniacolor (Italian), and

Cinephotocolor (Spanish).[33] He concluded that "Technicolor showed to less advantage," largely because "producers of a certain type of American film favour vulgarity of effect, in a deliberate attempt to cater for a low level of public taste."[34] Eastman Color was still relatively new as a cheaper stock, and Agfa and its derivatives were admired for their subtle rather than vivid colors. Anderson found the apparently decreasing number of black-and-white films "disturbing" and was concerned that color was too often substituted for style. In view of Anderson's own later use of color interspersed with black-and-white sequences in *The White Bus* (UK, 1967), *if...* (UK, 1968), and *O Lucky Man!* (UK, 1973), this might seem surprising. It is, however, the case that when discussing color in these films, he denied using it for symbolic intent, preferring audiences to see color instead as but one aspect of a film's overall "incitement to *thought*."[35] This denial of color's specific agency in bringing to cinema new impressions, techniques, and levels of intensity reflected his concerns that such effects might distract audiences from issue-based drama. When he reviewed the CinemaScope travelogue *Canzone di Lima/Empire of the Sun* (Italy, Enrico Gras and Mario Craveri, 1956), he thought that, although "magnificent," its use of Ferraniacolor was "ruined by persistent showmanship, without true feeling of concern for its subject."[36]

Another British filmmaker who discussed color in the pages of *Sight and Sound* was Tony Richardson, who directed *Tom Jones* (UK, 1963), a visually sumptuous, highly distinctive British color historical film. He described *Le carrosse d'or/The Golden Coach* (France/Italy, Jean Renoir, 1952), a film about an eighteenth-century French touring *commedia dell'arte* company, as "visually breathtaking," with color contrasts and decoration giving "the whole harmony an added strength and vibrancy."[37] The language used to describe these effects was quite specific in terms of techniques: "Renoir uses simple light settings, the interiors of pale and natural woods, the exteriors of mellowed plaster, and the costumes are in subdued violets, lemons, and blues."[38] The referencing of specific textures and materials featured particularly in reviews of Japanese historical films, but here Richardson uses his observations to foreground contrast and the interaction of colors with lighting, sets, and props: "Against these are set the bright scarlets, the sharp cobalts of the players," and how "in every shot there is some note off key—the decoration on a chair, the jewel on a cravat."[39] Writing about John Huston's *Moby Dick* (Technicolor, U.S., 1956), Richardson praised its "remarkable and original exploration" of grain and bleached-out effects. Richardson cited the exploration of a range of "cool" tones to give the film "an outstanding visual unity and beauty," although he considered less satisfying the "pure science fiction" vivid green glow used for the spectacular "St Elmo's fire" shot, which stands out as totally different from the film's otherwise desaturated palette.[40]

The critics' development of discourses during this period that favored "auteur" analysis led to some filmmakers being particularly associated with notable uses of color. Jean Renoir's first color film was *The River* (France, India, U.S., 1951),

FIGURE 11.1 Color contrast in *French Cancan* (Jean Renoir, 1954).

and he went on to direct a trilogy of musical comedies, *Le carrosse d'or/The Golden Coach*, *French Cancan* (France, Italy, 1954), and *Eléna et les hommes/Elena and Her Men* (France, Italy, 1956). Renoir reflected on how realism should not necessarily be pursued: "One has to retain the possibility of a transposition. One mustn't just copy, one mustn't imitate nature—luckily, colour processes aren't perfect and this copy of nature remains rather remote, so that in practice colour offers other means than black and white of effecting this transposition."[41] Catherine de la Roche had indeed noted this "transposition" approach when she reviewed *French Cancan*, noting its composition in "colour sequences rather than musical sequences."[42] Of the film's flamboyant opening featuring an Oriental dance in a fashionable variety hall, she noted "rich hues, black and white predominating," whereas for a sequence located in a "cheap dance hall," the colors were "lighter . . . brought here and there into relief by ink blue, and the range is simpler."[43] She also drew attention to how contrast is used in relation to the vivid costuming and presentation of the seductress character La Belle Abbesse (Maria Felix), who in one scene reclines on an opulent red and gold couch, colors that are especially striking since the other half of the frame is inflected with colder blue-gray tones (figure 11.1). One romantic scene is made up of pink shades to color roses, tree blossoms, fluttering lines of washing, and the dress worn by Nini (Françoise Arnoul). This "exquisite delicacy" was linked to the director's overall vision, as well as being an example of fine art direction by Max Douy and cinematography by Michel Kelber. The final Moulin Rouge sequence, which is notable for its stunning array of colors and sheer frenetic exuberance, was appreciated by de la Roche for how the dancers were accentuated by their brightly colored costumes in comparison with the tones of the set in the background. In this way the effects of color contrast emerge as a key attribute as a critic understands the impact of a fully "color-conscious" design.

Other key color films were identified by *Sight and Sound* critics. Russian films seen at festivals, as described in a report by director René Clair following a visit to Moscow in the mid-1950s, charted developments such as Sovcolor's ability to blend artificial light with sunlight when shooting exteriors. This represented a technical advance on Agfacolor from which the stock was derived.[44] *The Lesson in Life* (Yuli Raizman, 1955), for example, was identified by Clair as being "extraordinarily interesting" in terms of color and technique, with "sensational results" for exterior shots, made possible by the stock's rapid emulsion.[45] The filmmaker and critic Ivor Montagu appreciated Alexander Dovzhenko's *Michurin* (1948), his first color film, which exploited expressionist color contrast, such as by indicating a character's horror of death and loneliness through a black screen immediately following a normal color scene.[46] Films shown at festivals such as *Glinka* (Grigori Aleksandov, 1952) and *Sadko* (Aleksandr Ptushko, 1953) were noted for their "magnificent" color.[47] Lindsay Anderson's festival reports usually included references to new Russian films, and while "striking" color stood out for him in *The Forty-First* (Grigori Chukhrai, 1956), no further observations or specific details were offered, perhaps because of Anderson's overall reticence about color.[48]

Although color in many American films was dismissed by "higher-brow" critics as "gaudy" and "tasteless," some directors were credited with its creative deployment. Stanley Donen's films were well regarded in *Sight and Sound*, particularly the musicals *Funny Face* (1957) and *The Pajama Game* (Stanley Donen and George Abbott, 1957). *Funny Face* occasioned a detailed commentary by David Vaughan, who identified a striking sequence in which Fred Astaire photographs Audrey Hepburn at well-known tourist locations in Paris. The shots were shown in each phase of development, from negative to black-and-white positive, and then "with the addition of isolated or deliberately distorted colour."[49] Vaughan referenced the collaboration of the fashion photographer Richard Avedon with Ray June, the lighting cameraman, and Frank Bracht, the editor, in achieving "a sequence of extraordinary beauty and interest: the quality of light is often truly impressionist."[50] Vaughan also praised *The Pajama Game* for its "bold use of colour and neon fluorescent light."[51] Otto Preminger's *The Cardinal* (1963) was admired for Leon Shamroy's color cinematography in distinguishing different tonal sensibilities for depicting different locations, such as New England and Rome.[52] In this way, American films were not ignored, although they were clearly far from prioritized in terms of color commentary. Vincente Minnelli's Technicolor films were discussed by critics in *Sequence* and *Movie*.

But it was not until the 1970s, as auteurism became further entrenched, that the so-called lurid color values of Douglas Sirk's melodramas were positively reevaluated in publications, including *Oxford Opinion*, *Movie*, and Thomas Elsaesser's seminal article in *Monogram*.[53]

Japanese films received a fair amount of coverage in *Sight and Sound* when international film festivals screened titles associated with the Golden Age of the 1950s, including *Rashomon* (Akira Kurosawa, 1950) and *Ugetsu* (Kenji Mizoguichi, 1953). Donald Ritchie, an American writer who specialized in Japanese culture and cinema, reported on younger filmmakers who were coming into prominence at the beginning of the 1960s such as Kon Ichikawa, who directed *The Key* (1959), a contemporary Japanese "pink" film (a low-budget film with sexual content). Ritchie noted how its "muted" color created an atmosphere of "near-claustrophobic intensity," achieved through "that dark and keyholed and magnificently photographed house."[54] But it was a very different Japanese historical film that stood out as a marker of real significance in the greater appreciation of color by critics. More than any other foreign color film, *Jigokumon/Gate of Hell* (Kinugasa Teinosuke, 1953) received extremely favorable reviews, the majority of which pointed to color as a distinctive attribute from which other filmmakers could learn. As I have argued elsewhere, the film was an interesting case, since its reception was more positive abroad than with Japanese audiences and critics, and Kinugasa Teinosuke drew on both Japanese and Hollywood influences in his approach to color design.[55] *Sight and Sound* reproduced Danish filmmaker Carl Dreyer's extended article on *Jigokumon/Gate of Hell* in which he appreciated its careful color planning, use of warm and cold colors, and "profound simplification."[56]

Contemporary British reviewers in a wide range of publications also noted that the film's color was distinctive. Arthur Knight highlighted its emotional role, citing specific instances: "Fiery-red oranges dominate the opening scenes of chaos in the imperial palace, icy blue bathes the scene of the assassination—and when a soft yellow light breaks into it it suggests both the approaching tragedy and Kesa's purity. . . . Its delicacy, its subtlety provide an almost startling contrast to our Hollywood-conditioned concepts of colour in films."[57] *The Observer*'s film critic C. A. Lejeune noted its use of texture: "Every colour combination has its purpose, and the sense of texture, the changes of tone brought about by the use of gauze materials and translucent screens, the sudden glow or dimming of a lamp, are beauties that have to be seen to be appreciated" (figure 11.2).[58] It was as if the film's extraordinary color inspired critics to elevate their prose accordingly, mentioning specific colors, lighting, and textures more than in most other reviews of color films. While British critics admired the color in superlative descriptive terms, Japanese critics referred to specific knowledge of the film's intermedial connections, some of which explain the approach to color as related to national aesthetic traditions. The acting style, for example,

FIGURE 11.2 Texture and color in *Gate of Hell* (Kinugasa Teinosuke, 1953).

contributed to the prioritization of a color design that had a sense of depth, subtlety, and affect. A contemporary Japanese critic noted that the success of *Jigokumon/Gate of Hell* owes much to the Noh drama and Kabuki stage in the treatment of themes. The same critic, however, noted a negative aspect to this exhibition of exoticism, ritual, and the "trappings and symbols of old Japan."[59] Other Japanese critics shared this view, arguing that if Japanese films were to conquer overseas markets, they would have to "present new Japan and modern life."[60] The Western critics' concentration on exoticism was to some extent expressive of Orientalist sensibilities in which the East is evoked as a vibrant, exotic "other" as opposed to the more restrained chromatic preferences that dominated Western aesthetic taste cultures.[61]

Discussions of *Jigokumon/Gate of Hell* were part of a longer process of critical evaluation around what was considered to be pleasing, aesthetically distinctive color. While an orientation toward realism and "unobtrusive" color continued to influence critics such as Lindsay Anderson, and British directors such as Ken Loach were wary of color's tendency to "prettify" an image, at the same time some critics acknowledged and celebrated the power of color. For writers in *Sight and Sound* such as Penelope Houston and Tony Richardson, observing color trends invited discussion of mise-en-scène, as well as the collaborative contexts required to stage innovative color designs. Within the field of film criticism, color beckoned the creation of "a new position beyond the positions presently occupied."[62] As critics embraced it, their terminology expanded somewhat so that specific colors, textures, and aspects such as the interaction of color with lighting and film stock were taken into account. While the prevalent interest in auteurism resulted in some key directors being asked about color, it was rarer for a film to be discussed according to different cultural registers, a notable case being *Jigokumon/Gate of Hell*. Some critics clearly used well-known theoretical categories such as "warm" or "cold" colors, contrast, hue, and saturation. Yet they tended to shy away from detailed descriptions, often relying instead on prose that conveyed the *effects* of colors, using effusive language such as "visually breathtaking" or "a discreet, tasteful palette." Occasionally, an area such as the relation between color and class might be alluded to, as with Gavin Lambert's review of *Senso* (Italy, Luchino Visconti, 1954) that described the color and decoration as displaying "high aristocratic taste" that made "a curious contrast with the film's evident revolutionary sympathies."[63]

The relative novelty of color for much of the period brought new dimensions to topics such as the impact of stock and different release prints. When *Il Gattopardo/The Leopard*, a film shot on Eastman Color stock in Technirama, was first released, the French and Italian prints were processed by Technicolor, whose release prints were produced from matrices made directly from the original negative. But when Fox released prints in CinemaScope, they were processed by its subsidiary De Luxe Laboratories using a "dupe" negative. This resulted in a loss of color fidelity and definition, causing most of the interiors to "suffer from a bluish haze" that appeared "crude," as noted in *Sight and Sound*.[64] Similar examples of variable exhibition contexts created some awareness of color films' more vulnerable position in global markets. In the 1970s, when figures such as Martin Scorsese drew attention to the propensity for Eastman Color prints to fade, color films faced further problems in being presented to best advantage.

Critics played an important role in raising consciousness about color films during the global process of adoption across a range of popular, new wave, art, and postcolonial cinemas of the era. As global films were disseminated more widely, British directors such as Tony Richardson, Nicolas Roeg, Joseph Losey, David Lean, Ken Russell, Peter Watkins, and Derek Jarman were inspired to use color assertively to innovate genres, including historical/period films, fantasy and horror, and experimental cinema. "Europhile" aesthetic sensibilities influenced films such as *Joanna* (Michael Sarne, 1968), *Girl on a Motorcycle* (Jack Cardiff, 1966), and *Don't Look Now*.[65] Antonioni directed *Blow Up* (1966) in Britain, and Nicolas Roeg worked as cinematographer on François Truffaut's *Fahrenheit 451* (1966), films that are particularly notable for color. Even if finding the most appropriate language to describe color in films could still be elusive and challenging, critics' discussions undoubtedly enabled global frames of reference to be more visible, diverse, and accessible to color-conscious audiences and filmmakers.

Notes

1   Sarah Street, *Colour Films in Britain: The Negotiation of Innovation, 1950–55* (London: Palgrave Macmillan/British Film Institute, 2012), 258.

2   Dudley Andrew, "The Post-war Struggle for Color," *Cinema Journal* 18, no. 2 (1979): 47.

3   Sarah Street, Keith M. Johnston, Paul Frith, and Carolyn Rickards, *Colour Films in Britain: The Eastmancolor Revolution* (London: British Film Institute/Bloomsbury, 2021).

4   Tony Garnett, "The Wrong Kind of Bird," *The Independent*, October 1, 1999, 14.

5   Mattias Frey, "The Critical Question," *Screen* 54, no. 2 (2013): 206.

6   Pierre Bourdieu, *Distinction* (London: Routledge, 1984); Pierre Bourdieu, *The Field of Cultural Production* (Cambridge: Polity Press, 1993).

7   For useful applications of Bourdieu in relation to art cinema, see Barbara Wilinsky, *Sure Seaters: The Emergence of Art House Cinema* (Minneapolis: University of Minnesota Press, 2001); and Margaret O'Brien, "The Rise of Art Cinema in Postwar Film Culture: The Exhibition, Distribution, and Reception of Foreign Language Films in Britain 1945–68" (PhD diss., University of London, 2018).

8   John Ellis, "The Quality Film Adventure: British Critics and the Cinema, 1942–48," *Screen* 19, no. 3 (1978): 9–49.

9   Julian Petley, "The Lost Continent," in *All Our Yesterdays: 90 Years of British Cinema*, ed. Charles Barr (London: British Film Institute, 1986), 98–119.

10 Leila Wimmer, *Cross-Channel Perspectives: The French Reception of British Cinema* (Bern: Peter Lang, 2009), 189.

11 Frey, "Critical Question," 209.

12 Carl Dreyer, "Thoughts on My Craft," *Sight and Sound* 25, no. 3 (Winter 1955–1956): 128–129; Sergei Eisenstein, "Writings on Colour and Colour Theory," *Sight and Sound* 30, no. 2 (Spring 1961): 84–86, 102.

13 Guy Austin, ed., *New Uses of Bourdieu for Film and Media Studies* (New York: Berghahn Books, 2016), 8.

14 Bourdieu, *Field of Cultural Production*, 223.

15 Siegfried Wyler, *Colour and Language: Colour Terms in English* (Tübingen: Gunter Narr Verlag, 1992), 10.

16 Bourdieu, *Field of Cultural Production*, 224.

17 Bourdieu, 96–97.

18 John Gage, *Colour and Meaning: Art, Science and Symbolism* (London: Thames and Hudson, 1999), 22–23.

19 Gage, 163–164.

20 Siegfried Wyler, *Colour Terms in the Crowd: Colour Terms in Use* (Tübingen: Gunter Narr Verlag, 2006), 104–105.

21 Josh Billings, "Horrors of the Black Museum," *Kinematograph Weekly* 504, no. 2695 (April 16, 1959): 15.

22 Gavin Lambert, review of *Les Grandes Manoeuvres*, *Sight and Sound* 25, no. 3 (Winter 1955–1956): 146.

23 Pierre Billard, *Le mystère René Clair* (Paris: Plon, 1998), 356.

24 Christopher Wagstaff, "Italian Genre Films in the World Market," in *Hollywood and Europe: Economics, Culture, National Identity, 1945–95*, ed. Geoffrey Nowell Smith (London: British Film Institute, 1998), 74–75.

25 Josh Billings, "Look Out for Likely Prospects," *Kinematograph Weekly* 471, no. 2551 (July 5, 1956): 28.

26 O'Brien, "Rise of Art Cinema," 62.

27 Penelope Houston, Cannes report, *Sight and Sound* 33, no. 3 (Summer 1964): 120; Penelope Houston, review of *Il deserto rosso*, *Sight and Sound* 34, no. 2 (Spring 1965): 80–81.

28 Houston, review of *Il deserto rosso*, 1965.

29 Penelope Houston and John Gillet, "Conversations with Nicholas Ray and Joseph Losey," *Sight and Sound* 30, no. 4 (Autumn 1961): 183.

30 Penelope Houston, Cannes report, *Sight and Sound* 35, no. 3 (Summer 1966): 126.

31 Penelope Houston, review of *Fahrenheit 451*, *Sight and Sound* 36, no. 1 (Winter 1966–1967): 42.

32 Houston, 42.

33 Lindsay Anderson, Cannes report, *Sight and Sound* 24, no. 1 (Summer 1954): 6.

34 Anderson, 6.

35 Lindsay Anderson and David Sherwin, *if. . .* (London: Lorimer Publishing, 1969), 10.

36 Lindsay Anderson, report on Venice Film Festival, *Sight and Sound* 26, no. 2 (Autumn 1956): 86.

37 Tony Richardson, review of *The Golden Coach*, *Sight and Sound* 23, no. 4 (Spring 1954): 199.

38 Richardson, 199.

39 Richardson, 199.

40 Tony Richardson, review of *Moby Dick*, *Sight and Sound* 26, no. 3 (Winter 1956–1957): 151–152.

41 Jean Renoir interview, *Sight and Sound* 37, no. 2 (Spring 1968): 58–59.

42 Catherine de la Roche, review of *French Cancan*, *Sight and Sound* 25, no. 2 (Autumn 1955): 85.

43 de la Roche, 85.

44 "René Clair in Moscow," *Sight and Sound* 25, no. 3 (Winter 1955–1956): 130–131.

45 "René Clair in Moscow," 130–131.

46 Ivor Montagu, "Dovzhenko: Poet of Life Eternal," *Sight and Sound* 27, no. 1 (Summer 1957): 48.

47 J. A. Wilson referenced *Glinka* in his report on the Venice Film Festival, and Gavin Lambert referenced *Sadko* in his report on the Venice Film Festival; *Sight and Sound* 23, no. 2 (Autumn 1953): 58–59.

48 Lindsay Anderson, report on Cannes, *Sight and Sound* 27, no. 1 (Summer 1957): 28.

49 David Vaughan, review of *Funny Face*, *Sight and Sound* 27, no. 1 (Summer 1957): 40.

50 Vaughn, 40.

51 David Vaughan, review of *The Pajama Game*, *Sight and Sound* 27, no. 3 (Winter 1957–1958): 148.

52 Richard Roud, review of *The Cardinal*, *Sight and Sound* 33, no. 1 (Winter 1963–1964): 35.

53 Thomas Elsaesser, "Tales of Sound and Fury: Observations on the Family Melodrama," *Monogram* 4 (1975): 1–15.

54 Donald Ritchie, report on Japan, *Sight and Sound* 29, no. 2 (Spring 1960): 78–79.

55 Sarah Street, "The Monopack Revolution, Global Cinema and *Jigokumon/Gate of Hell* (Kinugasa Teinosuke, 1953)," *Open Screens* 1, no. 1 (2018), http://doi.org/10.16995/os.2.

56 Dreyer, "Thoughts on My Craft," 128.

57 Arthur Knight, "Japan's Film Revolution," *Saturday Review*, December 26, 1959.

58 C. A. Lejeune, review in *The Observer*, June 6, 1954.

59 Sakanishi Sjio, "A Dilemma of Japanese Film World," *Japan Quarterly* 2, no. 2 (1955): 219.

60 Sjio, 219.

61 Edward Said, *Orientalism* (New York: Pantheon Books, 1978).

62 Bourdieu, *Field of Cultural Production*, 106.

63 Gavin Lambert, report on Venice Film Festival, *Sight and Sound* 24, no. 2 (Autumn 1954): 58.

64 Brenda Davies, "Can the Leopard . . . ," *Sight and Sound* 33, no. 2 (Spring 1964): 99.

65 Street et al., *Colour Films in Britain*, 310.

12

All about Landscape

The Shift to Color in Australian
Film at Midcentury

KATHRYN MILLARD AND

STEFAN SOLOMON

This chapter explores the shift toward "natural color" in Australian film in the mid-twentieth century as the global industry and audiences embraced color film as a dominant aesthetic choice. Features shot in natural color arrived relatively late in Australia in comparison with many other countries; no feature films were shot in natural color in Australia prior to 1950. From the late 1940s onward, color wars between various North American and European companies played out on Australia's shores primarily in the realm of the feature film. To some, Australia was simply an exotic backdrop for runaway productions. Yet local filmmakers had long sought to project the distinctive hues of their landscape onto the big screen. Significantly, in the late 1940s, Australia—along with other former British colonies—began to more strongly assert a national identity. Filmmakers increasingly drew on a color palette derived from key moments in Australian painting to project this new identity. Location-based films led the way. While the celebrated new wave of the 1970s looked to historical palettes for inspiration, documentary and experimental filmmakers engaged with the work of contemporary artists. Drawing on case studies from documentary, features, and experimental films produced between the late 1940s and the 1970s, this chapter examines the starring role of the landscape in the new Australian color cinema.

Three features—*Kangaroo*, *The Queen in Australia*, and *Jedda*—all made some claim to being Australia's first film shot in "natural color."[1] *Kangaroo* (1952) was the earliest, albeit with Americans in the key creative roles and leading the cast. The film was edited and postproduced in Los Angeles under the supervision of the producer Darryl Zanuck. *The Queen in Australia* (1954), made with considerable input from British filmmakers utilizing Ferraniacolor and postproduced in London, was Australia's first "natural color" feature-length documentary. Shot on Gevacolor and processed in London, *Jedda* (1955) was the first "natural color" feature conceived of and produced by Australians, who starred both behind and in front of the camera. Of course, as in many fields involving new technologies and innovation imperatives, identifying a "first" can be difficult, since the criteria can be hazy. What is clear, however, is that these films sprang from a longer-term quest to capture and project Australia's distinctive colors on the big screen, and many involved collaboration beyond national borders.

Motion picture photography in color, which took many years and the efforts of hundreds of people to develop, was often referred to as "natural color" or photographic color and, at least partly, was associated with realism. In Australia, the term *natural color* was used longer than in many other parts of the world and was associated with landscape. Technicolor, which dominated global color production from the 1920s to the 1950s, was promoted as providing the finest natural color pictures ever produced. Given Australia's relatively small population, its distance from processing laboratories in the United States and Britain, and its particular climatic conditions, the challenges of shooting in color were substantial. Technicolor was considered too expensive for regular use in Australia. Consequently, in the 1930s, with minimal resources, two Australian cinematographers devised film stocks designed to be reliable and inexpensive alternatives. Commonwealth Film Laboratories invented a 35mm color process, Mal-com Colour, named after the cameraman George Malcolm, in 1937. A bipack process, Mal-com Colour was intended to be used for Australian color features. In fact, due to its cost, its use was restricted to cinema advertisements. Arthur Higgins invented Solarchrome, a bipack color film system also designed as an alternative to Technicolor.[2] One reviewer claimed that its colors were comparable to those in American movies, but Solarchrome found limited uses in advertising and documentary.[3] In the Solarchrome films we have viewed, warm tones—lemon, gold, orange, chestnut, and maroon—are especially prominent, as if Australians were living in an endless late summer. Kodachrome, intended primarily for amateur use, was used by Australian documentary filmmakers from the 1940s onward—notably, by the ethnologist and filmmaker Charles Mountford on documentaries, including *Tjurunga* (1946) and *Walkabout* (1946), and on Mountford's collaboration with Lee Robinson on *Namatjira the Painter* (1947), discussed later in this chapter.

In the postwar era, many more viable competitors to Technicolor emerged internationally due to industrial secrets obtained by the Allies as part of the spoils of war. In 1945, Nathan Golden led a delegation to Germany to interrogate color scientists being held in U.S. custody. He reported that Agfa color film was processed like black-and-white film and required less light. Compared with Technicolor, its colors were pastel-like. Within two years, the American-based Ansco developed a fast color film based on Agfa's system.[4] In Europe, too, competition was on the way. New processes such as the Belgian Gevacolor and the Italian Ferraniacolor were variants of the Agfacolor process. While some of these stocks were destined for feature film production, documentary was the immediate beneficiary of color film in Australia.

Painting the Outback with Albert Namatjira

One notable early example in this vein is *Namatjira the Painter,* which was shot on 16mm in Kodachrome in 1947 and screened for several years before being revised for further release in 1974 (figure 12.1). A documentary about the Indigenous landscape painter Albert Namatjira, the film was shot around the Hermannsburg Lutheran Mission near Alice Springs (Mparntwe) in the Northern Territory and was funded by the Australian Film Board, operating then under the auspices of the Department of Information. It shows the artist at work, with

FIGURE 12.1 *Namatjira the Painter* (Lee Robinson, 1947/1974).

his family, and in conversation with one of his champions, the Victorian artist Rex Battarbee. After visiting the mission in the early 1930s, Battarbee introduced Namatjira to the techniques of watercolor painting and organized the exhibition of the younger artist's work in Melbourne. Namatjira's landscape paintings from this period demonstrated an increasing proliferation of detail coupled with a command of extensive spaces.[5]

The documentary exploring Namatjira's career was an effort involving Charles Mountford, the cinematographer Axel Poignant, and Lee Robinson, a young director who later experimented with Gevacolor in his short documentary *Switch on Bigga* (1953). While the film initially played before selected screenings of *The Outlaw* (Howard Hughes, 1943), the inclusion of footage of a particular corroborree (a sacred Aboriginal dance ceremony) of the Arrernte people meant that it was later pulled from circulation.[6] It was three decades before the new version was released. Viewed in the 1970s, the film, which focuses on the transitions and disjunctions between pre- and postcolonial life, takes on a more melancholy tone. A voice-over tells us that, after a period of imprisonment and suffering from pneumonia, Namatjira died in 1959. Haunted by the artist's death, *Namatjira the Painter* registers the clashes of Arrernte and colonial ways of life. Practices once pitched as benevolent transfers of cultural knowledge are also expressed as a series of violent historical ruptures. The film creates a continuum that links Indigenous rock paintings to Namatjira's early pyrographic works—as seen in a mulga wood plaque of two emus running, made specifically for the film—and then to the watercolor landscapes that the artist would develop as his trademark.[7] Namatjira began his work with watercolors under the influence of Battarbee, and we are told by the (condescending) voice-over that it was his handling of color that justified Battarbee's tuition.

There is another link between Namatjira's watercolors and the color of the film in their depictions of the Central Australian landscape. One of the key effects that Namatjira utilized to add intensity to his colors was "luminosity." Theoretically, this is achieved when "light passes through transparent pigment particles, is reflected by the white paper, and passes back through the pigment particles a second time—as if through a stained glass window."[8] Kodachrome, a stock renowned for its well-defined hues, color accuracy, and dark-storage longevity, would seem well suited to accentuate Namatjira's radiant displays of color.

The film and its vivid palette were well received internationally. *Namatjira the Painter* screened at the Edinburgh International Festival in 1949, and the rights were sold to MGM for screenings in London. When the film was transferred to 35mm for domestic release, however, the color palette appeared degraded. In the process, wrote one Australian critic, "it has lost some of the brilliance and sharpness of the original photography."[9] The once lustrous watercolors now lend a desaturated and ghostly quality to the desert, rocks, and trees that populate Namatjira's paintings. In addition, the color of the film image is increasingly washed out as the horizon recedes, until the mountains in the background appear as if matte paintings or distant rear projection. Due to the optical phenomenon known as the Rayleigh scattering effect, the blues of the nearby MacDonnell Ranges (Tjoritja) are produced for the naked eye through a combination of naturally occurring ambient eucalyptus oils, dust and water vapor, and the short wavelengths of light that appear blue. The nebulous quality of the watercolors, as filtered through the equally ill-defined hues of the transfer, only redoubles the perception of these mountains as a seemingly composited plane on a more uniformly colored landscape.

Namatjira learned to take and develop his own black-and-white photographs in the late 1930s, and his practice as a painter was in part informed by his photographs of the region. As Lee Robinson suggested: "He framed the view with his hands like a modern cameraman—he squared it off—decided . . . how high he would take his sky—and from where he would take his foreground. Once he had that he could go somewhere else and paint it."[10] Namatjira's watercolors, then, are modeled at least in part on black-and-white photography.

The photographic index was instrumental in demonstrating the realism of color in the paintings of the region. In the postwar years, Battarbee began experimenting with color photography and reportedly made use of the images he captured to "convince the remaining sceptics who questioned the vivid colours in his paintings."[11] Robinson's film provided evidence of the fidelity of Namatjira's paintings to the appearance of Arrernte land. "Picture by picture," wrote one reviewer, "the Namatjira water-colors back up the film, ascribed to Axel Poignant and vice versa; either the Northern Territory is those colors, those reds and pinks and blues unseen anywhere else on earth, or the aboriginal [sic] artist and the Australian photographer are both liars."[12] Peering over Namatjira's shoulder, we watch pencil drawing turn to finished watercolor. As the camera pans up, we see the landscape rise in the background, mirroring the image captured by the artist on his canvas. Howsoever faded they might now be, "the rich reds, the deep violet-blues, the golden-yellows" were apparently once evident in both painting and film image.[13] From midcentury onward, an emerging national cinema would mobilize the "naturalness" of color as a bid for authenticity.

The Red Desert

While Robinson was shooting *Namatjira the Painter*, the race was on to make Australia's first feature-length film in "natural color." Technicolor's response to the threat from European competitors was swift. It ramped up activity, keen to exploit its market domination while it still could. Twentieth Century-Fox sent crews around the world to produce color features in "exotic" locations. Many of these films depicted frontier wars. Early in 1950, Fox announced that its upcoming feature, eventually titled *Kangaroo*, would be in Technicolor (figure 12.2).[14] The original plan was to shoot in northern New South Wales or

FIGURE 12.2 *Kangaroo* (Lewis Milestone, 1952).

Queensland, but this was problematic because both states were experiencing heavier than usual rainfall. Attention turned to South Australia.

That same year, Charles Chauvel and his wife and filmmaking collaborator, Elsa Chauvel, announced they would be moving their cameras to the outback to film what would come to be titled *Jedda*. America had more than its fair share of stars. For Australians, the landscape deserved star billing, and especially in color. Inspired by a yearlong trek across the country, the Chauvels prepared to make Australia's first all-color, all-Australian feature.[15] The duo initially looked to the United States for financial backing and color processing. In something of a David and Goliath story, the Chauvels' film *The Northern Territory Story* (aka *Jedda*) and Fox's *Kangaroo* slugged it out for the title of "Australia's first natural color feature."

Leveraging profits from exhibiting pictures in Australia during the Second World War, Twentieth Century-Fox secured generous support from both the Australian Commonwealth and South Australia governments and relocated its production to Port Augusta and the Lower Flinders Ranges in South Australia. Penned in Hollywood and transposed to Australia, *Kangaroo* was set around 1900, during one of the worst droughts since European settlement commenced at the end of the eighteenth century. In the storyline of postwar Australia, *Kangaroo* would break the nation's feature filmmaking drought. It is estimated that only twenty feature films were produced in Australia in the 1940s, with British and American companies the key investors. Most projects initiated by

Australian filmmakers struggled with extremely low budgets and limited distribution. Local and international filmmakers alike continued to express a strong desire to depict the antipodes in color. Carl Kayser—the cameraman on *The Overlanders* (1946)—expressed his regret that the film was shot in black and white. Amazed by the ever-changing hues of the Australian interior, Kayser longed to shoot the film in Technicolor.

On the outskirts of Sydney, men load bulky film lights into the back of a truck—the Technicolor process required large quantities of illumination to create its fabled silhouettes and sunsets. Trucks emblazoned with the Twentieth Century-Fox logo prepare to depart. As the convoy sets off, dust rises from the road. This image is from newsreel footage depicting the *Kangaroo* crew's epic journey across the interior of the continent as an advance party traveled from Sydney to Port Augusta. A film colony was established on the edge of town—one of the most desolate locations imaginable. The state premier visited and named this Hollywood Down Under Zanuckville. It was hoped that this first "natural color" feature would put Australia's colors on the world screen and attract tourists and migrants in great numbers.

If there is a single color associated with *Kangaroo*'s exteriors, it is red. Red earth. Red dust. Red haze. The country around Port Augusta and the Lower Flinders Ranges was notorious for its dust storms, or "whirly-whirlies." Early settlers reported they "could see nothing before us but a great wall of dust which seemed to reach from earth to heaven."[16] Later accounts echoed that view: "The gloom was eerie. People walked about in a red twilight."[17] Charles Clarke, the Hollywood-based director of photography, observed that, on location, dust was an unavoidable fact of life. There was no escaping it. His solution was to incorporate into *Kangaroo*'s pictorial design herds of cattle or mobs of kangaroos shot through clouds of deliberately created dust.[18]

The most striking scenes in *Kangaroo* are undoubtedly those that feature Aboriginal performers reenacting a corroboree. Charles Mountford, along with the production's research adviser, Colin Simpson, worked with the Indigenous cast to adapt such ceremonies and "magic songs" for the screen. Ceremonies that did not belong to this specific country were added for dramatic effect and to meet studio head Darryl Zanuck's constant demands for "local color."[19] A contingent of more than a hundred Aboriginal performers—mostly men from Ooldea Mission—were provided by the South Australian government. They usually wore Western-style clothing. The red garments they wore on camera were a response to the dictates of the Hays Code assessors. Nudity on-screen was not permissible, and red, of course, registered well on Technicolor.

Generations of artists and photographers have produced artworks depicting the area around the Flinders Ranges where *Kangaroo* was shot—so much so that the area is known as artists' country. Aboriginal Australians, keepers of the oldest continuing culture on earth, have made pilgrimages to the region for more than 40,000 years to source highly valued red ochre for important ceremonies. In the 1930s, the German-born artist Hans Heysen traveled to the region to learn how to paint a landscape he described as vast and ancient with an intensity of light: "Reds, ochres and chocolates are the dominating color schemes and the blue hills are the keynote."[20]

There is a story—possibly apocryphal—that during the shoot for *Kangaroo*, the city of Adelaide ran out of green paint. The production had bought up all available supplies to transform the subtle, grayer hues of the Australian bush into the brighter, more tropical-looking greens that would register better on Technicolor. Whatever the truth of that story, the color makeover failed. Despite a relentless publicity campaign, *Kangaroo* was dismissed by critics and spurned by audiences. The producers were asked to remove "The Australian Story" from the title.

The Colors of Colonialism

Before *Jedda* made it to the screen in 1955, there was another contender for the title of Australia's first "natural color feature." *The Queen in Australia*, produced by the Commonwealth Film Unit, portrayed a youthful Queen Elizabeth II on her first visit to the antipodes. The filmmakers trained their lenses and microphones on Her Majesty as she traveled the length and breadth of the country. Prime Minister Robert Menzies committed the Commonwealth Film Unit to completing the film by April 1954, just two months after the royal visit. It was an ambitious schedule. Color film of the era was especially sensitive to heat, and, as with *Kangaroo*, the logistical challenges were considerable. Since there were still no facilities for processing 35mm color footage in Australia, the exposed negative was placed in refrigerated containers ready to travel overseas.[21] *The Queen in Australia* was shot using the Italian-devised Ferraniacolor, with footage flown to Denham Laboratories in London for processing, editing, and postproduction.[22]

The Queen in Australia was released in cinemas in Australia and in other British Commonwealth countries as well as in the United States, and it was seen by many as an overseas advertisement for Australia. The documentary was lauded for its "superb colour,"[23] as well as the way it captured the "loneliness and heat-bleached colour of the Australian desert."[24] Royal tours, of course, had been one of the key subjects for natural color film stocks since the earliest days of cinema, as with Kinemacolor's association with royalty in Britain. The *New York Times*, while describing the documentary as rather uninspired, complimented its color palette: "The glimpses of cities, villages and the outback made fitting subjects for the Italian Ferraniacolor process. . . . Its panchromatic hues vary in shading from pastel to vivid."[25] British Pathé's *Welcome the Queen* (Howard Thomas, 1954), documenting the same royal tour via Eastman Color, makes a useful comparison. It registers a far more restricted palette, skewed toward blue.

In Australia, color and landscape remained an ongoing emphasis in documentary and feature drama production at midcentury.[26] When *Jedda*—Australia's first feature-length production using Gevacolor—finally did make it into production, it also faced daunting financial and logistical obstacles. As the unit moved from one remote location to another, exposed cans of film were packed in ice and stored in caves to prevent heat damage. Footage was sent to London for processing, and there were long delays in receiving rushes' reports.[27]

Watching the restored version of *Jedda*, one's eyes are initially drawn to reds: its opening titles, key items of clothing, the distinctive earth and rock formations of central and northern Australia. (Of course, this film, like many others, has been through successive restorations as technologies and viewing platforms have changed.) But just as red is the afterimage of green, the reverse is also true. As the film's story unfolds, a remarkable range of greens also registers on the Gevacolor stock, from the gray-green and sage green of eucalypts to the lustrous greens of tree ferns and water-lily pads.

Technicolor was not the only color system to arrive late in Australia. Although Kodak introduced Eastman Color negative internationally in 1950, it was not widely used in Australia until well into the 1960s. Anecdotal evidence from cinematographers suggests that stock availability was hampered by customs controls and distance. Moreover, cinematographers battled to get sufficient rolls of film from a single batch to maintain consistency of picture quality.[28] Kodak was seen as treating Australia as a dumping ground for old film stock. It was not until 1967 that the first Eastman Color feature was processed in Australia: *Journey Out of Darkness*, an attempt to tell a contemporary story about white Australia's troubled relationship with its First Nations people. The film's reception was marred by the casting of non-Indigenous actors and the use of blackface. Just as Technicolor and other old color film stocks and systems lived on in Australia long after their retirement elsewhere, so did blackface.

Sydney in Sunlight

Outside of feature film production, the affordances of color stock from the 1960s onward were explored in different ways, with urban as well as rural landscapes reflected in nonnarrative color films of the period. At the very beginning of his career in 1964, the avant-garde German émigré filmmaker Paul Winkler devised a theory of "chromatic scales" that matched emotions with particular hues and framed his portraits of iconic Sydney locations.[29] Elsewhere, the Melbourne filmmakers Arthur and Corinne Cantrill pursued experiments in two- and three-color separation processes from the mid-1970s onward, shooting numerous locations in New South Wales and Victoria using different color filters.[30] The experimental documentary *Sunshine City* (1973), by Albie Thoms, takes the Sydney landscape as its point of departure. Thoms was a member of the Ubu Films group, an avant-garde collective of filmmakers and artists who met at the

University of Sydney. The group were mostly known for their production of countercultural shorts—made in the tradition of Alfred Jarry's satirical proto-modernist play *Ubu Roi* (1896), after which they were named—and for their experimental works involving scratching, puncturing, and painting the film-strip. Ubu Films had a reputation as the purveyors of pioneering psychedelic light shows across the Sydney rock scene in the 1960s, a practice that also worked its way into their films.

Thoms expanded on these approaches in his film *Sunshine City*, which he saw as "a film of the artist turning out on the consciousness of his city."[31] Sydney was captured on film using the fast daytime stock Ektachrome, which was designed for use in home movies and allowed for shooting with minimal natural light. Even during the day, shadows abound in the film's mostly exterior shots, and people and places seem to merge. The experience of color in the film is also deter-mined to a large extent by its fascination with light, with the sunshine of the title dictating the colors we see. A title card at the beginning reads: "This trav-elog of my home town is a diary of the flickerings of my consciousness over two years." These "flickerings" are meant in a quite literal sense, since the film alter-nates between full color images of the city and its inhabitants and clear leader in varying patterns according to Thoms's theory of the "three frame unit." In search of a grammar of film, and directly opposing Christian Metz's theory that the shot is the single smallest unit in cinema, Thoms proposed three successive frames as "the basic unit of film."[32]

In *Sunshine City*, Thoms puts his theory into practice, inserting a full frame of light between single frame shots, three frames of light between three frame shots, and so on. We view Sydney as if through a thaumatrope, a proto-cinematic toy that oscillated between two separate images and suggested their combination. Here in the rapid frames of light, we see retinal afterimages of dif-ferent parts of the city, from Palm Beach in the north to Maroubra in the south, and Cammeray and the city center in between. These alternations between detailed colorful images of people and places, and squares of pure light only abate during the film's extended interview sequences, in which Thoms inter-views friends.

One of his final interviewees is the painter Brett Whiteley, who explains his artistic practice seated in front of one of his studies of Vincent van Gogh. Part of Whiteley's connection to the Dutch Postimpressionist is through color: specifically, the yellow of the South of France that for Whiteley also evokes the sunshine of his own city. "Yellow's the color of madness," he tells Thoms, specu-lating about the effects on van Gogh of living in a room painted yellow for six months. This was the color that lent its name to the "Yellow House" in Potts Point, inhabited then by artists like Whiteley and Martin Sharp, along with members of the Ubu Films group, and used as an exhibition space.

Whiteley also considers the connections of yellow to light and to God, a line of thought in sympathy with the most explicit formal innovation of the film: the anxiety-inducing flicker of the blinding three-frame unit. The most insightful connection of the film to the color yellow comes from Ubu Films member Gary Shead, who considered this association by way of Whiteley's famous wall-length collage, *Alchemy* (1973), a monumental work that was being completed at the same time that Thoms was finishing his film. Whiteley described *Alchemy* as a kind of mental landscape, a work about his own "inner paddock." For Shead, attending to the color scheme of *Alchemy* allows us to see it as a scenario for *Sunshine City*. The film follows the spatial narrative of the painting but also evokes through sunlight and color the changing appearance of Sydney over the course of a day. The colors of the film thus proceed in line with the "seven stages in the production of gold": from the black that heralds the first light of morning, an "indication that the experiment is going well"; to the purification of white as seen in the flickers of the three-frame unit; to the red of "ecstasy and revolution"; to the final golden sunset on Sydney Harbour.[33]

Sunshine City transmutes the darker tones of the Sydney cityscape by virtue of its use of Ektachrome; as a result, the geographic movements through the metropolis are also movements through the color spectrum, from the deep blues of the dark before the dawn, to the dazzling yellows of the full sun and its glare reflected on the harbor.

Unsettled Histories

A brilliant sun blazes in a blue sky above a panorama of red dirt, perhaps the quintessential Australian cinematic image, according to the film critic Sandra Hall. This is the opening of *Sunday Too Far Away* (Ken Hannam, 1975), the first feature film produced by the South Australian Film Corporation and one of the forerunners of the Australian "New Wave" of the 1970s. Shot in the far north of South Australia near the *Kangaroo* locations, the film was set in the mid-1950s during a shearers' strike. Like the Australian Impressionist painters of the 1890s, filmmakers of the 1970s sought to evoke the specific colors, light, and atmospheres of the antipodes. The scriptwriter John Dingwall drew attention to the "red earth road," the "shimmer of heat rising from the plain," and a "puff of dust" moving in the distance.[34] A new set of national myths was being authored—this time with celluloid and chromogenic dyes rather than canvas and paint.

As the nineteenth century ended, Australian landscapes and narratives were given a new significance and status. In the lead-up to Federation in 1901, Australians—the majority of whom were urban dwellers—became interested in depictions of their own environment. The art historian Ann Galbally writes that Australians "began to see merit in lyrical depictions of figures and scenes from their own immediate past . . . small settlers' farms being carved out of the wilderness."[35] The Australian Impressionists were painters who worked together at artists' camps around Melbourne and Sydney in the 1880s and 1890s. They sought to capture scenes of Australian life, the bush, and the strong sunlight that typifies the country—variously described as either harsh or dazzling. Among the movement's central figures were Arthur Streeton and Tom Roberts, and Streeton's *Golden Summer, Eaglemont* (1889) is often regarded as the epitome of Australian *en plein air* painting of this era. Streeton portrayed summer with a high-keyed gold and blue palette he considered "nature's scheme of colour in Australia."[36]

Much of *Sunday Too Far Away* was set in a shearing shed. According to John Dingwall's screenplay, when the shearers first enter the shed, we realize immediately that it is a cathedral, a magical place.[37] The shearing shed was also a brutal place as men competed to shear the most sheep and earn the most money and was a place from which women were usually excluded. One of the key visual influences on *Sunday Too Far Away* was *Shearing the Rams* (1888–1890), a painting by Tom Roberts based on drawings the artist made on site.

As we researched and wrote this chapter, it became clear that a chronological history of the development of color film technologies and aesthetics in Australia prior to 1980 almost inevitably privileges a succession of men: a succession of director-cinematographer partnerships, from *Kangaroo*'s Lewis Milestone and Charles Clarke to Peter Weir and Russell Boyd (*Picnic at Hanging Rock*). As feminists, how do we write about the history of an art form that is so gendered, an industry that restricted women's behind-the-camera roles to those of assistant while men called the shots? In the Australian context, much more work remains to be done. Nevertheless, recent work by art historians points to some new possibilities.[38] The lyrical bush paintings of artists like Tom Roberts, Arthur Streeton, and others have long held a powerful pull over the collective imagination. But attention is now being paid to their female contemporaries, artists like Jane Sutherland, Jane Price, and Ethel Carrick.

If we expand the frame, too, we can see the often unacknowledged contributions of women to the hues of the new wave of Australian cinema in the 1970s. *Picnic at Hanging Rock* (Peter Weir, 1975) was adapted from a novel by Joan Lindsay, who trained as a painter. Her novel is studded with evocative descriptions of color and the play of light. The many shades of yellow described in the book range from "dry-yellow" to "coin-yellow" and "starlight yellow."[39] It is therefore no surprise that yellow-gold is the film's dominant color. The cinematographer Russell Boyd recalled putting pale yellow netting (bought from the bridal section of a local department store) over the lens to re-create something of the "golden effect" of Australia's Impressionists.[40]

Dust gathers. The wind picks up pace. We are in the middle of a drought. It is the 1890s, and outside, farmhands are struggling to get weak and undernourished cattle to safety. Inside, people rush to shut doors and windows. Oblivious to the dust storm, Sybylla, the red-haired heroine of *My Brilliant Career*, paces the veranda as she completes her manuscript. "This story is going to be all about me. It is a story of my career," she soliloquizes.

My Brilliant Career would also draw on Impressionist and Postimpressionist paintings for its color scheme, with the director Gillian Armstrong, cinematographer Don McAlpine, and production designer Luciana Arrighi collaborating closely on the film's look and color schemes. The result in this instance is not only an expanded palette but also an emotional nuance that is rare in Australian cinema of the period. While Twentieth Century-Fox's *Kangaroo*—likewise set during the devastating drought of the 1890s—would signal a breakthrough for color cinema in Australia, *My Brilliant Career* and its chromatic palette broke another kind of drought: the absence of women from key creative roles in Australian feature films that had lasted for nearly five decades.

We close this chapter by pointing toward what remains missing in a history of Australian postwar cinema. Where the emphasis remains largely on the male feature filmmakers of the 1970s, an approach to that history that emphasizes the importance of the chromatic dimension in the national film culture, particularly as connected to its landscape traditions, might with further research serve to unsettle that emphasis. Some of the challenges for Australian historians of film color include a lack of access to materials and detailed archival records due to the chronic underfunding of the national film archives and other cultural institutions over many decades. It is clear that while the "color wars" between various North American and European companies played out on Australia's shores from the 1940s in the realm of the feature film, color was also important for documentary and anthropological filmmaking, as well as avant-garde shorts of the 1960s and 1970s and the new wave of Australian features. Considering the instability of color—and color film processes—we hope to have provided some suggestions for further research in this area, and to have unsettled some of the received touchstones—white, male, auteur—in favor of a range of different practitioners and film forms not often remembered in the established story of Australian cinema.

Notes

1 Some of the material discussing *Kangaroo*, *The Queen in Australia*, and *Jedda* was previously published in Kathryn Millard, "Indigenous Colour: The Quest to Make Australia's First Natural Colour Feature Film," *Screening the Past* 44 (2019), http://www.screeningthepast.com/issue-44-first-release/indigenous-colour-the-quest -to-make-australias-first-natural-colour-feature-film/.

2 *Sun*, Sydney, March 24, 1929, 14.

3 "Newsreel News," *Smith's Weekly*, Sydney, January 24, 1948, 17.

4 "Fast Colour," *Time*, March 22, 1948.

5 See Martin Edmond, *Battarbee and Namatjira* (Artarmon, NSW: Giramondo, 2014), 153.

6 See Edmond, 213.

7   Indeed, so renowned was Namatjira in this mode that a review of *Jedda* would describe that film as depicting "typical Namatjira country." "Talkies," *The Bulletin*, May 11, 1955.

8   Edmond, *Battarbee and Namatjira*, 147.

9   "Colour Film of Aborigine Artist," *Border Watch*, August 12, 1948.

10 Quoted in Edmond, *Batterbee and Namatjira*, 215–216.

11 Philip Jones, *Images of the Interior: Seven Central Australian Photographers* (Adelaide: Wakefield Press, 2011), 143.

12 "Namatjira the Painter," *Smith's Weekly*, Sydney, October 25, 1947, 25.

13 C. P. Mountford, *The Art of Albert Namatjira* (Melbourne: Bread and Cheese Club, 1951), 68.

14 "'Bushranger' to Be New Colour film," *Advertiser*, Adelaide, January 11, 1950, 3; "Colour Film May Be Made Here," *News*, Adelaide, August 2, 1950, 2.

15 Charles Chauvel, "Our Outback a Rich Field for Filmmakers," *Sydney Morning Herald*, August 31, 1950, 2.

16 "A Dust Storm," *Evening Journal*, Adelaide, July 29, 1869, 3.

17 "Red Dust Storm," *Port Pirie Recorder*, January 2, 1928, 3.

18 Charles G. Clarke, "We Filmed 'Kangaroo' Entirely in Australia," *American Cinematographer* 33, no. 7 (July 1952): 292–293, 315–317.

19 Papers of Colin Simpson, Box 41, National Library of Australia, MS 5253, Canberra.

20 Hans Heysen quoted in Lionel Lindsey, "Heysen's Recent Watercolours," *Art in Australia,* no. 24 (June 1928): n.p.

21 *Daily Mercury*, Mackay, Queensland, November 16, 1953, 16.

22 For more information about Gevacolor, see Barbara Flueckiger, Timeline of Historical Film Colors, accessed July 17, 2018, http://zauberklang.ch/filmcolors /timeline-entry/1312/#/.

23 "Press Reviews of Royal Tour Film," *Armidale Express and New England General Advertiser*, June 30, 1954, 12.

24 "Australia at Best in Royal Tour Film," *Sydney Morning Herald*, May 19, 1954, 3.

25 "Tour Documentary," *New York Times*, June 16, 1954.

26 Sarah Street, *Colour Films in Great Britain: The Negotiation of Innovation, 1900–55* (London: Palgrave Macmillan/British Film Institute, 2012), 13.

27 Susanne Chauvel, *Charles and Elsa Chauvel: Movie Pioneers* (Saint Lucia: University of Queensland Press, 1989), 152.

28 Martha Ansara, *The Shadowcatchers: A History of Cinematography in Australia* (Sydney: Austcine Publishing, 2012), 48.

29 See Norman Ingram, "Paul Winkler: Interview," *Cinema Papers* 7 (November–December 1975): 220.

30 See Tessa Laird, "Sonic Disturbance and Chromatic Dissolution: The Cantrills Remake Melbourne," *Senses of Cinema* 85 (December 2017), https://www.senses ofcinema.com/2017/screening-melbourne/cantrills-remake-melbourne/.

31 Albie Thoms, "Sunshine City: 1972," in *Polemics for a New Cinema* (Sydney: Wild and Woolley, 1978), 154.

32 Albie Thoms, "A Shot Is a Sentence, Three Frames a Word: 1975," in *Polemics for a New Cinema*, 274.

33 Gary Shead, "From *Blunderball* to *Sunshine City*—Side Lights on the Films of Albie Thoms," *Filmnews* (October 1, 1975): 6.

34 John Dingwall, *Sunday Too Far Away* (South Yarra: Heinemann Educational Australia, 1978), 5.

35 Ann Galbally, "Australian Impressionists: Critical Reception and Patronage," in *She-Oak and Sunlight: Australian Impressionism*, ed. Anne Gray and Angela Hesson (Port Melbourne, National Gallery of Victoria/Thames and Hudson, 2021).

36 Wayne Tuncliffe, *Streeton* (London: Thames and Hudson, 2020).

37 Dingwall, *Sunday Too Far Away*, 6

38 See Galbally, "Australian Impressionists."

39 Joan Lindsay, *Picnic at Hanging Rock* (Melbourne: Hill of Content, 1967).

40 "Russell Boyd: *Picnic at Hanging Rock*," *American Cinematographer* 57, no. 9 (September 1976): 1038.

13

Moving Monochromatics

Paul Sharits and Color Field Aesthetics in a Global Context

GREGORY ZINMAN

The art historian Thomas Crow writes that at Mark Rothko's first solo show at Sidney Janis Gallery in 1955, the scale of the artist's paintings was so large that the gallery put some on the floor, resting against the walls. According to Crow, the gallery "simply could not give the paintings enough room to breathe."[1] This observation brought to mind an experience I had four decades later with a friend, while looking at a number of Rothkos. Three separate canvases were hung on three walls in one of the rooms of the Yale University Art Gallery. I was an undergraduate and was under the influence of psilocybin mushrooms. It is perhaps a hoary psychedelic cliché, but, gazing on the Rothko canvases in our elevated states, my friend and I had the distinct impression that the paintings were, in fact, breathing. Gently contracting and expanding, rose and gold and lavender and orange hues exhibited an aggregate vitality in our eyes, as color filled our fields of vision.

Rothko's stacked blocks of color are not made from solitary hues but rather comprise intricate layers of color that fray the boundaries of the rectangular forms containing them. Crow writes that, after a while, a viewer looking at a Rothko can "see its surface in another register," that the paints in those signature rectangular forms reveal some of their layered qualities, causing the picture plane to become a "mesmerizing field of shifting tone and density."[2] Crow refers to the "field" rather than the "picture plane" or "canvas" to denote an area of activity not limited to a surface, but at play above and beyond it. This chromatic force may have been gathering before my eyes in the gallery, but the reach of color field aesthetics is far greater, extending from canvas to screen, and impacting art-making across media as well as around the globe.

I had a similarly colorful experience more recently, in early 2019 at the High Museum of Art in Atlanta, watching Paul Sharits's multiprojector work *Shutter Interface* (1976). "Version A" of *Shutter Interface* is presented as an automated, looping four-projector installation. On this night, however, "Version B" was presented, a two-projector performance version that features two reels of solid-color frames (red, purple, pink, orange, yellow, blue), with each color lasting between two and eight frames while being projected at twenty-four frames per second. Perceptually, then, these brief intervals of color act as bursts that can be difficult to identify in sequence due to their extreme rapidity. Single frames of black break up the flow of color and are accompanied by an electronic tone. The resulting soundtrack is rhythmic and repetitive, hypnotic but strangely buoyant, while the visuals flash and dazzle, producing eruptions of color that result from an admixture of the internal and external stimulation of one's nervous system.

In "Version B" of *Shutter Interface*, the projectionist gradually and manually merges the projection beams horizontally into one another, so that the viewer begins the piece seeing the two distinct images, side by side, and ends by seeing them superimposed. The resulting hues are luminous, shimmering, and difficult to name. Purplish? Coral? Lime? When I viewed the piece, I had a sense of the images contracting and expanding, and then, eventually, as the performance called for, meshing in order to create a new palette of vibrating chroma—mysteriously beautiful and entrancing (figure 13.1). Similar to the "mesmerizing field of shifting tone and density" that characterized Crow's experience with Rothko's paintings, Sharits took advantage of cinema's technical affordances in order to create unutterable, ineffable color.

The title *Shutter Interface* refers to the projector mechanism that makes a single film frame blink on, and then off, the screen—the foundational mechanics of the illusion of motion that makes up the cinematic moving image, wherein discrete static images on the filmstrip seem to move when animated by the apparatus. Throughout his work, Sharits was interested in making the viewer aware of the technological mechanisms that shape the moving image. Nevertheless, I am not convinced that understanding the workings of the cinematic apparatus is the main takeaway from watching the film(s). The movement perceived in *Shutter Interface* does not occur within the images on-screen; it appears in the change from one color to another. The lasting impression is of the blending and even confusion of color.

FIGURE 13.1 *Shutter Interface* (Paul Sharits, 1972). Two-screen 16mm film installation, color, sound, 32 min. (Courtesy of Christopher Sharits. Digital image © Whitney Museum of American Art / Licensed by Scala / Art Resource, New York.)

Sharits's interrogation of color stemmed from his interest in the mechanics of cinema and an interest in limits of perception and bodily stimulation. He described his first color flicker film, *Ray Gun Virus* (1966), as an "assassination of normative consciousness," while notes for other films of his referenced the onset of migraines or premenstrual syndrome. Sharits's *Piece Mandala/End War* (1966) and *T,O,U,C,H,I,N,G* (1968) were obliquely political films that combined color flicker effects with photographic imagery. As detailed throughout this volume, and as was the case with many postwar artists-turned-filmmakers, the increased availability of 16mm cameras due to World War II surplus and the proliferation of 16mm color stocks made Sharits's desire to experiment with color in time possible and allowed him and other artists around the world to rethink and repurpose the tools of mainstream, industrial, and hobbyist filmmaking as a means of conveying radical aesthetic, political, and ideological expressions.[3]

Sharits's exploration of color was further sparked by global filmmaking currents. In particular, Sharits was struck by Jean-Luc Godard's use of color in *A Woman Is a Woman* (1961) and *Contempt* (1963), writing in 1966 about how the French New Wave director's work implied "some system for structuring the colors" in the development of a chromatic leitmotif, one that was less concerned with any kind of representational naturalism in favor of a chromatic sensuality that produced affective responses in the viewer. In the same essay, he leaned on the ideas of the Soviet filmmaker and theorist Sergei Eisenstein, espousing the notion that "each film create its own 'functional' system of organization, using arbitrarily chosen but consistently recurring colors or values" in order to develop thematic and expressive patterns throughout a work.[4] Sharits thus aligned himself with the rule-flaunting tendencies of international new waves—which, as Elena Gipponi and Joshua Yumibe have noted, "helped define the chromatic landscape at mid-century"—and the revolutionary theories of early Soviet film in his attempts to think through cinematic color.[5]

Additionally, Sharits was immersed in specific countercultural conceptions of color at that historical juncture that found purchase in the pages of Marvel comics; the dazzling, even perceptually challenging colors of op art; the swirling psychedelic light shows that accompanied rock concerts; the pursuit of outwardly expressing an internally generated vision (Sharits once wrote, "yogic mediation generates another sense of inner color"); and the kaleidoscopic color effects associated with psilocybin and LSD trips.[6] With regard to this latter point, Bregt Lameris has written about how the psychedelic films of the middle to late 1960s provide a particularly strong illustration of cinema's long-running use "of colours that deviate from the common experiential norm to represent the hallucinatory and imaginary," while Kirsten Moana Thompson asserts that "in the 1960s colour was being unleashed especially in the psychedelic culture."[7] Sharits's experiences with hallucinogens inspired his pursuit of "three-dimensional" color effects, but on another physiological level, Sharits suffered from migraines, which can produce their own kind of not-unpleasant auras prior to an attack, and which subsequently became the subject of his *Analytical Studies I: The Film Frame* (1971–1976), a short series of what he dubbed "pure color studies" films.[8] Sharits was thus operating in a chromatic space shaped by international avant-gardes, homegrown counterculture, and individual malady, one that he was helping to "unleash" by pushing past conventional understandings and receptions of film color in favor of a restorative, illustrative, and even therapeutic cinema of perception that embraces sensuous experience as a rebuke to instrumentalized modernity, even if that experience is fleeting.

With that said, I would argue that viewing works like *Shutter Interface*, or Rothko's canvases, or other works that I will discuss in this chapter does not necessarily lead to learning or knowledge but rather to experience in and of itself. To experience "what it is to be, seeing," as Annette Michelson said of viewing *2001: A Space Odyssey*, may be one of the most valuable lessons that derive from looking at such works. Perhaps even more rich is how such works demand that we question what seeing does, how we should approach a film (or world) in which our eyesight is subject to manipulation and precariousness, and the extent to which we can ever know what we are really looking at—the consequences of which carry multiple valences around the world in our politicized mediascape.[9] That this series of questions can be asked across painting and cinema leads me to expand my own visual field to consider additional moving image artworks that, like *Shutter Interface*, employ single colors in relational patterns. In what follows, I offer a series of prompts about the relationship between color field painting and films that use monochromes via a consideration of works by Sharits, who explored the relationship throughout his career. These prompts are as follows: (1) Color fields are about perception, (2) color fields are about space-time, and (3) color fields are about relationships between media. In offering these prompts, my goal is to situate films of "pure" color within a wider sphere of artistic practice that came into prominence at midcentury. In so doing, I hope to productively challenge familiar high modernist shibboleths about object-hood, self-referentiality, and negation in favor of a more pluralistic approach to thinking about art across media.

History and Context

Color field painting developed in New York in the 1940s and 1950s. Considered a subset of abstract expressionism, color field painting was a parallel development to the gestural abstraction of Jackson Pollock, Willem de Kooning, and Franz Kline, characterized by planes of solid color that are painted across or stained upon a material support, usually canvas. Color field painting challenged viewers to consider the limit cases of abstraction and was by turns formalist, materialist, and philosophical. Its exemplars include Rothko, Helen Frankenthaler, Yves Klein, Morris Louis, Robert Motherwell, Clifford Styll, Agnes Martin, and Ad Reinhardt, among others. Although centered in New York, the movement carried international ties: its genesis can be traced in part to the zero-degree abstract works of the Russian painter Kazimir Malevich near the start of the twentieth century, such as *White on White* and *Black Square on a White Field*,[10] and Rothko (né Markus Yakovlevich Rothkowitz) was born in Latvia, while Yves Klein was French. Formally, color field painting was noteworthy for collapsing figure and ground into one and the same; thematically, it sought to extend Malevich's desire to imbue painting with a spiritual, even mythic, dimension—one that might provide a salve for the collective psyche of a nation still reeling from the horrors of the Second World War. Color field aesthetics thus asks what can be represented, and how color can evoke or produce states of mind that might be inaccessible via other artistic or visual means. While largely promulgated by midcentury artists in the United States, color field painting has been taken up around the world, though artists' methods, materials, and ideologies vary widely. Some notable contemporary examples of color field painting's global expressions include the German painter Günter Umberg; the Nigerian-born American artist Donald

Odita; the Japanese painter Hisashi Indo; the Mexican artist Bosco Sodi; and the loosely knit group of Dansaekhwa artists in South Korea, including Park Seo-bo, Lee Ufan, and Yun Hyong-keun, who first came to prominence in Korea in the mid-1970s as they synthesized Western abstraction and Korean traditions, and whose legacy of thinking through materials and repeated gesture persists in the work of a number of practitioners today.[11]

While several color field painters were captured at work on film or interviewed on film, they did not venture into filmmaking themselves, though Justin Remes writes that, in 1954, "Yves Klein himself had conceived of a film that would offer only a series of monochromes: white, yellow, red, and blue."[12] Several filmmakers, however, have adapted color field aesthetics to their chosen medium. In the French experimental filmmaker Rose Lowder's *Parcelle* (1979), a small, centrally situated flickering figure that changes from a circle to a square and back again is set against a field of wavering color that shifts from orange to royal blue to red. The work's title can be variously translated as "atom," "plot," or "allotment," all of which suggest color as a marker of territories both physical and perceptual, or as a building block for seeing, as viewers contend with the balance/imbalance between the central glimmering object and the throbbing ground on which it floats. And the Uruguayan filmmaker Eduardo Darino's *Cocktail de Rayas* (1964), or *Striped Cocktail*, was painted, stamped, scratched directly on 16mm film, and set to music by Charles Williams. Contemporaneous with the hard-edged abstraction of color field painters such as Kenneth Noland, Al Held, and Ellsworth Kelly, and notably influenced by the hand-painted films of Norman McLaren, *Cocktail de Rayas* provides a visual dialogue between North and South America, its sprightly pulses strongly resembling the multicolored vertical lines seen in the paintings of Gene Davis and Barnett Newman.

Sharits himself trained as a painter and, in the early part of his career, would enact a rhetorical pas de deux that sought to twist film away from painting before, in the end, finally allowing itself to be held once again in its metaphoric arms. Nevertheless, throughout the 1960s and 1970s, Sharits eschewed any comparison between the color field painters and his own color flicker films, insisting initially on the cinematic specificity of his work. In 1974, for example, he wrote to *Artforum*: "Others have construed in my works a likeness to color-field painting. I am aware of these strategies and styles and have great respect for many of the practitioners of them. However, my own strategy issues from an attempt to frame and analyze the fundamental propositions of traditional cinematic logic."[13] By the 1980s, however, the artist longed for painterly effects: "I wanted to bring to film a certain sort of consciousness associated more with painting. . . . I longed for the immediacy of the experience of painting, where everything was in my control, the image was exactly where it was, I could see it, I could respond to it, there wasn't anyone else getting in the way of it, and it was a more immediate process."[14] Comparisons to painting were never far from Sharits's thoughts. He peppered his writing and interviews with litanies of painters: Claude Monet, Mark Rothko, James Ensor, Ad Reinhardt, and Paul Gauguin, to name only a handful.

For Sharits, as well as a number of other moving image artists, the relationship between color field painting and the moving image was seemingly inexorable and necessitated a thoroughgoing investigation of film's potential for extending the possibilities of monochromatic abstraction. Sharits's films, in particular, call into question what we are looking at, on a number of registers: the object seen, the object filmed, the relationship between object and image, and the relationship between object/images—the camera, the profilmic, the projected, the apparatus, the screen/surface, between what we see and how we see it.

Color Fields Are about Perception

The curator Barbara Rose views the painted monochrome as a Schrödinger's box of meanings, simultaneously evoking "simplicity and unity, which masks a potential for multivalence and paradox," that is concrete yet metaphysical, material yet transcendent.[15] Such binaries are not always reconcilable, as is the case with Ad Reinhardt's black paintings. He painted twenty-five such works between 1953 and his death in 1967. They present an almost ludic optical experience, in which a discerning viewer, confronted by what appears to be a completely black surface, gradually becomes aware of geometric compositional elements and variations in hue (faint lines of blue or red, for example). These paintings were made in close parallel to the civil rights movement in which Reinhardt took part, and yet the artist was eager to de-cathect his work from outside contexts in favor of isolated objecthood, as if they (or, perhaps, the person who painted them) could exist outside of their surroundings, their beholders, or interpretation—a solipsism of technique and optics. As Reinhardt put it: "A pure, abstract, non-objective, timeless, spaceless, changeless, relationless, disinterested painting—an object that is self-conscious (not unconsciousness), ideal, transcendent, aware of no thing but art."[16] However "pure" (always a vexed supposition when dealing with blackness and Blackness as color and race) Reinhardt's conception of his paintings may have been, we can also understand them as what Yumibe terms "afterimages of the transformations in color culture" and culture more broadly, lingering traces of the abutment of modernist claims of medium-specific autonomy running up against the realities of contemporaneous politics, regardless of the artist's intentions.[17]

Reinhardt's "disinterested" color is at one end of the color field conceptual spectrum. On the other end, quite a lot of effort goes into convincing viewers that what they are looking at is in fact much more than what it appears—a painting of vermillion, or teal, or cornflower blue. If the work is indeed only a colored canvas, it runs the risk of being decorative or insignificant. Reviewing the exhibition *Ten Approaches to the Decorative* at Alessandra Gallery for *Artforum* in 1976, Jeff Perrone expressed the difficulty of overcoming the art world's stigma of decoration, writing that "'decorative' is about as pejorative a description as 'literary' or 'theatrical.'"[18] That stigma persists, and the decorative has often been associated with the feminine, with craft, and with unserious whimsy. Modernist precepts of materiality, self-referentiality, and negation, says the curator Anna Katz, obscure or outright obstruct readings of art having to do with issues of "identity, history, race, gender, the personal, the private." We invest a great psychic and personal energy in decoration and ornament, in creating overall environments in which to live and express ourselves. The idea that artworks must stand apart as objects somehow outside of context and environment seems at odds with the way most people use and appreciate art, which is relationally.

In attempting to fend off accusations of a childlike devotion to decoration or ornament, however, artists' stated schemas of "negation," "science," "math," and "perception" can function at odds with the fundamentally sensual nature of the work. The art historian Briony Fer sums up this tension between subjective and objective interpretations of color as "not entirely free from rules, but neither is it entirely systematic."[19] Color is both obvious and indeterminate, deceptively simple, and unruly. The minimalist sculptor Donald Judd wrote, "Color is like material. It is one way or another, but it obdurately exists. Its existence as it is is the main fact and not what it might mean, which may be nothing."[20]

In many ways, Sharits's use of color in his flicker films counters the ways that color can be said to "obdurately exist." Color, for Sharits, was more than an exercise in perception, as in Reinhardt's black paintings, and it meant more than "nothing," in Judd's terms. Sharits was searching for something beyond "pure" color, a new way of seeing that might reorient our relationships to ourselves and the external world. In his writing, he mentions closed-eye vision, a concept heralded by Stan Brakhage, in which phosphenes produce impressions of light, color, and form via retinal stimulation, even when an individual's eyes are shut.[21] Indeed, inner color is a key to understanding Sharits's works. "One of the reasons that I worked with color flicker was to create colors that were indefinite," he told an interviewer in 1983. "You're watching this shimmering effect, your mind cannot fix and say, that's either yellow or orange or purple, but that it's an impossible constant kind of fusion. . . . it's almost like trying to touch something to feel what it feels like."[22] Color here is something experienced but unknowable, just out of reach. In these films, color changes relationally—a synthesis of optic nerve, image, and afterimage that functions as a tool for testing the boundaries of what one sees externally, and of how one "sees" within oneself.

But what is the material nature of Sharits's colors? Little has been written about the imagistic basis of his color frames. Rosalind Krauss, writing in an 1976 exhibition catalog about *Ray Gun Virus* (1965) and *Razor Blades* (1965–1968), describes how, through "alternating passages of color-field and photographic imagery, Sharits created for himself a situation in which the cinematic field oscillated between the abstract, luminous flatness of the 'empty' frames of color (and the still emptier ones of after-image), and the aggressive three-dimensionality of the frames with objects."[23] What Krauss has not acknowledged, however, is that the color fields are also "photographic imagery." In a letter written in response to the review, Sharits claimed that he understood his work as "purely documentary," explaining, "Film strips are, I believe, quite as much 'external reality' as are movie actors, mountains, etc., and when one perceives clear images of them projected upon flat supportive surfaces, one is experiencing representations of them."[24]

Sharits also failed to mention that, among the representations of the material elements of film, there were also representations of another set of objects: the sheets of Color-aid paper that he photographed to produce those "empty" frames of color in *Ray Gun Virus*, *Razor Blades*, and various other examples of his early films. Color-aid paper is used in a variety of art and craft applications. The standard set consists of 220 matte-finish, interrelated colored sheets, available in two sizes (6 by 9 inches and 4.5 by 6 inches). The set comes with a booklet that formulates the Color-aid system, which is based on a categorization of color by hue, tint, shade, pastel, and gray. The contemporary Color-aid booklet for the full set (314 sheets, introduced in 1990) introduces the three dimensions of color: "When describing a color you need to give its hue, its saturation and its lightness. . . . Saying a color is red is not sufficient, you need also to say whether it is a light or dark red, and if it is a saturated (vivid) or desaturated (grayed) red. The proportions of these three attributes pinpoint where a color belongs within the three-dimensional color solid."[25] Now recall Sharits's comment about making color that produces the sensation of "trying to touch something to feel what it feels like." Even with their matte finish, Color-aid sheets have a velvety texture, a certain depth and richness to them as both colors and objects placed before a camera. Somewhat ironically, the paper, in longer sheets, was initially used as backdrops for photographic shoots. But Sharits made them the primary subject of his films. The filmmaker Bill Brand, who assisted Sharits on several films, writes: "He never liked the colors you could get by just working with filters. He would shoot these Color-aid papers, and he worked very intuitively, so he would go in a trance and shot these patterns and would be kind of making music."[26] This mode of creating was markedly different from other projects of Sharits's that were meticulously designed and scored on graph paper before filming or installation began.

Color-aid paper's main claim to fame, however, was its adoption by the painter and teacher Joseph Albers as an instructional device by which he could illustrate—and have students discover—the "relativity and instability" of the relationships he famously set out in *Interaction of Color* in 1963.[27] The sheets were easily manipulated and could be arranged in a way that obviated the necessity for students to master the intricacies of oil paint in order to engage in color theory. Linking photography (Color-aid's purported use) to painting (Albers's classroom) to music (Brand's analogy to describe Sharits's working method) to film (Sharit's flicker works), Color-aid paper was an unlikely connector of experimental media practice.

Color Fields Are about Space-Time

Much of the writing on abstract painting, and in particular writing on monochrome and color field works, tends to focus on the qualities of the painted surface and its physical presence in the space it occupies as a means of determining its effects. For example, Arnold Berleant wrote of color field painting that it was intended "to provide a feeling of openness leading viewers to experience a different aspect of pictorial space."[28] The reconsideration of pictorial space has to do with the relationship of a canvas to its surrounding wall, the surface texture of the painting, its finish (matte or reflective), and its shape. These effects, in turn, are largely determined by the length of a viewer's encounter with the work. Looking at Rothkos produces a variety of durational effects that are markedly distinct from the solidity of and declarative color relations within a Newman "zip" painting or one of Frank Stella's shaped canvases, for example. As Glenn Phillips contends, "The visual apprehension of a Rothko painting is a temporal experience; seeing a Rothko painting is a process that unfolds dynamically over time."[29]

This unfolding has led some critics to move past assertions of objecthood within a given space to claim the paintings as liminal, "portal experiences." Writing in 1953, Rothko himself offered: "Maybe you have noticed two characteristics exist in my paintings; either their surfaces are expansive and push outward in all directions, or their surfaces contract and rush inward in all directions. Between these two poles you can find everything I want to say."[30] This perceptual expansion and contraction of the image is familiar to anyone who has watched one of Sharits's flicker films. William Wees describes the experience: "As the light continues to flicker, the whole image may seem to expand and contract and even lift itself off the surface of the screen and hover disconcertingly in some ambiguous plane that is impossible to fix in space. In fact, it is not 'in space' at all. It is 'in' the temporally organized firing of brain cells. It is quite literally an 'internal time-shape,' as Sharits calls it, created by 'the electrical-chemical functioning of [the viewer's] own nervous system.'"[31] Many of these effects would be explicitly detailed and explored by international op art practitioners such as Bridget Riley and Victor Vasarely. Some monochrome artists extended the idea of painting as a passage even further, as in the case of Agnes Martin's decades-long investigation into monochromatic painting. Martin's *Friendship* (1963), for example, an enormous work measuring six feet on each side, is a grid made up of small rectangles, painted with gold leaf and gesso so that the resulting color resembles a shimmering sunflower. But Martin, with her transcendentalist outlook, likened looking at painting as a kind of inward traveling: "It is to accept the necessity of . . . going into a field of vision as you would cross an empty beach to look at the ocean."[32] The surface of the painting, for Martin, provides an invitation, or rather, a directive, to enter into another perceptual realm that is both subjective and elemental.

In his thoroughgoing exegesis of *Blue* (1993), by the English artist and film-maker Derek Jarman, Justin Remes coins the term *monochrome film* to describe the static titular field that makes up the image track, writing, "Drained of any visual content or movement, Jarman's film offers an ostensible void, an absence, a retreat from representation. . . . *Blue* becomes a conceptual waiting room."[33] For Remes, Jarman's blue is related to stasis and death, the latter being the subject of the film—Jarman's diaristic account of the AIDS-related illness that would claim first his sight, and then his life.

Sharits, however, was more pointed in his desire to draw viewers' attention beyond the screen by emulating the exhibition practices of painting. He said that he wanted "to create intensified places."[34] These "locational" pieces, as he called them, like the full version of *Shutter Interface*, or *Sound Strip/Film Strip* (1972), were intended to emphasize spatial relationships between projector, screening surface, and mobile spectators by positioning the projectors within the space of exhibition, so that viewers would have to consciously move around them while simultaneously observing the mechanical relationships between them and the resulting projections. "I wanted to bring film into sync with conceptual art; so I never totally left my first love, painting. I wanted to paint during the years 1964 to 1978 but was so busy with film and then film installations . . . bringing the act of presenting and viewing film as close as possible to conditions of hanging and looking at paintings."[35] In these works, the space in which the moving images unfolded was as important as the images themselves.

Sharits's *Sound Strip/Film Strip* is a four-projector installation. Its imagery is composed of a single pink hue, shot on film from a Color-aid sheet, that Sharits subsequently exposed "from white to black and all levels of pink saturation in between" in an investigation of the film frame and filmstrip. Evidently, Sharits also asked Brand to come up with a way to scratch a diagonal line in one direction across one half of a processed hundred-foot roll of 16mm color reversal film, and then scratch another line back across the second half. Accordingly, Brand fashioned a device that could scratch the frames precisely, using a cheap pencil compass to accomplish the task.

The piece utilizes four separate projectors housed in black rectangular plinths to throw the four loops, each ten minutes long, sideways. The resulting images are larger than human scale and present as four vertical rectangular forms with rounded edges reminiscent of film frames, separated by a little bit of black space.

Each rectangular form displays shifting registers of pink with visible sprocket holes running across the top of each at different speeds, creating a sense of movement from right to left as the sprockets pass by like windows of a moving train. Each rectangular image sports two scratches, one "real" and one rephotographed. The images are unsynchronized, and as such, their combinations do not repeat. The sound—a recording of Brand saying "miscellaneous"—emanates from four speakers, one for each loop, creating an impenetrable sonic overlap. The projected images of *Sound Strip/Film Strip* also appear, in their arrangement and texture, as a moving monochromatic quadriptych, wherein the texture of the photographed Color-aid paper lends it a painterly air even as the piece's sound, unexpected depth provided by the rephotographed film, and overall movement announce it as an immersive moving image installation wherein the briskly scrolling images, the sculptural presentation of the projectors, and the hard-to-decipher, ping-ponging soundtrack mark a deliberate shift away from a conventional cinematic experience toward a more thoroughly embodied encounter with space and time.

Conclusion: Color Fields Are about Relationships between Media

Sharits continued to seek out new methods for producing vibrational color. The video artist Woody Vasulka attempted to build a new device for his SUNY Buffalo colleague that would produce suitably brilliant hues for filming. Alternately called the Vasulka Color Generator, the Color-Frames-Analysis Machine, or the Vasulka-Sharits Stroboscope Project, the device was described in a National Endowment for the Arts grant proposal as a device for creating "color-field motion picture films," thus making its link to color field painting explicit.[36] Sharits completed a single video using the color generator, *Passare I* (1988), which was originally supposed to be a film, except that Sharits wrote that he "came to appreciate the special color luminosity of video."[37] Sharits considered *Passare I* to be a "chapter" in a visual novel of abstract color that had direct and specific correspondences to events in his life, particularly related to travel (other installments of *Passare* became works on paper)—yet another invocation of monochromes as passages, portals, places to cross.[38]

The Vasulka-Sharits collaboration may not have yielded much work, but the moving monochrome would not be abandoned. To consider the present: Jason Livingston's cameraless work in progress *On the Matter of Blue Lives* offers a speckled light blue array punctuated with an intermittent scrawl reading "F12" (internet slang for "f-ck the police"). The film was made with a cyanotype process, hearkening back to photography's origins as it presents an impression of the *stuff* and vim of contemporary political protest, some of which is more material (an orange mask that leaves only a white imprint, Goya salt, pepper spray) and some of which is more ethereal (such as the "Antifa Dust" listed as one of the film's components). This is not Derek Jarman's blue, or Yves Klein's blue, or the police's "thin blue line" stripe on its dark version of the American flag that once was intended to show support for law enforcement and now has been co-opted by far-right groups seeking to oppose racial justice movements, specifically Black Lives Matter. Livingston's modest but earnest rejoinder makes light of the positioning by police and media outlets obsessed with antifa, the antifascist and antiracist protesters who clashed with extreme right-wing groups and police throughout the protests that spread across the United States in the summer of 2020. At once suggestive and a mode of documentary—cyanotypes were methods of capturing nature by recording the physical impressions of objects onto photosensitive film—*On the Matter of Blue Lives* is a monochrome that explicitly engages with the politics of protest in a more pronounced fashion than in Sharits's color flicker works.

And where Vasulka's computer device may have failed, the color field has become algorithmic. The Austrian artist Rainer Kohlberger's deliberately trippy and destabilizing films and installations, for instance, have been described as "pure light generated by algorithms,"[39] and his exploration of cameraless digital abstractions builds on Sharits's preoccupation with overwhelming viewers' perceptual faculties by combining incandescently strobing smears, dots, and overlays of color with thundering electronic drones. More prosaically, over on Twitter, @vogon's automated @everycolorbot produces frames of solid color (oxcdo6ad is a bright fuchsia, for example) to "bless the timeline," as social media parlance goes. Joe Fox's bot colorschemer (@colorschemez) offers Newman-esque vertical bands of color in the manner of *Who's Afraid of Red, Yellow, and Blue IV* (1969–1970), with strange or even hilarious descriptors, such as "stichomythic light periwinkle/transcalent topaz/rueful purplish red."[40] Other stochastic compositions from colorschemer bear an arrested, lobotomized resemblance to Sharits's *Shutter Interface*. Machinic, shorn of autobiographical, philosophical, or scientific pretensions, these precisely calibrated percentages of red, green, and blue (Corn Yellow: hexadecimal color code: E4CDo5), totaling 16,777,216 possible colors in the sRGB gamut, are coldly declarative rather than searchingly perceptual, offering momentarily colorful interludes to break up daily doomscrolling. Even more so than in the films discussed here, the human hand is absent, and "pure" color not left to chance, relation, or interpretation. Note the thousands of videos on YouTube that display blocks of solid color, available to anyone around the world with an internet connection. These videos sport loglines ironically or counterintuitively expressing excitement for unwavering chroma: "watch beige for 1 hour of this incredible beige screen! . . . or light brown?" (figure 13.2).[41] Boasting more than hundreds of thousands of views, these putatively moving images do not betray visible motion or even change. Their only indications of time are the seconds ticking by on the progress bar—utilitarian stasis for, as indicated by the comments, sleeping or studying or lighting a video call or monitor calibration. On videos displaying color gradients, users indicate their favorite color combinations with timecodes. Deracinated from artistic

watch beige for 1 hour of this incredible beige screen! Or brown...light brown? balance monitorcolor

FIGURE 13.2 Video Game Philosopher, "watch beige for 1 hour of this incredible beige screen!" (2019), YouTube, screenshot.

history, global politics, philosophy, method, and modernism, today's color fields offer authorship without aura, data points and digital paint chips for surfaces that will never be touched by a brush. Perfect and empty, incidental, instrumental, and beloved. Color-aids, indeed.

Notes

1   Thomas Crow, "The Marginal Difference in Rothko's Abstraction," in *Seeing Rothko*, ed. Glenn Phillips and Thomas Crow (Los Angeles: Getty Research Institute, 2005), 26.

2   Crow, 26.

3   See John Powers, "A DIY Come-On: A History of Optical Printing in Avant-Garde Cinema," *Cinema Journal* 57, no. 4 (Summer 2018): 71–95.

4   Paul Sharits, "Red, Blue, Godard," *Film Quarterly* 19 (Summer 1966): 21–22.

5   Elena Gipponi and Joshua Yumibe, "Cinema and Mid-century Colour Culture: An Introduction," *Cinéma & Cie* 19, no. 32 (Spring 2019): 8–9.

6   Paul Sharits, "Notes on Films/1966–68," in *"I Was a Flawed Modernist": Collected Writings by Paul Sharits/Collected Stories about Paul Sharits*, ed. Sarah Markgraf (New York: The New American Cinema Group/The Film-Makers' Coop, 2017), 116.

7   See Bregt Lameris, "Hallucinating Colours: Psychedelic Film, Technology, Aesthetics and Affect," *Cinéma & Cie* 19, no. 32 (Spring 2019): 89; Kirsten Moana Thompson, "Falling in(to) Color: Chromophilia and Tom Ford's *A Single Man* (2009)," *Moving Image* 15, no. 1 (2015): 62–84.

8   Jean-Claude Lebensztejn, "Interview with Paul Sharits," in *Paul Sharits: Catalogue Raisonné 1962–1992*, ed. Susanne Pfeffer (Cologne: Walther König, 2016), 270.

9   Annette Michelson, "Bodies in Space: Film as 'Carnal Knowledge,'" *Artforum* 7, no. 6 (February 1969): 53–64, https://www.artforum.com/print/196902/nnette-michelson-on-stanley-kubrick-s-2001-a-space-odyssey-36517.

10 I have written about the troubling racist undercurrent of these early abstractions. See Gregory Zinman, *Making Images Move: Handmade Cinema and the Other Arts* (Berkeley and Los Angeles: University of California Press, 2020), 147.

11 See Joan Kee, *Contemporary Korean Art: Tansaekhwa and the Urgency of Method* (Minneapolis: University of Minnesota Press, 2013).

12 Justin Remes, *Motion(less) Pictures: The Cinema of Stasis* (New York: Columbia University Press, 2015), 124.

13 Paul Sharits, "Letter to *Artforum*," September 8, 1974, in *"I Was a Flawed Modernist,"* 176–177.

14 Lebensztejn, "Interview with Paul Sharits," 276.

15 Barbara Rose, "Pre-Malevich Monochromes and Chronology," in *Monochromes: From Malevich to the Present*, ed. Barbara Rose (Berkeley: University of California Press, 2006), 14.

16 Ad Reinhardt, "The Black-Square Paintings," in *Art-as-Art: The Selected Writings of Ad Reinhardt*, ed. Barbara Rose (Berkeley and Los Angeles: University of California Press, 1991), 83. Nevertheless, it is difficult to remain "relationless" when reflecting on how notions of purity run up against how Blackness was and is understood and constructed culturally beyond the context in which art is made, not to mention the wider art historical contexts of how art changes hands, how it ends up displayed, and how it is valued.

17 Joshua Yumibe to the author, personal communication, June 8, 2023.

18 Jeff Perrone, *"Ten Approaches to the Decorative* at the Alessandra Gallery," *Artforum*, December 1976, https://www.artforum.com/print/197610/approaching-the-decorative-37972.

19 Briony Fer, "Color Manual," in *Color Chart: Reinventing Color: 1950 to Today*, ed. Ann Temkin (New York: Museum of Modern Art, 2008), 28.

20 Donald Judd, "Some Aspects of Color in General and Red and Black in Particular," 1993, https://juddfoundation.org/artist/writing/some_aspects_of_color_in_genera_1993.

21 Paul Sharits, "Toward Meditational Cinema: Notes (c. 1970)," in *"I Was a Flawed Modernist,"* 116.

22 Lebensztejn, "Interview with Paul Sharits," 270.

23 R. Krauss, "Paul Sharits," in *Paul Sharits: Dream Displacement and Other Projects*, exhibition catalog, Albright-Knox Gallery, Buffalo, New York, 1976, reprinted in *Film Culture* no. 65–66 (1978): 100.

24 Sharits, "Letter to *Artforum*," 176.

25 "The New Color-aid Booklet," 6th ed. (Hudson Falls, NY, 2006), 3.

26 Bill Brand, untitled statement August 5, 2004, in *"I Was a Flawed Modernist,"* 377.

27 Joseph Albers, *Interaction of Color* (New Haven, CT: Yale University Press, 1963), 2.

28 Arnold Berleant, "The Visual Arts and the Art of the Unseen," *Leonardo* 12, no. 3 (Summer 1979): 233. My thanks to Jessica Storm for the reference. See Jessica Storm, "The Medium Is the Medium: The Complexities of the Preservation of *Rate of Change* and *Color Series*" (master's thesis, UCLA, 2011), 13. My thanks to Bill Brand for sharing this valuable resource with me.

29 Glenn Phillips, "Introduction: Irreconcilable Rothko," in *Seeing Rothko*, 2.

30 James E. B. Breslin, *Mark Rothko: A Biography* (Chicago: University of Chicago Press, 1993), 301n1.

31 William C. Wees, *Light Moving in Time: Studies in the Visual Aesthetics of Avant-Garde Film* (Berkeley: University of California Press, 1992), 147.

32 John Elderfield, "Transformations," in *Seeing Rothko*, 106.

33 Ann Wilson, "Linear Webs," *Art and Artists* 1, no. 7 (October 1966): 49.

34 Linda Cathcart, "An Interview with Paul Sharits," *Film Culture* no. 65–66 (1978): 104.

35 Paul Sharits, "Post-Expressionism" (1985), in *"I Was a Flawed Modernist,"* 134.

36 David Held, "Summary of NEA Services to the Field Grant: Vasulka/Sharits Stroboscope Project" January 12, 1985, 1.

37 Paul Sharits, *"Passare I,"* undated statement, accessed on November 22, 2023, http://www.vasulka.org/archive/Artists6/Sharits,Paul/general.pdf.

38 Paul Sharits, *"Passare I (Italia),"* in *Buffalo Heads: Media Study, Media Practice, Media Pioneers, 1973–1990*, ed. Woody Vasulka and Peter Weibel (Cambridge, MA: MIT Press, 2008), 357.

39 Stella Ammar, "Rainer Kohlberger's Visual Music, between Noise and Light," *Cercle*, no. 8, "Ghosts," September 15, 2020, https://www.cerclemagazine.com/en/magazine/articles-magazine/rainer-kohlbergers-visual-music-between-noise-and-light/.

40 @colorschemez, Twitter, September 11, 2021, 11:23 a.m., https://twitter.com/colorschemez/status/1436712130657460226.

41 Video Game Philosopher, August 31, 2019, YouTube, https://www.youtube.com/watch?v=iGr9Xkv5FyQ&ab_channel=VideoGamePhilosopher.

14

On Vivid Colors and Afrotropes in African and Diasporic Cinemas

JOSHUA YUMIBE

Chromatic Blackness

The saturated world of Black color design in film and media has profound yet undertheorized legacies in sub-Saharan African media of the 1960s and 1970s as well as in the ensuing South-North diasporic flows of chromatic style. In the context of the dominant transition to monopack color in global cinemas of the era, African and African diasporic cinemas pose an expansive range of styles and concerns through which to track color's relation to decolonial aesthetics.[1] From a decolonial perspective, the aesthetics of Black color design are remarkable and profoundly diverse, which creates critical opportunities for rethinking the various political and sensory potentials of color in postcolonial as well as diasporic cinemas.

This chapter takes up these issues through focused case studies of *Xala* (Ousmane Sembène, Senegal, 1975), *Touki Bouki* (Djibril Diop Mambéty, Senegal, 1973), and *Daughters of the Dust* (Julie Dash, U.S., 1991). As will be discussed, the globalized image of chromatic Blackness found in each of these films decolonizes color by adapting and reclaiming its diasporic history and effects. To frame these works' interventions broadly, the next section of this chapter historicizes the deployment of cinematic color across sub-Saharan and diasporic traditions.

The latter half of the chapter then takes up the varying color designs of each film. These are disparate works, yet each reflexively illustrates the global flows of color in their postcolonial and diasporic contexts. Through the circulation of vivid hues across the material, a chromatic afrotrope of cinematic effect can be traced that brings to the surface and reappropriates the violent legacies of color's colonial history.

A Revolutionary Upsurge

A common refrain in Western aesthetic theory associates color with race, asserting that so-called primitive cultures prefer bright hues. Johann Wolfgang von Goethe famously wrote that "savage nations, uneducated people, and children have a great predilection for *vivid colours*," which is part of the generalized chromophobic discourse that favors Whiteness—the absence of color—aesthetically as well as racially.[2] Goethe's treatise on color is centered on the implications of the visual afterimage, something that struck him initially while he was staring intently at a woman: "I had entered an inn towards evening, and, as a well-favoured girl, with a brilliantly fair complexion, black hair, and a scarlet bodice, came into the room, I looked attentively at her as she stood before me at some distance in half shadow. As she presently afterwards turned away, I saw on the white wall, which was now before me, a black face surrounded with a bright light, while the dress of the perfectly distinct figure appeared of a beautiful sea-green."[3] The anecdote combines scopophilia—the lurid focus on the woman's scarlet bodice—with an unexpected conjuring of race, a watercolor portrait of which Goethe also painted in 1810. After the woman moves away, the white wall that was behind her becomes a screen of inverted desire: as an afterimage her "fair complexion" transforms into a Black face surrounded by shimmering light as the watercolor makes clear. This phantasmagoric appearance in the midst of his desire brings to the surface the racialization of color in his theory.

In texts and illustrations such as Goethe's, colored skin as well as brightly colored fashion become synonymous with both desire and aesthetic vulgarity, the sensual opposite of the genteel taste cultures of the colonizing West that preferred subdued and subjugated hues, tasteful harmonies, and Whiteness. Such ideas that naturalize chromatic meaning along racialized geographies are worth interrogating, particularly given their continued influence, as well as subversion, in color design of the postwar era. Bright, living colors, vivid, Kool-Aid hues in decolonial and countercultural works develop a dialectical relationship with alterity, becoming an emblem as well as a revolutionary signifier for the oppressed and subaltern. In writing about the artistic changes emerging from a postcolonial "awakening of national consciousness," Frantz Fanon notes, "Colors, once restricted in number, governed by laws of traditional harmony, flood back, reflecting the effects of the revolutionary upsurge. Certain ochers, certain blues that were apparently banned for eternity in a given cultural context, emerge unscathed."[4] Vivid colors return and are deployed politically in a variety of decolonial works that interrogate race, primitivism, and modernity. From the color of skin to the saturated palettes of the mise-en-scène, bright, vivid colors are appropriated not as a naturalized emblem of difference but as discursive signs in a signifying chain of political and aesthetic resistance.

Indigo, Calico, Chattel Slavery

Discourses about color and race do not emerge in a vacuum. Indeed, they are aesthetic afterimages of the global transformations in the political economy of the time. Like the Black inversion of Goethe's desire, the ideological entwinement of color and race silently testifies to the colonial histories of extraction that connect modern color and slavery at a material level. Before the discovery of synthetic aniline purple (also known as Perkin's mauve) in the nineteenth century, natural dyes were imported at great expense from these very same, so-called primitive colonies—the cochineal reds of the Americas, the indigo blues of West Africa, and the indigos and calicos of India. Michael Taussig delineates how some of these colors—the calico prints that the British East India Company acquired in the eighteenth and nineteenth centuries—were in fact destined for subsequent export to Africa, to be used as currency in the slave trade through the bartering of calico prints from India for enslaved Africans destined for the colonies.[5] Continuing the cycle of global exchange, indigo plants were transplanted from India to the plantations of Brazil and the West Indies and eventually to South Carolina in the seventeenth and eighteenth centuries. Indeed, this nonnative crop in the New World fueled the rise of plantation slavery, allowing farms to begin with only a field of indigo plants and a few enslaved peoples, and then quickly expand off the profits by clearing more land and purchasing more slaves year by year—acquiring them from the very network of the transatlantic slave trade that Indian calico was simultaneously fueling.[6] Oppressively, color paid for slaves who were put to work making more of it, and indigo was also noxious to produce, as attested to by the common illnesses and premature deaths of dye workers.[7]

Given the global infrastructure of colorants and chattel slavery, the racist rhetoric of chromatic primitivism papers over the horror of colonial extraction and exchange that fueled the rise of global modernity and the emergence of new cultures of consumption. Such associations in Western color theory have been a means of ideological obfuscation, forgetting the colonial legacies that are the material grounds of color history and exchanging them with an aesthetic discourse that mythologizes those very hues through a primitivist logic that exalts whiteness aesthetically over the vividness of bright colors. Further, these aesthetic moves sublimate the supremacy of Whiteness in colonial rule and the enslavement of Indigenous bodies.

Color and the Afrotrope

In relation to the technical and aesthetic transformations in midcentury color cinema that this volume tracks, it is worth interrogating further the racial mythologies and materialities of color in African and diasporic cinemas from the 1960s forward, which resist and subvert the primitivist ideologies of color that have dominated Western aesthetics. The temporality of the 1960s and 1970s is crucial for this account, given the complex political and aesthetic revolutions that decolonialization fostered. In film history these decades coincide globally with the rise of new wave cinema and counter cinema, as well as various technical transformations, including the rapid adoption of monopack color technologies. These are fundamentally different spheres of change, yet they are also ones that intersect, as has been well charted in various accounts of global new wave cinemas.[8] The specificity of color in postcolonial aesthetics at the time allows for new insights into these intersections.

For the sub-Saharan and African diasporic contexts, it is useful to draw from Huey Copeland and Krista Thompson and to read color as functioning aesthetically as an "afrotrope" within a specific genealogy of global art cinemas. Theorizing the concept, Copeland and Thompson delineate the afrotrope as "those recurrent visual forms that have emerged within and become central to the formation of African diasporic culture and identity. . . . Their circulation thus illuminates both how black subjects have imagined themselves and reconfigured the visual technologies of modern cultural formation and image transmission more broadly."[9] For Copeland and Thompson, the neologism illuminates a way of tracking the provenance of African tropes as they circulate across time and space, particularly in diasporic contexts in which they transform and accrue various forms of aesthetic and political meaning. It is through this lens, as object and visual effect, that this chapter takes up cinematic color.

Mandabi and Color Balance

Color filmmaking in Africa was introduced as a colonial technology, as Jacqueline Maingard shows, from stenciled Pathé films such as Alfred Machin's safari expeditions *Chasse à la panthère* (France, 1909) and *La chasse au marabout en Abyssinie* (France, 1912), to Technicolor imperial epics like Zoltan Korda's Sudan-based *The Four Feathers* (Great Britain, 1939).[10] Monopack color filming in African cinema began with nonfiction and educational works during the colonial era, largely produced by non-Africans. This was the case, for example, with Jean Rouch's ethnographic works, as well as with features such as the fictional *Omaru: Eine afrikanische Liebesgeschichte* (Austria, 1956), which was filmed in Cameroon in Agfacolor by the Austrian director Albert Quendler, and the 16mm Kodachrome docufiction *Fincho* (Nigeria and U.S., 1957), which was set and filmed in Nigeria and directed by the UCLA-trained Israeli polymath Sam Zebba with a Nigerian cast and crew.[11] However, as with the other case studies in this volume, the primary era of monopack feature filmmaking in Africa began in the 1960s, with Ousmane Sembène's *Mandabi* (Senegal, 1968), which was filmed in Eastman Color.

As Manthia Diawara and others have discussed, this shift to color specifically in Francophone West African cinema was initially motivated by French neocolonial funding sources. Sembène obtained international financing for *Mandabi* through the Centre national du cinéma (CNC), and the assigned French producers, Robert de Nesle and Jean Maumy, insisted—among other stipulations regarding adding erotic scenes, which Sembène refused—that the film be produced in color to appeal better to international tastes.[12] Sembène initially resisted filming in color, as he believed it would make the film too sensationalist and exoticizing. He was also concerned about the film stock's sensitivity to Black skin tones under the West African lighting conditions. Sembène acquiesced to using Eastman Color for the film, but his hesitancy was understandable given the primitivist exotification of Africa in the Western visual imagination, as well as the technical White bias built into color film stocks.[13]

Yet Sembène's achievements with color in the film are remarkable and add another layer to his realist aesthetics of the time. Its opening shots directly refute Sembène's initial hesitancy: tilting down across a tree, set against a clear blue sky, the first shot centers on an everyday view of Dakar, with several men sitting in the shade of the tree while having their heads and faces shaved by outdoor barbers. After a cut in to a medium shot, the third shot of the sequence cuts in again, to a shallow focus close-up of the face of the film's protagonist, Ibrahima Dieng. The barber's skilled hand massages shaving lotion over Ibrahima's face, creating a resplendent yet naturalized variety of brown hues across the frame: the tan of the earth in shallow focus in the background, the darker tan of the barber's hand, and the reflective, oiled hues of Ibrahima's face. The everyday nature of the opening scene—Ibrahima getting a shave—pushes against the exoticizing gaze that Sembène rejected, and the movement from blue sky to the glistening face demonstrates the filmmaker's ability to recalibrate Eastman Color's chromatic bias (figure 14.1). Through lighting and costuming choices in the film and in his ensuing work, Sembène experimented with and demonstrated a masterful eye for color design as he expanded his stylistic range, pushing the boundaries of his initial realist mode through his use of color in later works. Parallel to global trends of the 1970s, most feature filmmaking in sub-Saharan Africa after *Mandabi* similarly transitioned to color.

Xala and Liminality

The film *Xala* (1975), which Ousmane Sembène adapted from his own novel from 1973, follows the plight of a corrupt businessman, El Hadji Abdou Kader Beye, who has had a curse (a *xala*) placed on him, rendering him impotent. Sembène

FIGURE 14.1 Ousmane Sembène's careful registration of skin tones on Eastman Color in the opening of *Mandabi* (1968).

uses El Hadji as a satiric metaphor for the neocolonial, independent government of Senegal, a parallel that the film draws out in its introductory, pre-credit scene, which is the focus here. Echoing *Mandabi*'s opening, the first shot of the film is a close-up of a man's face, dripping with sweat as he loudly plays a djembe drum among a crowd celebrating independence, the sound filling the score. The camera pans down from his face, along his vivid red shirt to the drum, connecting the African drumming to the red of revolution. A cut to a young woman in traditional beads, dancing joyously to the drum rhythms, provides a successive contrast to the red shirt as her head is draped in a green scarf. A third shot then pans across the scene to more beaded dancers and drummers, in contrasting reds and greens, partially echoing the hues of the Senegalese and other African flags of independence. The rhythmic drumming and movement correspond to the vivid red and green contrasting palette, using color to help signify the celebratory moment of Senegalese independence from colonial rule—a pictorial embodiment of Fanon's reflections that previously restricted color "flood back, reflecting the effects of the revolutionary upsurge."[14]

The film's next sequence shifts registers: with the revolutionary drumming in the sonic background, seven businessmen in traditional Senegalese costume—patterned shirts in restrained, lightly saturated fabrics of golds, blues, whites, and pinks—rush into the glaring white, colonial Chamber of Commerce and Industry, as voice-over narration explains that never before had an African assumed the presidency of the country's financial ministry. As the businessmen enter the office, they are confronted by the current French president of commerce and his two assistants, all dressed in black business suits. The French bureaucrats abdicate the office, and the Senegalese businessmen subsequently remove the room's decorations of colonial jackboots and white busts of French figures, most prominently of Marianne, the figurehead of the French Republic, atop an office cabinet draped in red and blue cloth (representing the tricolors of the French flag) and take the statuary outside to the revelers.[15] The French bureaucrats then leave the building, picking up the abandoned statuary as they depart. In the next shot, Senegalese gendarmes arrive outside the ministry to break up the revelers, to their surprise. The former bureaucrats then return, still in their dark suits, and upon entering the chamber of commerce, the Senegalese businessman have now changed their garb, from traditionally colored shirts to Western suits and tuxedos, all black and white, and the former French president of commerce now offers each a briefcase full of cash.

Xala's opening political allegory thus stresses how it is business as usual within liberated Senegal—colonialism all too easily transitions to neocolonialism for the financial management of West African resources. A crucial way in which this is articulated is through the scenes' gradated color codings, of the vivid reds and greens of African revolution, the attenuated hues of the businessmen's initial robes, and the desaturated blacks and whites of power and commerce. The restrained colors of the businessmen's initial traditional garb are situated between the revolutionary hues that open the film and the Western business attire that concludes the scene. This liminal in-betweenness foreshadows the ease of their subsequent costume change and connects the coded play with color in costuming to the politics of neocolonial resource extraction—transformed through Western hues, the businessmen can now take charge of Senegalese commerce.

To unpack the color design further, for modernism color played an instrumental role in the disruption of notions of mimetic realism. Emerging from their primitivist impulses, modernists working in the early twentieth century mobilized ideas about the language of color as a means of challenging restrained, naturalist aesthetics that favored pictorial verisimilitude. In the context of the political modernism of the 1970s—defined in film theory by post-1968 political commitments, the prioritization of Brechtian critiques of realist form and illusionism, and the rise of Third Cinema of which Sembène's work is an exemplar—color was still a language but one that was informed by semiotics. It was part of the sign system of cinema, related to the new wave aesthetics of the 1960s, as in Jean-Luc Godard's famous formulation in response to an interviewer's observation about the amount of blood in *Pierrot le fous* (1965): "Pas du sang, du rouge" (It's not blood, it's red).[16] Such an emphasis on the nature of color as a semiotic sign, rather than as a naturally occurring thing, helps to delineate the liminal function of color in *Xala*. While the hues of its opening allegory correspond to specific objects—a shirt, a headdress, Senegalese and European formal wear—the ways in which they signify larger tropes is what is vital here. To an extent the colors correspond to the association of vivid color with primitivism and desaturation with colonial, Western power, though this reverses the aesthetic judgment by prioritizing vividness and liberation over the economic oppression of the latter. The Senegalese business attire falls liminally in the middle, attuned to the potentials of both revolution and colonial power. Yet these variances are not naturalized in the scene; their performative and polyvalent nature as signs estranges the colors from an illusionistic realism that might otherwise equate such values with race. Instead, they foreground color as a discursive system of signs—not blood but red, and, vitally, a revolutionary one at that. Sembène thus strategically embeds an anticolonial politics into the semiotic system of modernist color design.

Touki Bouki in Red and White

A related discursive approach to color meaning can be found in Djibril Diop Mambéty's *Touki Bouki* (1973), which curiously reverses the stereotypical association of vivid imagery with African culture. Instead, the film ties color to European decadence during an era in which color's reach had expanded dynamically through global developments in consumer capitalism. A landmark of modernist and countercultural cinema, the film shares allegiances through its disjunctive editing patterns with new wave style, from Godard to Věra Chytilová, as well as a connection to Sergei Eisenstein's montage—particularly in *Strike*, given both films' brutal depictions of abattoirs.[17] *Touki Bouki*'s plot is a simple one: Mory, the rebellious hyena (the *bouki*) of the film's title, and his girlfriend Anta (a university student) aim to leave Senegal for Paris, a location idealized within the colonial imagination. They are eventually able to pilfer the money and clothing they need for the trip, as well as a car, from the wealthy and queer Francophile Charlie, who had been pursuing Mory romantically for some time.[18] However, upon entering the harbor to board the ocean liner to France, Mory decides not to abandon his homeland and leave, while Anta walks up the gangway alone and departs.

In terms of color design, *Touki Bouki*'s opening presents a useful comparison to *Xala*. Over the title sequence, the film begins with agrarian imagery of a young boy riding a cow toward the camera while shepherding a cattle herd, in two shots toward the camera, from extreme long shot into medium framing. The palette, filmed in Eastman Color, is restrained, emphasizing the naturalistic browns, greens, and blues of the rural landscape. There is nondiegetic sound of a West African Fula flute that accompanies the diegetic mooing of the herd. The cattle form a sound bridge over a shock cut, of a white zebu steer in close-up in a modern abattoir, being pulled forward onto the killing floor. Over a series of shots, the bull is slaughtered in modern, industrial fashion: its throat cut, with deep streams of crimson blood spilling across the image and splattering the white cowhide in terrifying contrast. The mise-en-scène of the space—white tile, brick, and painted concrete, with industrial hoists and steel wires for lifting carcasses as illustrated through a camera tilt—is a sharp contrast to the rural scenes surrounding the slaughterhouse, juxtaposing modern infrastructure with the pastoral.

A final shot of the abattoir reveals a half dozen more cattle waiting their turn, before the film then cuts back to the flute sounds and the bucolic scene of the young boy riding toward the camera. The crimson red has disappeared, but now the sound of a motorcycle accompanies the image as well, forming a new sound bridge—a sonic rack focus as Vlad Dima discusses in his study of the film—as the sequence cuts with a disjunctive match on action to Mory astride a motorcycle decked out with cattle horns on the handlebars, creating an association between the young boy and the young man, seemingly one and the same.[19] It is a following shot, filmed behind Mory's shoulder and interspersed with shots of the neighborhood he is riding through. No longer in the countryside and the bloodied whiteness of the abattoir, he is now in a poor, working-class neighborhood of Dakar, full of wood shacks, desaturated in browns and tans save for splashes of bright international advertisements pasted against walls, some fruit at a stand, and a few people robed in yellows, purples, and blues, whereas most are relatively muted in dress. The mise-en-scène of the neighborhood is neither the pastoral of the countryside nor the violent, modern space of the slaughterhouse.

As Mory rides out of the neighborhood, the final image of the opening sequence is a dramatic shot from his perspective, traveling along a highway. Preceded by a rhyming, high-angled shot that tilts to follow Mory on the motorcycle, with a pedestrian overpass in the background, the sequence cuts in to the final shot, to Mory's point of view. The camera is initially pointed down at the road's dividing lines before tilting up to focus on a different pedestrian overpass, just visible farther down the road in the previous shot, across which a vacation advertising sign reads: "Nice la Riviera et la Corse." What is startling about the sign, which concludes the film's opening sequence, is that it recalls the colors of the slaughterhouse: scarlet letters against a white background. Not only do these colors echo the abattoir, but the tilting camera, the steel overpass, and the power lines along the road also evoke the industrial infrastructure of the earlier mise-en-scène.

The disjunctive associations built into the vivid colors of *Touki Bouki*'s opening sequence—the scarlet blood in the abattoir and the lettering of the sign, both set off against white backgrounds—establish a running motif in the film related to travel and postcolonial modernity, which encompasses Mory and Anta's pursuit of a brighter, more vivid world in Europe, a common trope of colonial and postcolonial culture. Yet this imagined utopia is anything but idyllic; it is instead linked ironically with death in the film's disjunctive editing. The stylish clothes they later steal from Charlie are European: a suit, red and yellow tie, and straw hat for Mory, and a bright purple coat, green dotted shirt, and red hat for Anta.

Charlie's car, which they also steal to ride through the city and into the port, is absurdly painted in American stars and stripes, suggesting the growth of U.S. hegemony within the neocolonial system. Ironically and critically, the color-coded markers of Western affluence that adorn Mory and Anta allow them entry to the ocean liner, the MS *Ancerville*, which sailed between Dakar and Marseille at the time.

Recalling the cinematography and colors of the film's opening sequence, camera movement introduces the ship, tilting up from the water along its white hull to the ship's name, *Ancerville*, in deep red, as a crane hoists cargo onto the ship. The camera tilt and color scheme establish formal parallels among the MS *Ancerville*, the earlier vacation advertisement for France, and the slaughter-house, and Mory and Anta's arrival at the ship further cements these associations (figure 14.2). Mory's sudden decision not to board and leave Senegal is cued when the gangway and especially the sound of the boat horn remind him of the entrance to the abattoir, which returns visually through disjunctive editing from the opening of the film. The contrapuntal sound montage of horn for the mooing of a soon-to-be-slaughtered bull begins the connection; a visual cut to the lowing bull crystallizes the association, as do subsequent cuts between the harbor and the slaughterhouse. There is a density of meaning to this montage: the scarlet-white slaughterhouse of commodified meat and a boat passage that carries similar associations for Mory, of commodified bodies turned into chattel through the Middle Passage. Mory flees the port, seemingly sensing the danger, though abandoning Anta.

Touki Bouki's politics are far more oblique than *Xala*'s overt attack on neocolonialism, yet both films are clearly critical of their contemporary political and cultural climates. Like Sembène, Mambéty critiques a postcolonial longing for the Global North and its fashionable new waves of color design, though at the level of personal desire with Mory and Anta as articulated through their vivid French attire, as opposed to the neocolonial, structural power that *Xala* critiques through the black-and-white play of formal wear at its opening. Both films translate these stances into their opposing color designs that reassess and subvert primitivist stereotypes of color meaning, making color function as a trope of African postcolonial aesthetics. The vivid, revolutionary hues of the opening of *Xala* are reversed as neocolonial emblems of French modernity in *Touki Bouki*, disassociated from the more subdued and naturalistic backdrop of Senegal in the film. Despite these differences, each film centers color in relation to systems of extraction and global exchange: the Chamber of Commerce and Industry and the abattoir-ship passage. The vivid colors that illuminate the films and facilitate their circulation within global art cinemas of the time, per the French prescripts for *Mandabi*, function as infrastructural resources, yet ones that are mobilized critically via their discursive inversions.

FIGURE 14.2 The repetition of red and white in Djibril Diop Mambéty's *Touki Bouki* (1973).

Coda: *Daughters of the Dust*

To extend the analysis of vivid color design to the African diaspora, it is useful to conclude with Julie Dash's *Daughters of the Dust* (1991). The film is temporally and geographically distanced from *Xala* and *Touki Bouki*, but even as it is narratively centered in the Lowcountry of the American South, its historical and aesthetic imagination is expansive. *Daughters of the Dust* reflects deeply on the oceanic currents of both the Black diaspora and the colorant trade in ways that speak to the decolonial approaches to color found in the earlier films.

Stylistically, *Daughters of the Dust* operates in a distinct chromatic register. Set in 1902, Dash and the cinematographer Arthur Jafa crafted a lush naturalism into the vivid palette of the film to evoke the warm hues of the South Carolina and Georgia Sea Island communities. The film's attention to color has been commented on since its release, with Lizzie Francke, for example, noting in a review in *Sight and Sound* in reference to a scene that features a kaleidoscope that it is as if the film itself "is filmed through that magical" device.[20] Dash was dissatisfied with the look of the color prints of *Daughters of the Dust*, filmed with Agfa-Gevaert negatives, but originally printed in Eastman Color, when it was initially released. Due to budgetary constraints, the original palette from the Agfa negatives was never properly graded on the Eastman Color answer prints; indeed, Eastman Color, according to Dash (and echoing Sembène's earlier concerns about the film stock), is ill-suited for Black skin tones.[21] She and Jafa chose Agfa-Gevaert because, in her judgment, "Black people look better in Agfa."[22] As she explains in more detail in a recent interview about the 2016 2K restoration by the Cohen Media Group, "Agfa-Gevaert reads warm in the shadow areas. Kodak film stock is blue/green in shadows. It reads black people as shadows, so they look blue or green. Now that it's in a digital space, we were able to dial up the colors and make them come back to the way they were supposed to be. Now there's more *vivid colors* and you're better able to see into the faces. So, I'm much happier now. I just thought it was very murky before."[23]

Through these vivid colors, *Daughters of the Dust* recounts the multigenerational and matriarchal history of the Peazants, a Gullah family on an island off the Georgia coast in 1902. As Tiffany Lethabo King has eloquently described, the family members are formerly enslaved people and their descendants, many of whom worked in the indigo fields and processing plants of the region that were discussed earlier in this chapter.[24] To mark this history, blue runs through the film, sometimes subtly as the background tone of sky and water, and at other times overtly. The clearest example of this is a flashback scene halfway through the film, from the tombstones of the Peazants' ancestors, to the indigo work they carried out as plantation slaves on the island, manufacturing the colorant (figure 14.3). As Dash explains the scene: "This is a flashback to an indigo-processing plant where the Unborn Child watches her ancestors at work. The colour, which is in the bow in her hair and on the hands of the

FIGURE 14.3 Indigo processing in Julie Dash's *Daughters of the Dust* (1991).

ancestor, is my way of signifying slavery, as opposed to whipmarks or scars, images, which have lost their power. Processing the indigo plant was an African practice that became poisonous when transferred to the new world. The colour is a trace like a scar."[25]

The vividness of indigo not only colors the Peazants' family history but also is a ribbon that weaves through the longer chromatic trauma of colonial trade and chattel slavery. It is this violent trace of color that is so unsettling in *Daughters of the Dust*, as well as across the disparate works of postcolonial and diasporic cinemas discussed in this chapter. Color is both a heritage practice and a colonial poison that bounds aesthetic history and discourse. From the liminal hues in *Xala* to the scarlet-white of *Touki Bouki*'s abattoir, and here with the transatlantic movements of indigo blue, the vivid colors in these films resonate as an afrotrope that embeds a legacy of colonial extraction—of the entwined colored commodities of dyestuffs and of chattel slavery—into the post- and neocolonial systems of global capital.

The appropriation as well as inversion of the saturated hues of modernism and of primitivist color theory play out strikingly across these works, in ways that affirm aspects of Fanon's claim that postcolonial color upsets the rules of traditional harmony. Indeed, the turn in these films to vivid color does not affirm a naturalization of the chromatic order. Rather than normalizing the primitivist prescripts of aesthetic theory, color design here denaturalizes them, specifically through these works' emphasis on color as a part of a mobile and fluid discursive system, one that takes on the valence of a chromatic afrotrope in their respective postcolonial and diasporic contexts. As the variety of these films indicates, this is not a unified media practice per se, but one that shifts and varies across form and context. Across the diversity of examples, these films experiment with the signifying potentials of color as they radically code and recode the history of chromatic Blackness across their moving images.

Acknowledgments

This chapter grew out of collaborative work carried out by Nicholas Gaskill, Sarah Street, and Joshua Yumibe in their coauthored chapter "Literature and the Performing Arts," in *The Cultural History of Color: The Modern Age*, ed. Anders Steinvall and Sarah Street (London: Bloomsbury Press, 2021), 135–153. Specifically, the section on *Touki Bouki*, as well as the theoretical framing regarding Fanon, derive from that chapter.

Notes

1 On the work of decolonial aesthetics, see especially Walter Mignolo and Rolando Vazquez, "Decolonial AestheSis: Colonial Wounds/Decolonial Healings," *Social Text-Periscope*, July 15, 2013, https://socialtextjournal.org/periscope_article /decolonial-aesthesis-colonial-woundsdecolonial-healings/.

2 Johann Wolfgang von Goethe, *Theory of Colours* (Cambridge, MA: MIT Press, 1989), 55 (my italics). Also see David Batchelor, *Chromophobia* (London: Reaktion, 2000); Richard Dyer, *White* (New York: Routledge, 2017).

3 Goethe, *Theory of Colours*, 22.

4 Frantz Fanon, *The Wretched of the Earth*, trans. Richard Philcox (New York: Grove Press, 2004), 175.

5 Michael Taussig, *What Color Is the Sacred?* (Chicago: University of Chicago Press, 2009), 134–136.

6 See David McCreery, "Indigo Commodity Chains in the Spanish and British Empires, 1560–1860," in *From Silver to Cocaine: Latin American Commodity Chains and the Building of the World Economy, 1500–2000*, ed. Steven Topik, Zephyr Frank, and Carlos Marichal (Durham, NC: Duke University Press, 2006), 53–75.

7 Tiffany Lethabo King, *The Black Shoals: Offshore Formations of Black and Native Studies* (Durham, NC: Duke University Press, 2019), 112.

8 See, for instance, James Tweedie, *The Age of New Waves: Art Cinema and the Staging of Globalization* (New York: Oxford University Press, 2013).

9 Huey Copeland and Krista Thompson, "Afrotropes: A User's Guide," *Art Journal* 76, no. 3–4 (October 2, 2017): 7.

10 Jacqueline Maingard, "Screening Africa in Colour: Abderrahmane Sissako's *Bamako*," *Screen* 51, no. 4 (December 1, 2010): 397–403.

11 Jean Rouch briefly discusses *Omaru* in "The Situation and Tendencies of the Cinema in Africa," trans. Steve Feld, *Studies in Visual Communication* 2, no. 1 (May 17, 2017): 58n11. On *Fincho*, see Sam Zebba, "Casting and Directing in Primitive Societies," *The Quarterly of Film Radio and Television* 11, no. 2 (1956): 154–166. Also, for examples of color filming in the British colonies, see Tom Rice, *Films for the Colonies: Cinema and the Preservation of the British Empire* (Berkeley: University of California Press, 2019), for instance, regarding Norman Spurr's experiments with color through the Colonial Film Unit on page 83.

12 See Manthia Diawara, *African Cinema: Politics and Culture* (Bloomington: Indiana University Press, 1992), 32. Also see Maingard, "Screening Africa in Colour"; James E. Genova, *Cinema and Development in West Africa: Film as a Vehicle for Liberation* (Bloomington: Indiana University Press, 2013), 138–139.

13 On the White bias of film stocks, see, for example, Lorna Roth, "The Fade-Out of Shirley, a Once-Ultimate Norm: Colour Balance, Image Technologies, and Cognitive Equity," in *The Melanin Millennium: Skin Color as 21st Century International Discourse*, ed. Ronald E. Hall (Dordrecht: Springer Netherlands, 2013), 273–286.

14 Fanon, *Wretched of the Earth*, 175.

15 David Murphy, *Sembène: Imagining Alternatives in Film and Fiction* (Trenton, NJ: Africa World Press, 2000), 110–113.

16 Jean-Louis Comolli, Michel Delahaye, Jean-André Fieschi, and Gérard Guégan, "Parlons de 'Pierrot': Nouvel Entretien avec Jean-Luc Godard," *Cahiers du Cinéma* 171 (October 1965): 21.

17 See Vlad Dima's extended discussion of Eisenstein's notion of "intellectual montage" in relation to the film's opening and closing sequences, in *Sonic Space in Djibril Diop Mambéty's Films* (Bloomington: Indiana University Press, 2017), esp. 44–45.

18 See Kenneth W. Harrow, "The Queer Thing about Djibril Diop Mambéty: A Counterhegemonic Discourse Meets the Heterosexual Economy," *Paragraph* 24, no. 3 (2001): 76–91.

19 Dima, *Sonic Space in Djibril Diop Mambéty's Films*, 46.

20 Lizzie Francke, "*Daughters of the Dust*," *Sight and Sound* 3, no. 9 (1993): 44. For the most extensive analysis of the film's colors, see Diana Pozo, "Water Color: Radical Color Aesthetics in Julie Dash's *Daughters of the Dust*," *New Review of Film and Television Studies* 11, no. 4 (December 1, 2013): 424–437.

21 Maori Karmael Holmes, "Invisible Scratch Lines: An Interview with Julie Dash," *Film Quarterly* 70, no. 2 (2016): 51.

22 Zeinabu Irene Davis, "An Interview with Julie Dash," *Wide Angle* 13, no. 3/4 (1991): 115.

23 Andrea Davis Kronlund, "Julie Dash on *Daughters of the Dust* and Speculative Fiction, Part 3," *Krull Magazine*, March 8, 2017, https://krullmag.com/blog/julie-dash-on-daughters-of-the-dust-and-speculative-fiction-part-3/ (my italics).

24 King, *Black Shoals*, 111–140.

25 Quoted in Karen Alexander, "*Daughters of the Dust*," *Sight and Sound* 3, no. 9 (1993): 20–23. Also, see the lucid description of the scene in the published screenplay, Julie Dash, *Daughters of the Dust: The Making of an African American Woman's Film* (New York: New Press, 1992), 133–134.

Acknowledgments

Global Film Color began with an idea for a panel coordinated by the editors at the Society for Cinema and Media Studies conference in Chicago in 2017 titled "A World of Color in Film and Media." We copresented with leading color scholars Kirsty Sinclair Dootson and Kirsten Moana Thompson. Thus began a conversation and realization that there has been little scholarship to date regarding the global history of color in cinema. In July 2019, Sarah organized a related conference, "Global Color and the Moving Image," at the University of Bristol, which was attended by a number of this book's contributors. The conference was an output of The Eastmancolor Revolution (2016–2019, a project funded by the Arts and Humanities Research Council, with Sarah Street as primary investigator). The event gave a real sense of global film color's many fascinating aspects, as well as the potential for future explorations. As we discovered, film color's political and ideological underpinnings had, and continue to have, ramifications all over the globe, regarding asymmetrical access, cost, and cultural expression. These tendencies—particularly the ways in which filmic technologies and production practices were developed and applied implicitly as well as explicitly to establish hierarchical and discriminatory associations of color with race and ethnicity—were first flagged by a number of pioneering scholars, and in light of losses in our discipline we would particularly like to acknowledge the late works of Edward Branigan, Steve Neale, James Snead, and Brian Winston.

With our deepest gratitude, we would like to thank the authors who responded enthusiastically to our proposal for an edited collection, which will enable us to put global film color more centrally on the map of color studies. We hope that this work inspires further, new research into the multiple contexts and varieties of color expression in film and media that continue to make the subject so fascinating and, indeed, necessary. We are extremely grateful to our editor, Nicole

231

Solano, at Rutgers University Press for being so encouraging and enthusiastic about the book throughout its production. The anonymous readers of the manuscript offered useful insights and suggestions we found very helpful in bringing it to its final stages. We would also like to thank the University of Bristol and the Humanities and Arts Research Program at Michigan State University for subvention support on the project.

By means of personal acknowledgment, Sarah would like to thank Sue Simkin for her wonderful support, as always, for what has now been a very long fascination with and foray into color. And Joshua would like to thank Juliet Guzzetta, as well as Livia and Raffaella, for exploring the world in all its remarkable hues lovingly together.

Notes on Contributors

WILLIAM CARROLL is an assistant professor in the Department of East Asian Studies at the University of Alberta, where he teaches on contemporary Japanese film, media, and culture. His first book is titled *Suzuki Seijun and Postwar Japanese Cinema*. He is currently working on a book about cinephile culture and film production in Japan from the 1980s through the present.

PHILIP CAVENDISH is a professor of Russian and Soviet film studies at University College London. His main research interests lie in the visual poetics of cinema and the relationship between film technology and aesthetics. He has published widely on prerevolutionary Russian cinema, the Soviet avant-garde of the 1920s, the theory and practice of camera operation, and the history of color film during the Stalinist era. He is currently working on early Russian and Soviet experiments in the sphere of color photography.

JOSEPHINE DIECKE is an assistant professor of film studies at the University of Zurich. She has conducted extensive research on the history of color film technologies, moving image preservation, and digital methods for computer-assisted text and video analysis. Her expertise stems from her work as a research associate on the "Filmcolors" project (University of Zurich), as the academic coordinator of the "Digital Cinema-Hub" project (Philipps-Universität Marburg), and as a film lab technician for various service providers. She holds a PhD from the University of Zurich, having written a thesis on Agfacolor and Orwocolor, and is coeditor of the *Open Media Studies* blog.

KIRSTY SINCLAIR DOOTSON is a lecturer in film and media at University College London. Her work on color has appeared in *Screen*, *Film History*, and *British*

Art Studies, and she is the author of *The Rainbow's Gravity: Colour Materiality and British Modernity*. With Professor Ranjani Mazumdar she leads an international research network exploring the history of color in Hindi cinema.

RAFAEL DE LUNA FREIRE is an associate professor at Fluminense Federal University, in Niterói, Brazil, where he is the director of the Audiovisual Preservation University Lab (LUPA-UFF). In 2019, he organized the First BRICS Audiovisual Preservation Meeting, bringing together film archivists from Brazil, Russia, China, India, and South Africa. As a film scholar, he has published widely on Brazilian cinema. His most recent book is *O negócio do filme: A distribuição cinematográfica no Brasil, 1907–1915*, a pioneering study on the history of film distribution in Brazil before the First World War.

ELENA GIPPONI is a research fellow at IULM University of Milan, where she received her PhD in communication and new technologies. She teaches courses in film criticism and color cultures in cinema and media. She has written a number of articles and essays on color and, with Joshua Yumibe, edited "Cinema and Mid-century Colour Culture," a special issue of *Cinéma&Cie: Film and Media Studies Journal*. Her book on the transition from black and white to color in the Italian modern media landscape is titled *Una rivoluzione inavvertita: Dal bianco e nero al colore nello scenario mediale della modernità italiana*.

HEATHER HECKMAN is associate dean for information resources and technologies at the University of South Carolina Libraries. She previously served as director of the Moving Image Research Collections at the same institution. She holds a PhD in communication arts (film studies) from the University of Wisconsin–Madison.

LAURA MAJOR is the library manager at the Moving Image Research Collections at the University of South Carolina. Previously, she worked at Colorlab, a motion picture film preservation laboratory, and specialized in film-to-film preservation. She sits on the boards of the Film Exhibition Fund as well as Mono No Aware.

RANJANI MAZUMDAR is a professor of cinema studies at the School of Arts and Aesthetics, Jawaharlal Nehru University. Her publications focus on the cinematic city, spatial aesthetics, and techno-urbanism. She is the author of *Bombay Cinema: An Archive of the City*, coeditor, with Neepa Majumdar, of *A Companion to Indian Cinema*, and guest editor of a special issue of *Bioscope* on cinema and techno-materiality. Her current research focuses on globalization and film culture; intermedial encounters; and the intersection of technology, travel, design, and color in Bombay cinema of the 1960s.

KATHRYN MILLARD is a writer, independent filmmaker, and emeritus professor of screen and creative arts at Macquarie University, Sydney, Australia. Her body of screen work spans award-winning feature dramas, documentaries, and essay films. She is the author of *Double Exposure: How Psychology Fell in Love with the Movies* and *Screenwriting in a Digital Era*.

LYDIA PAPPAS is the assistant director of the Moving Image Research Collections at the University of South Carolina and is the Curator of the Chinese Film Collection and the Regional Film Collections at MIRC. She has a background in Libraries and Archives, both in the United Kingdom and United States.

KAMALIKA SANYAL is currently pursuing her PhD on the introduction, evolution, and acceptance of photographic color film in Sweden. More specifically, she explores the transition-stage issues and critical reception of color in the art as well as the business of Swedish filmmaking between the 1930s and 1960s. She has published her findings on Swedish color remakes of the 1950s and has presented her work on early photographic color Swedish shorts, and the role of color in Swedish film promotion at various conferences. For her master's thesis, she studied the Scandinavian cultural influence on Ingmar Bergman's work between the 1950s and 1970s.

STEFAN SOLOMON is a senior lecturer in media studies at Macquarie University in Sydney, Australia. He is the author of *William Faulkner in Hollywood: Screenwriting for the Studios*; coeditor, with Alix Beeston, of *Incomplete: The Feminist Possibilities of the Unfinished Film*; and coeditor, with Lúcia Nagib, of *The Moving Form of Film: Historicising the Medium through Other Media*.

SARAH STREET is a professor of film at the University of Bristol, UK. Her latest books are *Chromatic Modernity: Color, Cinema, and Media of the 1920s* (2019, co-authored with Joshua Yumibe), winner of the Katharine Singer Kovács Book Award in 2020 and the IAMHIST-Michael Nelson book prize 2021; and *Colour Films in Britain: The Eastmancolor Revolution* (co-authored with Keith M. Johnston, Paul Frith, and Carolyn Rickards, 2021).

JOSHUA YUMIBE is a professor of film studies at Michigan State University. He is the author of *Moving Color: Early Film, Mass Culture, Modernism*; coauthor of *Fantasia of Color in Early Cinema* with Giovanna Fossati, Tom Gunning, and Jonathon Rosen; and most recently of *Chromatic Modernity: Color, Cinema, and Media of the 1920s* with Sarah Street, which won both the Katherine Singer Kovács Book Award in 2020 and the Michael Nelson Prize, International Association for Media and History in 2021.

LINDA C. ZHANG is an assistant professor of film in the Art and Media Studies program at Fulbright University Vietnam. She is currently completing a book project on media histories of modern Chinese animation, visual culture, and popular science texts from the early Maoist era. Her work has appeared in the *Journal of Chinese Cinemas*, the Association for Chinese Animation Studies, and RadiiChina. She has served as an academic contributor and translator for film events with the Berkeley Art Museum Pacific Film Archive, the China Film Archive, the Wattis Institute, Duke University Libraries, and the Mill Valley Film Festival.

GREGORY ZINMAN is an associate professor in the Department of Film and Media at Emory University. His writing on film and media has appeared in the *New Yorker*, *The Atlantic*, and the *Journal of Cinema and Media Studies*, among other publications. He is the author of *Making Images Move: Handmade Cinema and the Other Arts* and coeditor, with John Hanhardt and Edith Decker-Phillips, of *We Are in Open Circuits: Writings by Nam June Paik*.

Index

Page numbers in *italics* indicate photographs.

Printed and bound by CPI Group (UK) Ltd, Croydon, CR0 4YY

02/10/2024

14567339-0001